ABYSS
TO
Bliss

*My Healing Journey
into Wholeness*

TALCYONA NOVA

BALBOA.PRESS

A DIVISION OF HAY HOUSE

Balboa Press books may be ordered through booksellers or by contacting:

Balboa Press
A Division of Hay House
1663 Liberty Drive
Bloomington, IN 47403
www.balboapress.com
844-682-1282

Print information available on the last page.

ISBN: 978-1-9822-6839-8 (sc)
ISBN: 978-1-9822-6841-1 (hc)
ISBN: 978-1-9822-6840-4 (e)

Library of Congress Control Number: 2021909265

Balboa Press rev. date: 05/11/2021

Contents

Introduction

Come follow me, if you will, back to the land of the living—or at the very least, to a life of empowerment that no one can take from you, a most joyous and self-aware place to be. I feel energized to my core just thinking about sharing my journey back to myself— my physical, emotional, and spiritual wholeness. The journey is one that begins with years of illness and disconnection from spirit but emerges, through many healing modalities and much expansion of the mind and spirit, into wholeness and reconnection of my mind, body, and spirit, along with a rediscovered sense of life force energy and well-being. There can be no greater gift. It is my goal to help you learn how to reach this place of empowerment in your life, regardless of your circumstances, and to help you to learn how to change your inner landscape to make major positive changes in your entire life, especially your health.

This book is about my experiences dealing with severe health issues that were improperly diagnosed and managed by the Western health care system, and then my subsequent reliance on my intuition to move through it all with grace, which eventually healed me. I wrote it because so many people are still suffering terribly and not receiving the help they need from allopathic medicine, and sometimes even alternative, holistic medicine cannot do what you can do for yourself. Many have asked me to write this book, knowing that the process was far more involved than what may be imparted in a few simple conversations.

My hope for anyone reading it is that you will gain the tools to deepen your intuitive powers and deal with the intense emotions and opportunities for spiritual growth and empowerment when facing a crisis. My hope is for you to know that you are never a victim of anything happening to you, even though it may seem to be that way at first. In moving away from the perspective of being a victim, you become truly empowered, and true freedom can result. I feel that the wisdom I've gained in my journey can be helpful for almost any difficult life circumstances, helping to bring you through any dark abyss into the light of day. It is not for the faint of heart, however; it is for those willing to do the deep soul-diving. The rewards of doing this are profound. Not only will you find your own healing on all levels, but you will set the stage for your evolution in consciousness.

Why should you do this? By doing some or all of the practices I speak of in this book, you will gain clarity of mind, focus, inner strength, conscious control over your thoughts and emotions, courage, and compassion. You will also learn how to trust yourself and become more disciplined in achieving your goals. All kinds of blocks in your life may dissolve. And you will surely learn that everything in the universe is working in your highest good—always. My hope is that you will also begin to have a sense of feeling truly empowered and free to live a life of peace, joy, and well-being. A good part of this is done by changing subconscious thought patterns from negatively held beliefs to more positive ones—in essence, reconnecting to and embodying your authentic higher self, or spirit.

My credentials are as follows: I have a BS in psychology, I am an RN, DiHOM, CCHT, and Reiki master-level practitioner of Usui, Arolo Tifar, and kundalini Reiki. I am a shamanic practitioner and a practitioner of Marconic Recalibration and QTTT (quantum time travel technique) for healing core emotional traumas.

Heading for a Fall

Not one person has crossed through the dark abyss, faced
their inner shadows, dropped all their fears, liberated
and freed themselves at the end of the process …
and ever regretted it. The way out is through.
—Xoana Ra, @Xoana_Ra on Twitter

What I was dealing with when my journey started was literally caused by a misalignment of my spirit with my body. It's not something that is unique to me; it is a major pandemic happening in our world and has been for a very long time. It may be unique in how it presented with me. Being out of alignment with one's spiritual self is one of the primary causes of physical illness. Sadly, this is something that still goes unrecognized in our world. It is certainly not something we are taught is of major importance in life. If we all understood the absolute power that results from this connection, it would be the very first thing we would teach our children. In my health decline or state of dis-ease, back in 1990, the first thing I became aware of was that I was having real trouble tolerating any harsh chemicals in my environment.

Severe health issues and symptoms became my norm. I was affected primarily physically. Others may have mental issues or issues with abundance, relationships, or any number of manifestations. I had severe migraines, fibromyalgia, rashes, problems digesting food, severe burning nerve pain, joint pain, at times a racing heartbeat and skipped heartbeats, and a general cytokine storm state of affairs. I had a very overactive immune system, which saw everything as an invader and tried to fight it all off relentlessly. The cytokine storm is a form of agony and a literal hell on earth. Back when I first became ill, not much was understood about this or how to halt or subdue it. It was not easy to live any sort of normal existence. It became up to me to help myself through a long, slow, trial-and-error course of eliminating virtually everything humans use or eat in their lives.

As mentioned in the introduction, I have a BS in psychology and a BS in nursing. I worked with women on a gynecology unit, a step-down unit from ICU, and a cardiac unit during my career as an RN. When I became ill and allopathic medicine had very little to offer me, I began researching on my own. I found that alternative medicine had much more to offer that was helpful for me, and I eventually became a homeopath. I have since become a certified colon hydrotherapist in addition to the other forms of energy healing I listed in the introduction. Energy healing is a profound type of healing since it heals one on all levels—spiritual, etheric, mental, emotional, energetic, and physical.

Many years ago, when I was in my twenties, I began to experience unbelievably severe headaches, known as migraines, after using a toxic pesticide known as Quell body lotion for scabies, which I got while on a cross-country camping trip. Migraines are neurological in nature, and the organochlorine pesticide in the Quell lotion is known to be a neurotoxin, meaning it is quite toxic to the nervous system. I would have one of these migraines every ten days like clockwork, and with them would come a couple of days of being unable to eat, many times vomiting, complete with dry heaves. I was often unable to keep down water for twenty-four hours. This rapidly developed into chemical, pollen, and mold sensitivities, causing not only migraines regularly but other symptoms as well, such as all-over severe muscle pain for which there seemed to be no relief. Many thought I was talking about the kind of muscle pain one incurs after intense exercise. This pain was very different; it was a severe burning pain, as if I had acid inside my muscles, on fire in a sense. I now know this was most likely a cytokine storm. It is called a cytokine storm because substances called cytokines rampage through the bloodstream. These are small proteins that carry messages between cells to increase or decrease the immune response. If you happen to have underlying infections of any kind, this will most likely trigger increased immune activity. This can become catastrophic, causing blood vessels to leak, blood to clot, and blood pressure to drop, and as your own immune system attacks your organs, they can begin to fail.

By the time I was in my early thirties, I'm pretty sure I was in an immune cytokine storm much of the time, although back then, in 1990, doctors weren't familiar with what that was. I was in agony. The best diagnosis I got was fibromyalgia, and I don't think anyone knew how dreadful that was back then. It is severe burning, acidic pain and prevents you from focusing on your life and living it. Then there came the hives and skin breakouts, which I am now fairly certain was my body's attempt to rid itself of the poisons that had overwhelmed it. Luckily, hives weren't my biggest issue. I had so little energy it was hard to stand up many days, so raising my two young children was close to impossible at times. I had severe hypotension or low blood pressure, and it was documented several times that my oxygen levels were not sufficient or normal. I believe it is a miracle I lived through years of this.

The red blood cells lose their ability to carry enough oxygen when the body is overwhelmed by toxins and poisons. This also happens in a cytokine storm. I used to feel as if I were having internal bleeding and had frequent nose bleeds as well as bleeding from other orifices. No one understood or believed how sick I was, because I couldn't get a diagnosis other than allergies from a doctor. Therefore, people simply didn't believe me. Many thought I was trying to get attention or a hypochondriac. Nothing was known about what was going on with me back then. Suffice it to say, I was sick enough to die—and almost did several times—and still no proper diagnosis was made. I finally received a diagnosis of multiple chemical sensitivity, which to this day I feel is a misnomer, due to the fact that it is really a sign of being chemically poisoned and unable to eliminate chemicals safely from the body. The name gives the impression of simple allergies to chemicals. While in some cases this is true, for the most part, it is an issue of severe toxicity from poisoning.

That was simply the result of having Lyme disease go undiagnosed and untreated, another disease of biowarfare origin. This is the kind of world we've been living in. A world where biowarfare and chemical poisoning have been perpetrated on a vastly unsuspecting population. There is no doubt in my mind that those responsible for this sort of thing have been purposefully doing it. And so, when we have pandemics such as the coronavirus, it's no wonder to me that some have had severe and fatal cases of it. Every toxin, chemical and emotional, that came before that was not successfully cleared created a perfect environment for a catastrophic result in the well-being of the physical body. That includes electromagnetic radiation poisoning. Most of us have been accomplices in this, simply going along, sleepwalking and numb to the overall detrimental effects of all of this. Realizing your responsibility in this will help keep you out of the victim role. It is tempting to wallow there for a while, but it does nothing to help you climb out of that abyss. The real answer is for as many as possible to step up their game and stand in their power to create a new life of vibrant health and well-being. In doing so, you help the entire planet raise its frequency into that of love, harmony, peace, joy, and abundance.

That being said, this is not exactly a step-by-step book explaining exactly how you are going to get well and heal your life. It is meant as an inspiration and to share with you the story of the many ways I have been inspired to heal. In reading it, I hope you are inspired and motivated to begin or continue your own journey toward exquisite bliss and joyful wellness. You may feel this is not possible for you, as I, myself, honestly felt many years before. If only I had known that nothing could've been further from the truth. Healing is always possible—and even more so when we refrain from placing limits on it or deciding how it must look. It begs not only for an open mind but a very open heart. Some of the ideas and experiences I've opened myself up to along the way would have seemed quite foreign to me, based on the way I was raised to think and the paradigms and societal rules ingrained in my being from a very early age.

You know, the rules such as "If you're sick, go to the doctor and follow his advice to the T, regardless of whether it is actually making you feel worse—because the doctors know best." Well, as I found out, *no*, they do not know best. In the end, as it is your body and you are the one inhabiting it, *you* know best. Toward the beginning of my recovery, I went to a shaman, which some religions tell us is sacrilegious, and it was one of the best decisions I ever made.

Thankfully, I have a very open and inquisitive nature. I was wired to always be seeking something new, something different, something that worked for me. This is the story of my journey and the ideas and concepts that have worked very well for me in going from a place of what appeared to be a dark, dismal abyss to a state of profound inner knowing and bliss. They say that to truly know the light, one must also know the dark. Having come through this very long, dark abyss, or night of the soul, I now experience my life from a place of serenity, trust, expansiveness, openness, joy, surrender, gratitude, abundance, and a blessed knowingness that a greater power always has my back—regardless of how any outer circumstances may ever appear. As I now know, my healing, well-being, and sense of connection come from within. It is a place of great inner peace and acceptance of what is, which opens the doors to all of creation and wholeness.

I was the firstborn child of my parents, who were in love and happily married at the time. My father was a cook in the US Army when they were first married. He had been a cheerleader and a bass singer in high school, always very social, and he needed to travel often for work. He later became a traveling salesman for IBM. Because of this job, he was often gone, and my mother became lonely and overwhelmed at times, especially with four young children. My mom was in school to become an RN when she got pregnant with me, and she received her RN diploma before my birth.

I was born within eleven months of my parents' wedding day. My next brother came one year later, so we were dubbed "Irish twins." My sister was born three and a half years after him, and my youngest brother another year and a half later. When I was just six years old, my siblings were five, eighteen months, and newborn. We were all born between 1956 and 1962. Neither of my parents had hit the age of thirty yet. They were, perhaps understandably, somewhat immature and quite dysfunctional, as were many parents at that time.

My mom described herself as that proverbial tomboy growing up. She would beat up all the boys in her neighborhood when they dared to offend or bother her. She shared with me about a time when she was five years old and a boy was bothering her playmate, so she socked him in the nose, giving him a bloody nose, and he ran home crying. Another time, when she was eight years old, some of the boys were teasing her about the space between her two front teeth, calling her snaggletooth. It hurt her feelings badly, so she beat them up. She also recalled that being forced to eat vegetables before being allowed to leave the table as a kid gave her intense anger issues. She was extremely strong-willed and hated being controlled in this fashion.

In high school, she played basketball on her school team. She was considered a jock and very competitive for a young girl growing up in the 1940s. Therefore, she was labeled incorrigible, difficult, and different and never got any praise from either parent, perhaps giving her a huge inferiority complex. Boys were either not attracted to her (she claims) or perhaps were threatened by her, although she was a stunning beauty. She became an RN in her early twenties and worked in a labor and delivery unit for many years, where she could use her power and abilities in a more constructive fashion.

My dad traveled a lot, so he wasn't at home very much to help my mom with all the young children underfoot. He was out of town maybe half of the time, and when he was not, he often would not get home until all of us were in bed. One can just imagine how difficult this made life for my mother.

Like many of their peers, my parents enjoyed partying and drinking on weekends. I should mention here that it was discovered much later that my father had a real problem with alcohol and was actually what is considered an alcoholic. This partying lifestyle continued throughout my high school years, although by that time, it had definitely slowed down some, as my mom had begun working full-time in an effort to keep up financially. That never stopped my dad from stopping off at bars on his way home or going off for weekends to party with his drinking buddies. There were some loud parties that we were subjected to—as if we were going to be able to sleep through that kind of raucous laughter and noise. This was probably more difficult for me, a very sensitive double water sign, to endure with grace and ease. At an early age, I began to learn how to subdue my needs and learned they actually weren't considered much priority at all.

It definitely had a long-lasting effect. It's a pretty big need of most children—to be treated as if they are important, and their questions are important enough to be answered. They need to be treated with respect, not as if they are stupid for asking questions. I understood very early on that it was better to just keep quiet and try to go with the flow. This led me to want to read all the time. I was learning something about how things worked and got to be in my own private world instead of in a world that seemed like chaos, where no one actually cared. It's pretty hard for me to even remember a conversation from that time in my life. As I said, I learned early on to stay quiet and was in my own head most of the time. This is how many highly sensitive children living in a home environment of that type end up behaving.

When my siblings got a bit older, they and my parents enjoyed playing board or card games. My sensitive nervous system had serious issues with the loud carrying on of five people all trying to talk at the same time, and the repetition of the games bored me greatly. They all enjoyed watching sitcoms as well. I've never liked watching a lot of television. This sensitivity and need for expansive learning was not recognized in my home, so I spent many happy hours holed up in my room, living in a fantasy world, reading whatever books I could get my hands on. I loved mysteries and anything about outer space. I read lots of biographies and autobiographies of famous people. For this reason, they treated me as if I were a very odd bookworm. The funny thing was that on Saturdays, I'd be the only kid outdoors wandering through the woods, riding my bike as far away as possible to my secret places. The rest of my siblings and neighborhood kids were indoors watching cartoons. I couldn't stand the cartoons and never understood the draw.

Living in an alcoholic home with three younger siblings and being the black sheep of my family, I got saddled with the responsibility of many things that were not really mine. If something wasn't cleaned in the house perfectly, it was my fault. I was a Cinderella of sorts. If my sister damaged my belongings and I dared retaliate, then it was my sister who was considered the victim. This probably goes on in many families, but it doesn't make it right, and it creates seething resentment. When I was old enough to know better, I joked somewhat bitterly that it seemed I'd been born with a sign on my forehead that said, "Place all blame here." Anything painful others didn't want to or couldn't deal with seemed to come flying my way. After I left home, I had to learn how to let go of that and allow others to learn their own lessons the hard way. It was unhealthy for me to continue taking on that responsibility for them.

As well as feeling intensely responsible from a very young age for anything not being quite right, I also seemed to be the one who felt everything so intensely. I tried to squelch this from an early age, as it clearly was not accepted in my family. Not only was I incredibly emotionally sensitive myself and able to key into others' emotions with ease, I was sensitive to everything, including itchy wool and netting fabrics on my skin. I hated lots of foods, including eggs, pasta, bread, and milk—all foods that I was later tested for, the results showing me to be allergic. When you are born this sensitive, you just want everyone around you to be happy, because when they're not, it can have a devastating effect on your well-being. I didn't discover until much later that I am an empath, someone who can easily feel the emotions and physical maladies of others. I would venture to say that many who get sick with unexplainable illnesses or symptoms are empaths. I am also an INFP Myers-Briggs personality type.

I cried too easily, according to my mom and grandmother. I distinctly remember being told to keep a stiff upper lip by my German grandmother. As a child needing to express feelings, this felt very invalidating and unaccepting, although I did have a fairly close bond with my grandmother. She was the one who encouraged a lot of my special abilities. She had a piano at her house, and when she noticed I loved sitting at it and playing whatever I could play, she had my mom sign me up for piano lessons. She also had a room in her house with lots of craft and art supplies that she set up just for us kids, and I remember being the one most interested. She let me help her in the kitchen, making fun things like cookies and hot chocolate, which I loved doing.

Astrologically, I have a very splayed chart, meaning I have planets in almost every house, spread out—Gemini rising, Mercury conjunct Chiron, and Pallas in Aquarius in the ninth house, which sets me up to be able to teach and help others heal on a spiritual level. A good part of the rest of my chart is in fire signs, which gives me a lot of passion. Thank God for all the fire in my chart. I can see now that it was a saving grace for me in the family I grew up in, although when I was young, that fire energy was vastly subdued. My natal Mercury-Chiron conjunction didn't help me out much either. When one is born with Mercury conjunct Chiron, one has serious impediments in communicating one's thoughts verbally.

Chiron is known as the wounded healer, and thus you are wounded in being able to access the energy of the planet it conjuncts. You end up healing others as you grow older through the very means by which you are wounded. And ever since my own healing and awakening, it has been difficult at times to stop expressing myself and sharing my knowledge. Here I am now writing a book to help others heal themselves, something I never could've imagined being able to do when I was younger. In fact, I had an eighth-grade English teacher who told me, in quite a disgusted tone, I would never be a writer. This is just an example of the type of trauma or insult one endures while growing up with a Chiron conjunction.

I also think I had a lot of trouble being here and understanding how things worked on this planet. I didn't understand why everyone didn't communicate telepathically. I felt I couldn't easily find the right questions to ask, and there was no one who could help draw me out. Many times my mom would say things like, "Chin up; you need to grow a thicker skin," or, "You ask too many questions." I felt her profound exasperation with me. I basically just wanted to have a greater understanding of how things worked and why they were the way they were. I was a very curious child, and many things here made no sense.

I was labeled a complainer early on because I refused to let things that bothered me slide. I did learn how to say, "I don't like that," or just let out a good whine, which was probably annoying. I mastered facial expressions as a way of communicating. I've always had an easy connection to my feelings and emotions. I was physically, emotionally, mentally, and psychically sensitive from birth, and no one knew to tell me it could actually be a *good* thing—a gift, in fact—to be so open to the flow of all the energies in the universe. My sensitivity was seen as a character flaw, so I learned to keep quiet. Expressing myself did not come easily, and it didn't seem acceptable to most when I did. As a result, no one knew the level of my sensitivity, because I kept it well hidden, which wasn't hard to do in a family with four children. There was so much going on all the time, so it was easy to be overlooked. However, by the time I was about fourteen or fifteen, I began to become aware of having prophetic dreams, dreams that would later happen in waking life.

Most were commonplace dreams, such as my dad's car being sideswiped on a certain block in the city we lived in. He was stunned when I told him my dream and said, "I can't believe you dreamt that. It just happened today, in the exact place you said it did in your dream." Another major one was I dreamt I saw my first high school boyfriend in a coffin when I was sixteen. I told him about the dream the next day. He got very quiet and then told me for the first time that his kidneys were only functioning at 17 percent, due to having diabetes from the age of four, and he would need a kidney transplant in the next year or so. He could indeed die as a result. He did have the transplant about two years later and died within about four years from the time of my dream.

I now understand that my childhood experiences happened for my highest good, as during the many years of simply observing others, I gathered a huge amount of knowledge and understanding of them—wisdom of a certain kind. I now know there are many out there who are psychic, very intuitive, or empathic to the extreme and made to feel as if they are misfits. Some of us just learned to keep quiet, and while I did this to a degree, I could never completely hide who I was. If you are interested, it may be very helpful to get an in-depth astrological reading of your natal chart done, as our astrological chart is a map that shows much of what we came here to learn and how things may play out for our highest good.

What a blessing for me to have learned about my astrological life map! Everything changed once I understood the map of my life and my soul's path. I began to step into my own empowerment and felt free to be exactly who I came here to be. My prayer is that there is an awakening to the fact that more and more children are being born now who are very open to their gifts, and this awakening helps create a society that not only accepts but also nurtures and values these gifts. They are beautiful and worthy gifts that can benefit not only oneself but the world.

I recall tiny four-year-old me watching my poor mother cry at the kitchen table and feeling profoundly her sense of unhappiness. Of course, being able to sense her unhappy state made me feel extremely sad, almost bereft. I felt so small and powerless and without proper emotional sustenance and nurturing for myself. I am sure this played a big part in my beginnings of lacking self-esteem and a feeling of worth as a human being. As you can see, abuse and neglect do not have to be severe to have a strong impact, especially on the more highly sensitive child. It is a distinct memory, which I recalled, precisely as it had happened, in a trance state during a shamanic ceremony. With the typical psychology of a child, I decided it must have been my fault; after all, she had expressed what I felt was her displeasure over who I was enough times. I loved her and wanted her to be happy, so I made the decision right then and there to stop being so sensitive and to be who she wanted me to be—whoever that was. In my four-year-old mind, I truly thought I was the cause of her unhappiness. I thought if I could just do what she wanted me to do, I could help her and make her happy, and of course, she would be better able to provide for my needs.

I think many sensitive young children fall into this terrible trap. I now know this was the pivotal moment, spiritually, that led to my illness. In deciding to stop being who I really was, I was cut off from myself in a true spiritual sense, and when that happened, I was no longer connected to Source or my own spirit. This left me feeling in a state of complete aloneness in the world and, as a result, a huge amount of fear—pure and simple. Because I felt fear most of the time at this very basic level, I didn't know anything else. I could not have even pinpointed that underlying, fairly constant anxiety as fear; it was just too much my constant companion, my sensitive being struggling to be here and feel safe and loved and important and cared for deeply. Fear became most of what I knew about being here in the world, to the point where I could not really identify the emotion of fear in my being until it became escalated to the point of pure terror. Terror is a sort of acute state of spiritual illness, as opposed to the chronic spiritual illness I usually lived with.

Before the spiritual part of my healing, if someone had asked me if I felt the emotion of fear regularly or often, I would've told them that I rarely felt it. I was that out of touch with the feeling of fear, which was in truth my constant companion. That is a testament to the adaptability of the human being. We can adapt to almost anything over time, even if it is not healthy, functional, or in our highest good. When I speak of the spiritual part of my healing, some of you may be asking yourselves, "Healing from what?" To that I would say healing from the fear that is programmed into us from the time we are born. Fear of being judged, fear of never being good enough (as if we aren't perfect already in God's eyes), fear of not having enough money, fear of having bad things happen to us, and on and on. It's insidious.

If I'm completely honest with you, that is the state most humans live in without realizing it, as most are so ingrained with it from an early age. We are actually taught to be fearful of so many things in order to stay safe, to stay alive. In this process, we disconnect from our spirit. A big part of that happens to fit into a dysfunctional and maladapted system and world. Are you ready to uncover what is maladapted in you? To shed everything that is not who you really are? Because that is what true healing is about. And when we face ourselves in this way and heal our own maladaptation, we help to heal the world, literally.

It is true that we help to create our reality with our mental thought projections. Little by little, from the time I was young, the world seemed to bring me more and more things that I could be scared about. It became a scary, unwelcoming place that literally seemed to attack me as the years went by. Because I'm such a good manifestor, my perpetual state of fear began to create my world, a world in which there were obvious reasons for me to be in fear and a state of dis-ease. By the time I was six years old, I started having alopecia areata, which is now known is an autoimmune disorder. I would lose small patches of my hair, never more than the size of a quarter or fifty-cent piece at a time. This happened periodically, maybe once every year or two, and I was fortunate that the hair always grew back. In retrospect, I can see it happened many times in the summer months, usually when pesticide use was more rampant. You may be able to imagine the level of anxiety I would have as a preteen and teenage girl about losing hair! It only happened about once every couple of years, but for months after, I would stress out terribly and feel so abnormal.

For the most part, it stopped after I left home in 1974 for college. I was able to finally put this together when, twice as an adult, I knew I had been exposed to a large amount of pesticide. A lot of other symptoms ensued, and I again lost a patch of hair. By the time I was in my early teens, I was having issues like eczema from wearing wool clothes, having a dog in the house, and most likely eating foods such as eggs, peanuts, dairy, and pork. My mother finally took me to an allergist when I was fifteen, and he diagnosed me as allergic to all of those things. In addition, I was quite fortunate (as he was ahead of his time back in 1971) that he told my mother to get rid of any scented personal products she was using in our home. He advised her exactly what soaps and laundry detergents were safe to use. Maybe because of this, I didn't develop the most severe levels of sensitivity to scents that many with MCS (multiple chemical sensitivity) do. I did, however, have severe sensitivities to petrochemicals such as gas, exhaust and oil fumes, pesticides, and formaldehyde, among other things.

I most likely had these food allergies at an even younger age too. As I previously said, I had foods I intensely disliked when I was young. I could not understand why everyone raved over pizza and spaghetti and bread (all wheat). Oh, I grew to like it all, to my detriment, as I got older. But my pristine young self knew better. I remember being forced to eat eggs and drink milk. Many mornings were very rushed trying to get out the door to school. The chaos and tension was high in my home with four kids, and I would get sick to my stomach after many such mornings and vomit up the eggs at school. No one ever put anything together, as it was not an everyday occurrence.

My early life and the beginning of my illness also included swimming every summer day in chlorinated pools, living in a home with a monthly pesticide service, using Quell body lotion twice for scabies, flea bombing my home, and moving into a new home with unfinished, exposed particleboard rooms. All of these were exposures that had serious and noticeable consequences for my health. As an example, after flea bombing my home while on vacation for a week, I came home with my husband and six-month-old baby, I became extremely brain fogged, to the point I couldn't function at all. I literally couldn't get off the bed and unpack my suitcase. I wasn't too tired physically, and my brain could not function well enough to think of what actions to take. I was thirty years old; it was in 1986, and that was the beginning of some scary times and symptoms.

By the time I was about fifteen, I was having some serious sciatica and hip joint pain. I am almost sure this was caused by the beginning stages of Lyme disease, unknown to me at that time. It wasn't until I was fifty-two years old that I finally had a

Lyme test done, and even then, according to some standard set by the CDC, I was negative. However, according to Lyme-literate doctors and what is now understood about the progression of Lyme disease, I had evidence of a very longstanding infection with the Lyme spirochetes, or bacteria. I recall visiting with my cousin when I was about eight years old. She lived out in the country in Virginia, and we would just wander around for hours, playing in the woods. I remember one evening coming in, and her father, my uncle, checked us for ticks. He found a few on me and pulled them off with tweezers. I spent a lot of time outdoors the entire time I was growing up, often in the woods, which always seemed to be right next door to wherever we lived. So, there were at least a few tick incidents.

When I was twelve in the late sixties, my family moved into a brand-new house built primarily with plywood, the fabulous (or so many thought, due to the lower cost than the higher-quality, solid wood two-by-fours used prior) new product being used in construction. Engineered wood products such as plywood, particleboard, or pressboard, including OSB (oriented strand board), are all pieces of wood held together with glues, which are most often quite toxic and laden with formaldehyde. This creates a very toxic internal situation for someone with Lyme disease.

Whenever any Lyme bacteria dies, which they will, even if you aren't purposefully trying to kill them (the immune system is always trying its best), they create a very toxic by-product known as aldehydes, which the kidneys primarily have to deal with and eliminate. Aldehydes in too high concentration cause untold misery for the body they inhabit. They are known neurotoxins, or nerve poisons, and they cause the sick hangover feeling we experience after drinking too much alcohol (acetaldehyde is produced in many fermented products, which has an effect on red blood cell structure). This is why living with any amount of formaldehyde in your environment creates such a toxic situation, not to mention for someone who has been exposed to an infection of Lyme spirochetes.

The reason I disconnected at such an early age was because I felt that the way I had come into this life, capable of the most exquisitely profound feelings of all sorts, was just not acceptable. I didn't understand that I had perhaps a greater degree of this inborn ability to experience things so deeply and with so much more passion than many people. Or perhaps I just couldn't shut it off as well as most. When I was five years old in 1961, my mom made me a dress with netting material inside to make the skirt poofier, and I couldn't stand the scratchiness. I whined until it was off of me. She was so upset, as she'd spent a lot of time and effort making it and wondered what was wrong with me. I felt I was an odd duck, a problem, or a hindrance. Hence, being supersensitive, I disconnected to try to fit myself into the round hole everyone else seemed to fit into with great ease. I became as small as I could. While others my age were playing with their dolls and watching cartoons or TV, I was lost in my books and my imagination, wanting to be outdoors playing in the dirt or sand, feeling the wind on my face, my legs and arms or moving or floating through refreshing water at the ocean or pool. I wanted to be as active as I possibly could. I loved roller skating, playing kickball and baseball, swimming, and riding my bike around the block dozens of times and through the trails near our house. I found it hard to sit still for any length of time unless a very good book captured my imagination. School was rough for a child like me.

There was virtually nothing that held much interest for me there. I was so in my own world, or what I know now to be the world of imagination or spirit, but I never verbally expressed it. It wasn't a thing that was encouraged, taught, or accepted; rather, it was dismissed by everybody—society, teachers, my parents, grandparents, and peers. I seemed more tethered to that world than to this one. The main thing I did that people could outwardly see was spend as much time reading as I could, mostly fantasy and fiction. I was fascinated by children's stories of the Bible. I loved playing outside in the woods as much as I could, as there was so much freedom in that. I didn't know anything about astrology then, which could have helped me understand so much about why I was experiencing life the way I was. I was the kid who never spoke in school and spent a lot of time staring out the window and daydreaming. Most of the things taught in the school system bored me terribly. I was the child who was considered spacey or in outer space. I just couldn't make myself fit into the box that was considered the normal way to be. If only I knew then what I know now. There is no normal; each and every one of us is entirely unique, whether we are raised to understand that or not.

The home I grew up in had the somewhat typical issues of addiction and codependency. I have Pluto and Jupiter in the fourth house, conjunct the IC in my natal chart. No wonder I spent hours alone in my room, reading or in a fantasy world, or outdoors. I never did quite fit into any one group of people. I was an extreme empath and a loner child. I did the best I could to treat others with kindness and compassion, never understanding why others seemed either not interested in doing the same or incapable of it. I was a to view many things from a higher perspective, which made me seem even stranger and more like the proverbial space cadet to many.

By the time I left home, I realized that I wasn't thrilled about life and was somewhat depressed. I think I realized this for the first time when I was in nursing school in 1985, and the stress of that made me seek out counseling. There wasn't anything that happened other than growing up in an alcoholic home, which does have an effect on children that is not simple to rectify. It basically creates a state of PTSD, which when not dealt with at the time can affect your entire life.

Something else that could've been a contributing factor was that I went on birth control pills right around that time, and I could not tolerate the hormones in my body. I recall sobbing every day while on them for two solid months. I was told this would eventually get better, but I saw no improvement, so I stopped taking them. Whew, relief! After I got married at twenty-eight and had my first child at thirty, I went on a beach vacation with my mom, who had divorced my father seven years prior. She seemed so different from her usual self, so very happy and bright. I asked her what she'd been doing, and she said she had found a really good therapist to help her recover from the trauma she'd been through. I took note, got the therapist's name, and couldn't wait to dive headfirst into intensive therapy with a very gifted COA (children of alcoholics) licensed therapist.

I do believe if I'd known ahead of time how painful all of that work was going to be, I wouldn't have jumped in so eagerly. But the results were above and beyond worth it. After a year of working very hard with this therapist, I felt as if a two-hundred-pound burden had been lifted from me. I could actually smile and laugh, and I felt so much lighter. That turned into group therapy, then marriage counseling and twelve-step programs for COA and Al-Anon. These were all crucial in helping me regain my emotional equilibrium after such a childhood. And, as it so happened, this all became a solid foundation for the beginning of my spiritual path. It was profoundly helpful in dealing with the physical traumas that began to occur in my life, which I will share in the next chapter.

Dwelling in the Abyss

The wound is the place where the light enters you.
—Rumi

Two of my siblings and I decided to take a cross-country trip together when we were all in our twenties, in 1980–81. It was a wonderful trip full of growth opportunities and learning experiences. My sister and I decided to stay in Southern Florida to live, work, and play for a while. It was a somewhat idyllic time, as we camped in the balmy island weather and began to eat a healthier diet than we'd been raised with. We rode bikes all over the island, played tennis, took up jogging, and had new experiences in a locale very different from where we'd grown up. I particularly loved snorkeling, swimming in the crystal-clear blue/green sea among all the exotic coral and fish, and learning to catch lobster by gloved hand. We learned to live off our daily seafood catch or that of the local fishermen, and supremely delicious bananas and coconuts were ours for the taking as they fell from the trees. Lots of time was also spent swaying in our hammock, sunning on the beaches, and swimming in our little natural pool of water from the sea at the camp.

Quite unfortunately, toward the end of our stay there, we both ended up contracting scabies. A tiny burrowing mite that is very contagious and itches quite badly finds a home, mostly under the skin in places like knees and elbows. We were given a toxic body lotion at the Public Health Department, an organochlorine pesticide (a potent neurotoxin), to apply all over our bodies and sit in for twenty minutes (twice) before showering and washing it off. Being vastly ignorant of the repercussions, we followed the instructions to the letter, which included washing every bit of our clothing and bedding in the same chemical poison. Within a week of doing this, I started having the first real migraines of my life. They would come upon me suddenly and severely. I was completely incapacitated from the pain, nausea, and light sensitivity. I had no understanding of why it was happening. I certainly didn't connect it to the remedy to end our suffering from the tiny mites. I thought I had a brain tumor to have such severe pain and terrible symptoms. I was twenty-five years old.

From that point on, I had a migraine approximately every ten days. Not long after the migraines started, I also began to notice feeling emotionally haywire in public places like churches and moldy underground buildings. I was unable to stop talking to people around me in these places, and I would start crying or get upset when they would try to quiet me. It was quite bizarre. I remember being in church, and the amount of perfume people wore there severely affected my brain, always causing a migraine later. But the first symptom I had was to become a chatterbox. I remember sitting next to my sister in church and whispering to her repeatedly and her shushing me. There is very little understanding, even to this day, about how toxic chemicals and mold can affect different areas of the brain. I am sure some of you have experienced this direct and unpleasant effect yourselves, maybe not even realizing what the culprit was. Those around you assume you have mental or emotional problems, which can make them less understanding when you try to explain that you have a toxicity issue creating neurological and chemical imbalances, not only in your brain but your entire body.

I was still living a normal life, doing all the things that one would normally do, for the most part. I was in nursing school, had my own apartment, and was working at an insurance company part-time. I had a boyfriend whom I would marry in a couple of years, and we spent a lot of time together. We loved spending weekends at his parents' river cottage in the summers. We'd spend the entire weekend boating and waterskiing and having barbecues. So much fun!

One day about a year after the scabies treatment, I decided to go for a jog in the park near my apartment. This was in 1982. I rode my bike over and began what was to be a short jog, about a mile. It was a muggy August evening in Virginia. I remember on the news that day, they had cautioned older, sick people and people with babies to remain indoors because of the high air pollution index. I certainly didn't think any of this applied to me, being healthy for the most part and about twenty-six years old. Not very far into the jog, I felt extremely weak, so I sat down in the middle of the path, as opposed to keeling over on the spot. I proceeded to lose every ounce of energy. I lay down and could not even manage to speak. I was still conscious and watched as people simply walked, ran, or rode bikes past me.

The most amazing part was that no one stopped to ask if I needed help. That still stuns me to this day, but I know it was spirit's way of basically initiating me into the path of becoming a healer. I couldn't call for help. I couldn't even whisper, though I was trying with all I had left. I thought I might die right there, without anyone noticing or helping. After twenty or thirty minutes of lying there, unable to move, I had a small surge of energy. I sat upright, and when I did, I started to sweat so profusely it was as if I was standing in the shower with the water running full force over me. I had never sweated like that. But it did what it was supposed to do—kept me alive instead of dying from heat stroke. I suddenly felt very cool and was able to get up and gradually make my way back to my bike, sitting and resting for a few minutes every ten steps or so until I finally made it back to my apartment. I am certain I had help from God. It was a harrowing experience, and that was not the end of it. I believe it was this very experience that shut down my body's ability to sweat for a long time.

For this reason, sauna as a form of detox was never an option for me in my healing process. After that, sitting in a sauna never made me sweat. I would leave dry as a bone and sick as a dog from all the toxins that had been pulled out of my cells and were now in my bloodstream. My body was simply unable to sweat them out. My body temperature would soar to 101+ degrees, and I would become very lethargic, as if I were sick with a fever, which I was. I could have killed myself trying to detox that way. I have since read that the body's thermostat mechanism can be damaged permanently by heat stroke or heat exhaustion. Fortunately, I finally recovered the ability to sweat more after addressing the Lyme disease and other coinfections that a weakened body usually becomes a host to. I feel sure this is what led to the recovery of the proper functioning of my body's thermostat, as I finally regained my ability to sweat a year and a half after beginning a protocol for Lyme disease in 2006.

In 1990, my health started to decline. My daughters were four years old and eight months old. I rarely had enough help with them, considering the condition I was in, and the effort required to take care of their needs exhausted me to the point I could barely think. Much of this was exacerbated by the fact that we had bought a fairly new home in Richmond, Virginia, that still had an unfinished room, garage, and attic with walls of particle board, plywood's more toxic cousin. Most of the time in this house, I felt far sicker than one feels with a very bad hangover. I would wake up some days feeling as if I had acid coursing through my bloodstream, burning my blood vessels and the surrounding tissues. Many days, I either had a migraine, was nauseous, or was in excruciating pain all over. I had little to no energy and some crazy rages due to extreme liver toxicity.

By this time, I most likely had such a proliferation of Lyme spirochetes that many had morphed into the cell-wall-deficient type that hide out in the very immune cells designed to eliminate them, so my body's immune system was at a loss to even detect them, let alone effectively deal with them. This is what causes the infected person to begin to develop other symptoms affecting the autoimmune response that no one can properly diagnose. Thus, health professionals can have a very hard time getting to the root cause of the many issues that result.

The two years our family spent in this toxic house was a nightmare for me. Very quickly after moving into it, I began having horrifying rage attacks. I had a huge outbreak of acne on my chin (I now know this was my body's attempt to get rid of toxins) and discovered that I had many food allergies. All of this was an indicator of a liver that was seriously toxic, overwhelmed, and screaming out for help. I discovered that removing sugar, dairy, and chemical additives from our diets changed a lot overnight. Not only were the rages fewer and further between, our oldest child who'd been diagnosed with ADHD became very easy to discipline, loving, and peaceful, and she could sit still for more than a few seconds. As if being very sick with two young children to raise was not enough, our oldest child with ADHD had some severe food allergies and behavioral issues from them. Apparently, I chose the deep dive spiritual fast track in this lifetime.

Sadly, the change in diet alone was not to be the cure-all for me. I did calm down considerably and became more able to handle my emotions. However, I was still physically reactive to many things and places and becoming more so the longer I stayed in that house. Soon after we moved in, we gave our oldest daughter a doll for Christmas. It was filled with water and had been treated (I later found out) with antifungal chemicals, much the same as grass seed is to keep it from growing moldy after being watered. I became so reactive to that doll I wanted to fling it out the car window as we were driving down the road one day. All I knew was that every time it was around, my eyes would burn and sting so badly that I couldn't keep them open. It was excruciating. Much to my daughter's extreme disappointment, we had to get rid of the doll. She was understandably very upset. Many things like that continued to happen. We had to let go of many items, large and small, over the years. I had become so sensitized it was nearly impossible to detoxify them adequately.

Many social and family relationships underwent extreme testing, and most didn't make it, as most could not deal with my severe limitations. Some of these were life-and-death issues, but most people cannot understand when they've not dealt with it. I recall my grandmother visiting for my child's birthday party, and she'd used a hairspray that I'd previously said caused symptoms for me. I couldn't be in the same room with her for more than a minute. My eyes would sting and burn so badly I had to run to the bathroom to rinse them out. It was almost as painful as when you accidentally put contact lens cleaner into your eyes instead of pure saline. It was many years before my family understood that they would have to stop using some of the fragranced personal care products (with lots of other chemicals) in order for me to be around them without becoming ill or incapacitated. I had to opt out of society. And thus began my life as a hermit, which wasn't that different from my life as a child.

It has fortunately gotten much better in some sectors of the population, but still not enough people understand the severe, devastating, and life-altering effects of living a toxic lifestyle. The effects may not be the same for everyone, but I feel certain many diseases and maladies, including cancers, could be prevented by simply cleaning up the diet and environment. Much work still needs to be done at the foundation of our society and world, which is becoming obvious as we deal with things like the coronavirus and the severe effect it has on people whose immune systems are overburdened by all the toxic chemicals, heavy metals, and radiation exposure in our world.

A couple years later, I realized that I was not only having severe allergy-type symptoms, but I had lasting symptoms of toxicity anywhere from one to five days after this type of exposure. Like I previously stated, they would range from migraines, nausea, and vomiting to severe fibromyalgia or muscle pain all over, to intractable nerve pain in my back and legs, to severe insomnia and extreme fatigue. On some occasions, the exhaustion was serious enough to make using my chest muscles to breathe very difficult. My skin was also affected by terrible eczema, and like I said previously, my muscles burned as if acid was in them at times. I had trouble exercising, as any repetitive movement brought on severe muscle burning. I now know it was a lot of poisons being released at once into my muscles.

People often told me it was normal lactic acid buildup from exercise and that the soreness would go away in a couple of days. Having been a competitive swimmer from the age of nine to twenty-one, I knew what sore muscles from too much exertion or exercise felt like, and this was completely different. My "soreness" was an excruciating and unrelenting pain, nauseating in its severity, that would last a day and then be gone. At times, I screamed and cried in agony while living in that house.

We finally moved out of that toxic house after two years, in 1992. Nothing I had tried while living there worked to help me feel better. Ultimately, even the dietary changes didn't do much. I tried an allergy food rotation diet, avoiding all chemicals like the plague, killing candida, energy healing, allergy shots, and more. But I was basically in a sea of formaldehyde. We lived in that toxic house for two years, long enough for me to be seriously poisoned.

It is extremely hard to pull yourself up and out of this kind of abyss alone. At the least, you need someone with a functional and probing medical mind to help you sort things out. Honestly, your best person would probably be someone who's quite knowledgeable medically, emotionally, and spiritually and has been there. You become quite incapable of thinking through complicated things, especially an extensive protocol designed to help you regain your health. I would highly recommend finding or hiring someone you trust to work with you and not against you.

If you can't afford this, pray, set your intention to find this help, and see if you can find support from someone willing to do those sorts of things through a local church or place that helps those who are disabled. Other than that, it's really up to you to do the research, develop your own intuition, and develop your spiritual side. I did a lot of this myself in the days before computers, as my journey with MCS, or undiagnosed Lyme, started in 1990. By the time computers were a thing, I was so sick I couldn't be on one due to the electromagnetic radiation exposure. I think it's what forced me to develop my intuition and trust in myself. There was nowhere else I could turn to for good answers most of the time.

During the period of 1990–1992, I gradually eliminated every chemical contaminant from my life. This included all personal care products, such as makeup, shampoo, soaps, detergents, and household cleaning products. Everything was switched over to natural products with no chemical or toxic ingredients. I didn't even wear makeup for years. Unless it was a necessary product, I eliminated it. Certainly nothing like hairsprays or other hair products got any consideration in my world. No fabric softeners at all. Everything was fragrance-free. Most are artificially created chemical fragrances and quite nauseating for the very sensitive. I recall times I would run out of a public restroom with potent fragrance diffusers, gagging and retching as if my body was trying to vomit up the fragrance.

I would avoid going to places with a lot of people, who'd likely be overloaded with perfumed products, or with pesticides, weed killers, new construction, asphalt, exhaust fumes, or mold, which meant anyplace outdoors after a good rain. This meant the only safe places outdoors for me were in isolated areas, which was fabulous for enjoying peace and quiet in nature but pretty minimal for socializing and being part of society. I did not really go anywhere other than the grocery store or the doctor's office, as this kept my toxin exposures to a minimum.

Doing more than that would put my toxicity level over the top, and I would be inundated with symptoms that made it impossible to function well, even just at home. Many public buildings often have too many toxic products being used far too regularly for those who have faulty detox pathways or those who've been poisoned. More and more people seem to be falling into this category, unfortunately, and more will until our society begins to live more in accordance with nature.

Not only did I practice this type of avoidance stringently, but I also began to eat only organic food, substituting nongluten grains for those such as wheat. Sugar, chemicals, dairy, eggs, soy, peanuts, and many other highly allergenic foods became foods of the past. When one first embarks on this type of dietary regimen, the feeling is, *What will I eat?* But there is plenty, and healthier you eat and the more fruits and vegetables, the less hungry you are, since your body is being nourished with far more vitamins, minerals, enzymes, and nutrients. Amazing how that works.

We ended up moving to an apartment, where I spent a lot of time with severe insomnia, which I now realize was my natural detox from that horrendous nightmare of a house. We then moved into another house in 1993, which turned out to have a bad mold problem. Unbelievable, right? Back in those days, not much was known about the toxicity of mold in homes. I wished I'd known when I moved in that a musty smell in a house does not get taken care of by simply removing carpeting and drapes. Knowing what I now know, I would've immediately vetoed that house. When you are that sick, almost anything can become a severe problem to live with. During the summers in Virginia, the mold count would rise extremely high, and I would become practically comatose. I could hardly make myself get out of bed all summer. I lay around in a hazy stupor for most of the summer, barely able to do much more than get up for bathroom breaks and prepare the most basic of meals. I couldn't always manage even meal preparation.

My husband and I finally made a trip to Arizona one spring, and lo and behold, I felt like a different person the minute I stepped off the airplane. The weight I had felt in the mold-ridden house simply lifted off me. I felt as if my body was filled with air instead of wet sandbags. I knew I had to move there. I schemed. I knew I had no energy to carry something like this through in the manner that one would hope to be able to. I was in survival mode, almost like someone planning an escape from prison. The typical way for me would've been to plan it out in advance, perhaps having a place lined up to live in once I got there, or at least reaching out to some Realtors or apartment owners. I would've planned a date for my departure and left on that date. I couldn't begin to do these things, however, as I never knew how I'd be feeling from one moment to the next. I learned how to live flying by the seat of my pants. The extent of my planning was that the very next time I had any energy at all, I would use it to pack three suitcases, sleeping bags, and pillows, one for me and one for each of my daughters, who were six and ten at the time. I was not leaving them behind. They were my heart, my soul, my pride and joy, my reason to be and stay alive.

I asked my husband if he would help us drive to Arizona after I did that, and he agreed to. We left the day after I packed the suitcases. Now it seems ridiculous to have left the city where I had family and friends. But many family and friends simply thought I wanted attention or was a bit weird—a hypochondriac or a complainer. My sister told me that she and others in my family thought I was trying to get attention at first, and years later, they began to understand. My mom and my sister later began to have similar symptoms, although not as severe. I think this helped them to believe the truth of my situation more. Many simply had no idea how severe my condition was, as it wasn't even understood by the medical system.

I was so ready to try living in a place that was less moldy and had fewer industrial chemicals, lawn chemicals, and agricultural pesticides. I figured if I felt better, I would be happier and could do a better job raising my children. My girls and I ended up going alone. My husband was not ready to leave his secure job, so we went without him. We lived apart for a year and a half until he finally felt safe enough with a severance package to come.

I didn't realize I would be gaining another bonus. Arizona was far more progressive with natural, alternative energy and spiritual medicine, modalities that were much more suited to my needs. Allopathic medicine didn't seem to have much to offer me beyond chemical medications, which I was unable to tolerate. Honestly, some of the medications I tried before finding alternative medicine made me feel sick enough to die. What I now understand is that a person with high levels of sensitivity is usually empathic and very sensitive to energy, and vibrations, so how are they going to feel when putting dense, heavy synthetic substances into their being? Not the best, and your body is going to let you know when something is not right for it. I became sensitive enough to detect the vibration of certain chemicals. For example, homeopathy is energy medicine, and in some potencies, there is no original detectable substance left in the remedies, just the vibration, yet those particular ones are the most potent. Some people are sensitive enough to receive medicinal effects from holding a tube of homeopathy or the pellets without even ingesting.

The trip to the Southwest was not without incident. Our older model Honda lost its transmission in the middle of Texas farmland country. We had to be towed to the nearest city, which was Dallas. The first hotel we tried must've just had pesticide service because every time I tried to go into the room, it felt as if a bucket of fire ants had been dumped over my head and were slowly making their way down my neck and shoulders. I had never before had such a bizarre and excruciating reaction.

We realized that Dr. William Rea's environmental clinic (the Environmental Health Center in Dallas, Texas) and hotel accommodations were in this city, so we found out where the hotel was and were able to get a room there while our car was being repaired. Dr. William Rea (now deceased) was a cardiovascular and general surgeon with a well-developed interest in the environmental aspects of health and disease. I also went to an urgent care, as my time in the very toxic hotel had intensified an already existing rash to a state that was unbearable agony. Of course, they prescribed steroids, and I took them, not knowing what else to do. I have since learned that steroids are contraindicated in Lyme patients. Even though it was a very small 5 mg a day dose, my head looked and felt like it had swollen to pumpkin size within two days, and I felt as if I might have a stroke or brain aneurysm when I bent over.

My husband drove us to Tucson and left us in a hotel there that was tolerable, then returned to the East Coast to get back to work. I was far too sick to work, and fortunately my children were six and ten at this time, so they could do a lot to help at home. I called the prescribing doctor the next day, and he told me since it was a small dose and I'd only taken them two days, I could go off without tapering. So wrong. The day after stopping them, I felt yet again as if I might die. Even though I had so little energy and could barely hold my head up, I got my kids in the car and drove to the local ER, where I was treated as if I simply had allergies.

People wonder how we afforded all of this, as I couldn't work. My husband had a fairly well-paying career as an engineer, but still we went into debt. We never owned our own home outright even though we were married for twenty-six years. Nor did we go on exotic vacations or anything of the sort. We bought clothes from the thrift store, as so much of our money went toward trying to keep me alive. There were doctors' bills, oxygen, supplements, organic foods, and natural products. Needless to say, our lives were focused very differently from most others. I am now sixty-four and have never owned my own home outright. It's just not a possibility when you've been this sick and cannot get the help you need covered by insurance. Lucky for me, I came to the realization long ago about what you need in life to be happy and secure.

Not a thing was said there about my oxygen level being only eighty-six! I found this out later, after I left and read the paperwork. In the ER waiting room, I lay across several chairs, having virtually no energy to sit up. My children were the only ones with me, as I knew absolutely no one in Tucson, having just arrived the day before. I was referred to an allergist, which didn't help a thing. I know now that my adrenals were unable to handle getting off the steroids so quickly, and I almost had adrenal failure, which can be fatal.

Even with the extreme effort it took to drive myself to the ER, something in me would not allow myself to call an ambulance. I was so torn with not wanting to frighten my children.

Also, I was tired of people treating me as if I was a wimp, so I tended to do far more than what I was capable of at times. It is a terrible form of invalidation when people refuse to believe what you say your experience is.

I nursed myself back to health. This was still in the days before much internet access was available, so as soon as I felt OK enough, I went to the health food store and asked for help in the supplement department. I ended up getting watermelon seeds to help my body release the excess fluids the steroids had caused me to retain. I rested for several days in the hotel room while my kids quietly played together. We then found an apartment to rent, which actually catered to disabled people, so they were willing to rent an apartment without doing all the usual toxic things like carpet shampoo, paint, and pesticides.

My girls and I had arrived with nothing but a suitcase and sleeping bag for each of us. About a week after moving into the apartment, one day on a walk around the complex, one of the girls saw a woman putting a lot of her kitchenware and furniture on the sidewalk. My daughter asked what she was doing, and she said she was getting ready to take all of it to the thrift store. She then asked if we could have it, and the neighbor very willingly said, "Of course, take it!" So we got a lot of our basic necessities for free in one fell swoop. I was just beginning to see how spirit works in your favor when you follow what is right for you, as hard as it may be.

The next amazing thing was that I found a homeopath, and he prescribed a couple of remedies that cleared up my rash significantly, leaving me in a much greater state of comfort. I felt such great relief soon after taking the pellets. He first had me take the homeopathic remedy Ledum to clear toxins, including those from vaccinations. The next day or two, I began the specific remedy for the rash, and within two days, I was significantly improved and much more comfortable. This would not have happened back in Virginia, not then anyway. Spirit was showing me I had made the right choice and was coming into alignment by the little miracles that began occurring. Miracles, time and again, showed me I was on the right path.

Calling for a Lifeline

May all your hopes, dreams and prayers be carried
upon the wings of eagles, high into the air, and there
to fall softly, upon the ears of the Great Spirit.
—William Purcell

The soul always knows what to do to heal itself.
The challenge is to silence the mind.
—TheRandomVibez.com

I grew up being a swimmer but was terrified of the water as a very young child, until my mom thought it might help to push me into the deep end of a pool. I was eight years old in the summer of 1964, and we were members of a private swim and racquet club in Richmond, Virginia. She was exasperated and didn't know what else to do. While this was harsh and I reacted by feeling terrified and losing some trust in my primary caretaker, I made it out by frantically dog-paddling to the edge of the pool. It actually worked and quickly helped me progress beyond my unreasonable fear. I became an avid swimmer grew to love the water.

I believe that experience taught me to jump in where angels fear to tread and to have faith that everything will work out beautifully, or at least as it is supposed to. After all, it sure has worked for me that way many times. Early on in my unwell days, with this sink-or-swim mentality and knowing I had nowhere else to turn, I acquired the habit of asking for God's help, especially since most of the other help I was offered made me feel far worse. When asking for spiritual help, I always included all of my spiritual helpers, ascended masters, and archangels in my prayer, as I figured I needed all the help I could get. The ascended masters comprise what is known as the spiritual hierarchy of earth. They are believed to be spiritually enlightened beings who have been human in past incarnations but have undergone a series of spiritual transformations called initiations.

From the first time I asked for help from this realm, I received the help I needed—help that had not been available to me here on this earthly plane. There are those of us who go through something severe as a way of finding our unique spiritual path. Of course, I can easily say I wish it weren't so, but a way to reach that state of surrender seems to be through some of the most severe trials and tribulations life can offer.

Once when my children were very young, and we'd recently moved into the previously described toxic home, I was having a particularly frightening and dreadful day. I blacked out every time I tried to stand up. I felt really sick, as if I had almost zero life force energy. Doctors did not know what was wrong with me. The only diagnosis I received at that time was severe allergies with the highest eosinophil (white blood cells) count my doctor said he'd ever seen. I was most likely in a highly inflammatory state due to all the bacteria, coinfections, and the die-off poisons created from those, in addition to a mounting chemical overload in my body.

The primary cause was a toxic slew of ingredients and not allergies. It took about five years after that to be diagnosed with a severe environmental illness (multiple chemical sensitivities, or MCS), along with systemic candidiasis and other bacterial, viral, parasitic, and mycoplasma coinfections that had almost completely overwhelmed my immune system. My doctor had put me on Nizoral to kill candida at the time, and the die-off was so severe I couldn't stand up and remain conscious. I quit taking it after three days. No doctors or medical professionals knew how severe the die-off, or herxheimer, reaction could be in people who were very sick. The herxheimer, or die-off, is probably well known to many. It is the effect on the body of a large amount of pathogens dying and being released at once, which can create unpleasant symptoms. The most common are headaches, fatigue, nausea, and brain fog. In the early nineties, many health professionals seemed to lack any knowledge of more gentle ways to deal with eliminating this kind of heavy infectious load.

Most of what I found out in those early days was from my own experience, using myself as a guinea pig. I didn't even have access to many alternative health professionals when in Virginia. Most allopathic medical professionals didn't have a clue about chemical poisonings, toxicity, or Lyme disease. I did find a clinical ecologist, who was known as a glorified allergist. He knew a lot about living in a cleaner environment without all the chemical toxins but was still treating to a large degree for allergies, which just didn't work for me. However, I did receive validation from him on the chemical reactions, in addition to support for receiving disability benefits. I also found out some interesting things, such as my body had become reactive to my own progesterone. I've never been able to tolerate even a drop of any progesterone or herb that increases progesterone without some ill side effects. In fact, menopause was a huge blessing for me; as my progesterone levels dropped and stayed low, I felt better and better.

A major reason so many in our world are now sick with autoimmune disorders, cancer, and heart disease is the way our society lives, totally out of alignment with nature and the natural order of things. It does not contribute to good health in any way. We become overloaded and overburdened by the plethora of toxic substances that ultimately lower the body's ability to fight off infection. Add vaccines, electromagnetic radiation, being super sensitive to energies that are out of alignment with the natural order, childhood trauma, ingrained false thought paradigms (*I'm not good enough* and poverty consciousness are examples), and genetic snips in detox pathways, and you have the ingredients for a slow decline into dis-ease of all types. It was only much later that I realized the die-off or toxic load the body is attempting to eliminate can actually kill those as ill as I was. Because of this, it is crucial to learn how to detoxify your body as slowly as you need to. I will talk more about how to do this later—under the supervision of a really good health care professional who understands this premise, especially if you are extremely ill.

I was beside myself with terror that I may not be able to survive to take care of my children. I knew this terror was creating huge unrest in me. I fervently prayed to God to give me that peace that passeth all understanding, which is spoken of in the Bible. Within a few minutes, I felt a miraculous peace descend over me and envelop me, and I knew I had been heard. I suddenly felt extremely calm and beyond peaceful. It was indeed a peace that passed all understanding. I was unable to feel the extreme worry and stress I had just been feeling a few minutes earlier. It felt as if angels were holding me in their wings. It was so beautiful and such a profound respite. And then I actually heard a voice say to me, "You are *alive now. Now* is *all* you have, so do not worry about the future."

I call it my *Power of Now* moment, as it is pretty much exactly what is spoken of in the book *The Power of Now.* I understood it on a level that is hard to explain, but it gave me such great peace to realize I *was* alive and there was nothing else to think about except being here now and being in utter gratitude for that. It changed my outlook. My life became a meditation of moments. I knew from the profundity of that experience that it was time to stop stressing over the future, which didn't even exist yet, since there was not a lot I could do about anything that hadn't yet happened. It was time to start living in the present. This helped me to calm my terror, as that terror had been all about what might or might not happen in the future.

There is nothing to be gained from placing your attention in the future, because it doesn't exist yet. All there is, all you really have, is the present. The past is gone and unchangeable, other than to rescript it in your mind or heal its traumas. Mindfulness is being aware of what thoughts are in your mind as much as possible and to redirect them to a place that is current with exactly where you are at this moment. This is what brain retraining helps you do. It can heal you on the deepest levels, even on the physical level. Healing often comes from a higher place, not easily understandable for the human intellect.

Every malady and illness and even injuries have spiritual causes that have been determined quite correctly, and if you are honest with yourself, you can often see these reasons have been emotions or ways of thinking you have stubbornly held onto for many years, resulting in your body becoming ill or starting to break down. An example is liver problems; a spiritual cause is repressed rage. I have had issues with liver toxicity due to my illness and a lot of repressed rage from my childhood. This is why once these spiritual/emotional causes are addressed, many seem to have miraculous or faith healings, as they reach a place where they have no other options than to let go and surrender to Spirit. To allow your mind to be in any place other than the moment in front of you is a huge waste of energy and creates a lot of unnecessary emotional and mental trauma. It is without merit and has zero productivity. This kind of mental trauma greatly reduces your body's ability to heal.

After that major spiritual experience, I knew I would continue to seek whatever treatments might help me regain my health, but I would no longer spend time freaking out over my current condition. I learned to ask myself, "Do I have everything I need right here and now?" from a point of view encompassing life or death. The answer was almost always "Yes, I do." For sure, I would no longer stress out about my future. I still wasn't ready, even at this point, to take on full responsibility for my health. I wish I could say that was when I started to tune into my own intuition about my body, but I was still choosing to leave my treatment up to my doctors.

I had been trained from birth, like most of us, that the "authorities" or someone who knew more than I did would take care of me and would have my best interests at heart. In the long run, I found out no one could know more about my body than I did. All the tests did was show numbers that medical doctors had been trained to believe meant certain things. It didn't always work and often had detrimental effects on me.

For an example, valium and Benadryl both have agitating effects on me. I could forget about sleeping whenever I took either. Restless, crawling sensations in my muscles made sleep and relaxation impossible. Many drugs have the opposite effect on me. I once tried one-tenth of a dose of a sleeping medication, and the next day, I could not formulate words or sentences. Episodes like that with synthetic medications were quite scary, and after numerous and various tries with different meds, I finally gave up on that avenue of help. I later realized that even if the drug didn't have an immediate side effect, it was another poison in my system.

As another example, it's common for doctors to think that too much sodium is bad for anyone. There is a lack of understanding that, in many diseases, especially those of the immune system or toxicity, the cells become more permeable, causing inability to hold onto enough sodium. Some people, such as myself, desperately need extra sodium in the form of sea salt. Especially when I was very sick, I needed it; otherwise they had trouble getting a blood pressure reading. It behooves you greatly to listen carefully to your body. No one knows it like you do.

More than likely, because of being a sensitive, I came into this world to live in alignment with my spirit and the natural order of things and guide others on that path. For the most part, that is not stressed as important in allopathic medicine. Yet it's the most important thing that will help you on any path, spiritual or recovering your physical health. At the time, I still believed that God was an authority who resided outside of myself. Even naturopathic doctors and those trained in other fields of alternative medicine didn't seem to have answers for me. I had to come so close to death numerous times before I finally understood I was on my own but could always call on the help of the spiritual realm. It didn't seem like a lot at first, but it was all I had, and it turned out to be *everything* I needed and more. You see, when you connect to the unseen, you are connecting to your own spirit. We all have this connection, as we all have a spirit form.

Eventually, I made the decision in 2008 to ignore any medical advice and to tune into myself for my answers about what to do to get well. I made this decision after another close call having to do with a bad dental infection that became systemic. I began to understand how much the medical field perpetuates fear in people—fear that if you don't do as they say, you will die; fear that your condition is progressive and fatal; fear that there is nothing that can be done for you. We have been living in a world programmed by fear.

For the most part, as a whole, allopathic or conventional medicine in the West ignores the spirit and the spiritual causes, as well as the help available from this realm. No longer would I be at anyone's else's mercy, health professional or not. I would take the reins of my life, and if I failed, I would have no one to blame or look to but myself and Spirit. In essence, I was taking complete responsibility for my health and well-being and invoking the help of the spiritual realms. This was the best decision I made for not only my healing but my entire life.

It was stunning how rapidly I started to improve. Within a week of tuning into what I should do for myself, I noticed I no longer had any anxiety and was sleeping much better. This change came from making my diet a 100 percent organic, raw, vegan diet. It was quite noticeable within three days. The changes over the next few months were profound. My body was finally getting the nutrients it needed to function well. My energy levels skyrocketed. I felt so calm and clearheaded. The best part was that it opened me up even more on the spiritual level, and my ability to just know things I needed to know increased. It really does open you up spiritually to detoxify your body in a way I couldn't have predicted.

Little did I understand then that my spirit connection would never steer me wrong, as long as I took the time to tune into the information I received and not what my head intellectually and logically assumed or thought was correct for me, like the doctors had been doing. From that point on, I never again listened to any fear-based tactics. A fear-based tactic is medical professionals pushing things like vaccinations on their clients, telling them that if they don't, they are at much greater risk for contracting illnesses. This puts a person into a state of fear, and from here, you aren't even to access your intuition easily, which always has the best answers for you. It would be better for them to help their clients to understand that the body has its own excellent capacities for staying well and healing. There are many natural proactive things one can do to optimize the health of the body. Introducing foreign, man-made substances is not one of those things and has a very detrimental effect on many.

I am now completely turned off by fear, as fear is what strips us of our true freedom in life. When I finally made the conscious effort not to succumb to fear or the what-ifs that may or may not happen in the future, I began to hear my inner voice speaking loudly and clearly to me. Yes, dropping the fear is what set me free and made a place for me to step into my own power, to stop being anyone's victim, and to hear that tiny voice inside that has only grown louder and more and more consistently validated ever since. We are a society that has been schooled in fear. We're so used to it we accept it as normal—when it is anything but and so out of alignment with universal laws. When you live out of alignment with universal laws of nature, you open yourself up to disease and the opposite of what you're taught you will have if you remain fearful.

We fear economic collapse, illness, global warming, Armageddon, terrorist attacks, alien invasion, and natural disaster. Then there are the more personal fears, such as getting fired from a job, having a close relationship end, losing our looks as we age, or being shot, mugged, or raped. We are told from a very young age that we have to do everything according to societal standards, and because it is in us from a young age, we never question it. We take it as the law for what we need to do to be safe and secure and have a good life. We do many things without thinking about whether or not we want to do them. We sometimes end up behaving in ways that are inauthentic to who we really are and doing things we normally wouldn't do to hang onto a relationship, simply out of fear that we will be left if we don't. Yet that might be the very best thing that could happen! If you look deeply within, there is usually some illusory reason for the fear, though it seems very real.

Anytime you do anything on this premise, you are more than likely giving up a part of your true authentic yourself. And the sad fact is that we've been taught to fear doing things based on our innermost longings and authentic selves. It's a pervasive technique that's been designed to keep us under control and going along with what those we have perceived as authorities or in control of us tell us we need to do. So many things we are taught to do are rooted in fear, from the very beginning of our lives. We are trained to look outside ourselves for everything and to operate from logic and the left side of our brains. And the fact is nobody can take control of you or has any authority over you without your consent.

We run to the doctor for anything wrong with our bodies and are told that the doctor knows best when it comes to our health. We are taught from early in our lives to listen to authorities or those we deem have more power or knowledge in certain areas. There is a belief in the supremacy of allopathic medicine, and the belief is also that it will save us if we need help. We've been trained to look outside of ourselves for help, which takes us that much further away from inner wisdom, and this is where you will always find what's best for you. It just takes practice, and confidence grows over time through repeated successes.

My naturopath found, at one point, that I was low in B-vitamins and suggested I begin eating more red meat. Instantly, I felt my whole body go into the gag reflex. I had been noticing when I cooked meat the smell was like rotting flesh and repulsed me. The very next day, instead of doing as he had suggested, I began eating a totally raw diet. I had been eating two raw meals a day for almost a year at that point, but I took the next step and took it to 100 percent raw. Within three days, my severe anxiety was gone, as well as a few other symptoms that had plagued me for a long time. This let me know I was finally on the right path for myself, and nothing needed to make medical or logical sense anymore in order for me to follow what my body knew it needed.

From a spiritual standpoint, looking back on all that has happened in my life, I believe that my being had been in a process of ascension, or purifying on all levels, mind, body, and spirit, and I was finally helping it along by lightening my body's load in the way I intuited was best. This is what has been and is being required by many at this time, to help in healing not only ourselves but the entire planet—radical self-responsibility, self-love and self-care. It is so true that what you do for yourself, you do for everyone else as well. It ripples outward.

To place any focus on what you do *not* want draws it to you automatically. This is true in every area of life. It is so important to lift your vibration up to include only that of the light, that of good and that which you *do* want. This is a powerful thing to know, to have faith in with all your heart, and to fully understand. Not only will this begin to help heal you, it will lead you into a more pure Christ consciousness. Jesus said in the Bible that we would do the same as He did (as far as healing and miracles) and more. It is time for that now. We all have this power, and we are all capable. You must start to believe in yourself first and foremost. *I am that I am.* Really ponder what that means. The translations are "he who becometh" or "I will create whatever I will create." And you can and will.

This is part of how I started to grow spiritually and how I began to understand that the direction I chose to focus my mind and thoughts was of crucial importance in my times of greatest need. I started to really understand that we are not alone here and that we have everything we need at our disposal, even when it seems we do not, through the power of our minds and our connection to the spirit realm.

I remember once asking Spirit to help my P450 pathway enzymes to function efficiently, to remove whatever toxins were in my system, making me feel sick at the time, and lo and behold, I felt much better within about thirty minutes. I began to understand that if we can change what's going on in our bodies, that which medical science has told us is permanently damaged or broken, then we most likely have the power to change our DNA. There is now evidence beginning to support the truth in that.

When you are so far down the rabbit hole, with seemingly intractable symptoms, to the point it's difficult or impossible to live with any normalcy, let alone work and support yourself, it's hard to remember the spirit world and ask for help. So, may I impress upon you to start making it your daily habit to ask for help in as many situations as possible when you are feeling well. This way, not only will it be less likely to come from a place of fear; it will become ingrained in you and be so automatic that on days when you are not all there, it will come easier. Also, you can ask for spiritual help ahead of these times. Those in the spirit realm will understand and be there to help you, regardless of whether you are in your right mind enough to remember them. I used to place Post-it notes all around my house—on the fridge, on the bathroom mirror, and next to my bed. I would write my prayers and what I needed to do for myself in times of crisis when I couldn't think. I began to remember to look at the notes after several times.

Countless times, I pray, asking for God, Jesus, all my spiritual guides, angels, counselors, teachers, doctors, and nurses. Every time I ask, I also thank them and give them my utmost gratitude, even if I can't know with my physical senses that help is there for me at that precise moment. I act as if. I operate on faith. I believe, and because I believe, this asking has never failed me, not once. They *are* there. They *do* help. *Ask*. Ask, and it shall be given. The spirit world is far more advanced vibrationally and in a place of pure, unconditional, high-vibrational love we cannot imagine.

It is crucial to pay serious attention to the spiritual side of yourself. As anyone who has been sick or debilitated for a long time knows, this state of ill health or dis-ease can be devastating to your mental, psychological, and spiritual well-being. There is little that can lift your spirits and emotional health as much as knowing that you are supported by the spirit world with profound love and healing. It is yours for the taking. One thing that exacerbates poor health is shutting your heart down, as when you do this, your entire physical being follows suit. Opening your mind, heart, and being to the fact that there is more than what we've been taught there is is so important in healing your body. The longer you put this off, the more traumatized your body and psyche are likely to become.

I feel that brain retraining or serious, in-depth spiritual work/ healing of some kind is crucial for recovery from MCS, FMS, CFS, Lyme disease, and many other illnesses (especially the autoimmune illnesses or any other dis-ease state that medical science alone is unable to cure). The more committed you are to this concept, the greater your chances of becoming healed, whole, and healthy once again. It *can* happen, with your determination, focus, trust, faith, and discipline. Each of us has an amazing ability to heal ourselves. When we get into a state of fear and distrust, we move into feeling helpless and frightened, and we lose sight of this ability.

When we're calm and centered, we have much better access to our internal wisdom. This is why meditation can be so helpful. I had extreme trouble meditating when I was at the height of the illness, as my body and mind were in such a terrible state of unrest and mind racing, which so many reactions and neurological symptoms seemed to escalate. I learned to use the time when I would wake in the morning or the middle of the night, when I was more at peace, to try to tune into my inner self. I always asked my spirit guides for help with this, as it seemed so hard at first. Often, especially when we first get sick, we look outside ourselves to others, especially those in the allopathic field, to help us heal.

However, doctors cannot do the crucial groundwork you need. It is a shame that we are led to believe someone else can do it all for us—and should. It is true that we come into the world alone, and we go out alone. We also heal alone primarily, with the help of our inner wisdom or higher self or God, whichever you choose to call it. Of course, you need the help of others, but when you put yourself in charge and depend on your intuition (not what your mind tells you makes sense, or what others tell you that sounds logical), you will drastically increase your chances of success. It's an inside job. Your management and your own personal CEO resides within you. Pay attention to yourself. Tune in, trust yourself, and make yourself your first priority.

I hope you are starting to see how important the spiritual component is. Religion is great but most often teaches us that all of our power comes from outside ourselves, from God, who is separate from us. But God is not separate from you. Religion, from my standpoint, often seeks to control, primarily through fear tactics. Fear is not love or loving. Fear robs us of our peace and joy. Love covers us in peace and joy and everything of the light. If we are all one and God is the Father, and we are his children, then we are all part of God, sparks of God's creation. He cannot be separate, apart from, or outside of us. He has given us the power and free will to use as we please. Why not take this God-given power and learn how to use it to heal yourself?

As Jesus said, "You shall do this and more." He was speaking truth when he said that. You can learn to harness this power and use it for good. How do you think folks miraculously heal themselves from cancer? They have learned how to harness and direct this power we all have. You simply must believe, as Jesus also said. It was truly wonderful that an ascended master such as Jesus incarnated in the flesh to try to teach the world universal and sacred concepts. And there have been many other ascended masters, each teaching in their own ways. However, it is time for many to awaken to the fact that all is not as it seems with religions. Many organized religions, for the most part, do not want us to know we actually have the power within us that we have. That's too bad, because people are awakening to their own power and connection with God, Source, and All That Is.

It took me two long decades of being extremely ill until I finally made the choice to surrender. I wish with all my heart and soul I had decided to do this letting go earlier. Of course, I wouldn't have learned many things if I had. It was not completely a conscious choice either. One day in 2010, after having done a protocol that helped me tremendously to eradicate the Lyme, I decided that I had spent entirely too much time striving for good health and still had not been able to make it to that golden 95–100 percent that I wanted so badly. I thought, *I am fifty-four years old, and I may have only twenty more years here on this planet. Do I want the next twenty years to be spent stressing and striving over what I don't have that I want so much? Or do I just want to enjoy every moment I may have left to the greatest degree I possibly can?*

As I lay there on my bed one day, it just happened organically, and it seemed such an easy choice, in part because I was absolutely bone and soul weary from the constant striving. I said to Spirit, "OK, I get it. I finally get it. I get that in this life, I came in to experience being sick, and so I just accept that now, but I'll be damned if I am going to let that take my soul, my spirit." In this moment, I knew that my soul wanted more than anything else to live from a higher-vibratory state of joy, peace, and love, regardless of all outer appearances, meaning how I thought anything should be in my life in order for me to experience happiness and joy.

Within a very short time of this surrendering process, I also decided to let go of needing anything to be other than how it was before I could experience true joy and happiness. It was as if I had decided to grab that proverbial brass ring for every bit of what I was worth for the rest of my time here. I gave up needing to be well and needing anything outside myself to be any certain way I might think it should be in order to be happy. In essence, it is letting go and going with the flow of how things are in the moment and being in absolute gratitude for everything. If you stop and notice how you're feeling while you're holding onto a thought such as *As soon as I no longer have chronic fatigue or severe pain, I can begin living my life*, you will notice you feel as if you're striving for something different from what you have. If you simply look around at what is and feel a sense of gratitude for what is there, it takes you into a very different state of being, one from which healing arises.

I truly believe that letting go in this moment of ecstatic revelation was the ultimate path to my healing. That was the beginning of my true spiritual awakening. I have since told many people a profound healing can result from letting go of the intense desire and need to heal—which can result from knowing you have everything you need within you and that God has a reason for everything being the way it is, a perfect plan for your life.

This is a spiritual truth that I now understand, and it can change anything in your life. Let go of the need for anything to be any certain way before you can reach a state of happiness, peace, or joy. The truth is it all comes from within, which is why the gurus say you have everything you need within you, the entire universe. Within a short week of this surrender, I had a spiritual kundalini awakening and what seemed a miraculous return to wholeness and my true state of being. Kundalini is a latent female energy, or shakti in Hindu, that lies coiled at the base of the spine. When it awakens, it begins to move upward through the seven chakra centers and out through all the nadis, another Indian term. The nadis are nerve channels or meridians all over the body through which prana or life force moves. This is what leads to an expanded state of consciousness.

I can now see my journey has been a personal spiritual quest with deep insights and meaning and growth that I can now share with others on a similar path. There are still days that are hard, as it's a never-ending journey. However, the more backup one has on the spiritual level, the easier it becomes, and the more sure and unshakable you begin to feel with this solid foundation beneath and all around you.

A Thought Map to the Light

All healing is essentially a release from fear.
—*A Course in Miracles*

Positive self-talk is one of the most important things you can do when you are recovering and have gotten into a state of doing the opposite. Keeping your focus on how bad things are (and I know they can be) will not help your recovery. It serves to pull you down further into a state of fear and misery. Disciplining yourself to practice positive self-talk will improve not just your health but your entire life.

During my time with severe MCS, I would worry about a certain toxin being present in a place I would be going, and I would actually start to experience the symptoms of that exposure before I got there. And often, this place would have the exact toxin I'd been reacting to before I even arrived! I realize I could've been psychically picking up on the toxin ahead of time, but it was amazing how the psychic knowledge could also create the physical symptoms, although not as severely.

If I was going to a park, for example, and had any fear about there having been fertilizer recently used on the grounds or too many people with heavy perfumed products or fabric softeners permeating the air, I often began to feel sick with a headache before even arriving!

I now know I was helping to create the possibility that I'd receive a certain exposure with my focus and thoughts on the feared toxin. It is hard to fathom how that happens, but I've noticed it enough times to know it's true. It is still not completely understood how much control our minds have over our lives and bodies. There are well-known professionals who are aware of this and doing their best to educate society. Dr. Bruce Lipton and Dr. Joe DiSpenza are two such well-known public figures, and they have some very good videos on YouTube.

I have since come to learn that I must be exceedingly conscious and careful of my thoughts. As I know now, after having consciously watched what happens, my thoughts do help to create my reality. A part of it has to do with what you are saying to yourself on a consistent basis. Becoming aware of your internal dialogue is crucial. It can be a game of sorts, where you begin to pay close attention to your internal messages on a daily basis, especially during times when you feel stressed. It is so important to stop and ask yourself, "What is the voice in your head saying to you?"

For example, before arriving at the park, I might think, *I wonder how many people will be there today with heavy perfumes on?* There would then be the resulting feeling of tension or stress in my body just wondering about it, as I knew from past experience how awful the effect could be. In retrospect, the healthier option would've been to focus my thoughts on all the fun I was going to have being outside and in the fresh air.

It is a far healthier option emotionally, physically, and spiritually to focus on what brings you joy, peace, happiness, and pleasure. It is terribly unhealthy for you to stay focused in the past or the future. Be present to what is right in front of you. I know firsthand how difficult the constant looping is to extricate yourself from, but it is your most important ally, Spirit aside, in recovery from any illness. In great part, that precipitated your dis-ease to begin with.

So, stop. Ask yourself in stressful moments, "What am I saying to myself?" You will find that often there are negative, fear-based, old-paradigm, disempowering thoughts that continually loop in your brain in response to trying or challenging situations, which bring up fear or feeling like a victim of circumstance. I urge you to begin focusing your thoughts more positively; instead of focusing on and repeating to yourself how you can't tolerate pesticides or whatever other chemical seems to abound, focus on what you are able to tolerate and how thankful and grateful you are for its presence in your life.

And if there is nothing, focus on what you would like to be present. Sooner or later, you will be drawing whatever your focus is to yourself. It is the same as when you are buying a new car and have decided which model you want. Suddenly, because this is your focus, they start showing up all over the place. Maybe they were there all along and you just didn't notice, or maybe they weren't. They certainly weren't part of your reality before your new focus.

It is this crazy power we all have. You don't have to believe it's true to start. You only have to want the change badly enough and want to take steps away from feeling like a victim. When I was extremely ill, my thoughts were based on how I couldn't tolerate any number of chemicals, places, or people without becoming even more sick. It was a terrible way to live and had a devastating and limiting effect on my reality. Although it was my truth in reality, it didn't help me with my level of peace or happiness or my ability to recover. I began to understand this concept when I began a brain retraining protocol and started writing down all my thoughts when I was stressed. I was stunned by the level of negativity and fear behind my thoughts.

When I started to choose positive thoughts more consistently, I saw how much better I started to feel emotionally and how much happier I was, and in turn, my reactivity level began lowering almost immediately. I cannot begin to tell you how empowered and free I felt. I was happier, more functional, and eventually healthier and less reactive. You can choose to examine your thoughts and the emotions that follow in every situation. Ask yourself how you can change your thoughts, which in turn change your reality.

For example, you have an event you are excited about, and the day arrives, but due to unforeseen circumstances, you are unable to participate or go. You may feel very disappointed and sink into negative feelings. But you can choose to think something like, *It must be in my highest good not to go to that event today. I don't know what the reason is, but I will accept that this is so.* Your mood and emotions won't spiral out of control. We are all in charge of our thoughts to a much greater degree than we know. It is a superpower to be harnessed.

We need to step into our responsibility for our lives, health, and recovery to a much greater degree. I understand that horrifically terrible things happen to people. After all, I was bitten by an infected tick, undiagnosed for decades, and subsequently had mutations in my detox pathways, causing me to become poisoned by the slightest whiff of a chemical toxin anywhere I went. I cannot begin to impress upon anyone who hasn't experienced that particular sort of awful chain of events just how devastating it was. But it helps the situation not one iota to stay in a state of blaming or bitterness. It activates and changes everything to step into your own power and responsibility for yourself.

It is not my intention to make anyone feel blame. My intention is to help you feel more empowered in your life and begin to change the seemingly unchangeable effects your particular situation may have had on your mind and psyche. Honestly ask yourself if you want to continue to be a slave to your thoughts. That is what you're doing when you allow them to run your life. You have become a slave to your ego or mind. It doesn't bode well for a happy, high-vibrational life, let alone an optimal state of health or peace of mind. Never let your mind run haphazardly or without direction.

Be the master of your own mind. Discipline it just as you would a dog you don't want ruining your house. Keep it cleaned up and pruned as if it is your most prized and beautiful garden. The fruits and flowers it will bear for you are golden. You do this by becoming aware of your thoughts, paying attention to them, and writing them down. Decide whether or not you like having those thoughts and the resulting feelings. Then create sentences that you would like to be thinking and hence creating in your life.

Decide you will think these more positive thoughts like mantras or affirmations as much as you possibly can. Then make the effort to carry it out whenever you are thinking about it. This exercise has the effect of making you more aware of what you are thinking in any given moment. It is up to you to reformulate what you want to be thinking and then to put it into action by chanting it out loud or thinking it repeatedly, as it will help to reprogram your brain.

It is incredibly powerful. It is the way it works, but we are taught early on that our outer reality controls us and that our thoughts are not controllable, that we will think certain things because of what is happening. The only thing wrong with this is that you perpetuate issues by operating in that way. This is where our power as humans lies. We have this incredible power to program our minds. This is what we should be teaching young children.

I am the owner of a house built specially for those with chemical and mold sensitivity. I have rented out a room in my home to a number of people who have been ill. All of them lived with some level of fear, seemingly because of their illness and all the chemical atrocities of the world perpetrated upon them, all things happening outside themselves. One photographer friend, Julie, came to visit from Washington state. Before she came, she stated several times, "I'm very worried (worry = a minor state of fear) about the roads being too muddy to travel in and out easily by car." I said to Julie, "You really don't need to worry. This is Arizona and the middle of winter, and we rarely have enough rain to make the roads muddy for more than a few hours."

However, the day of Julie's scheduled arrival, it had poured nonstop for two days, and by the time of she got here, the roads were just as she had feared. I had never seen them so flooded, with mud thick and deep. Not once in twelve years of living there had they ever been as difficult to drive as they were for the exact length of her ten-day visit. Never again have they been like that, and this was nine years ago. I would say that was some pretty powerful creating. If I hadn't witnessed it firsthand and known the conditions prior to her visit and since, I may have thought it just a coincidence. Nothing is a coincidence. Everything that happens is divinely orchestrated by unseen vibrational energies all around us. It was a lesson to me to be aware of the thoughts, energies, and vibrations I am emanating.

Another woman with MCS I rented to, named Marianne, was worried about animal droppings and the infectious issues they might create, although I had no known infestations of anything at the time and communicated this to her. It almost seemed like she was actually trying, through her excessive fear over it, to create the exact thing she was worried about. During her stay, she found all kinds of bugs in her room, and by the time she left, I had begun to find animal droppings all over my house, in drawers and closets and corners. In the years I had lived here, I had not seen that before, and since she left and I cleaned them all up, I haven't seen a single animal dropping anywhere in the house.

The same thing happened with dogs in my neighborhood. Marianne was terrified of barking, vicious-appearing dogs, and when I went on a couple of walks with her, the dogs came out in numbers. Each time a dog approached us, Marianne's face turned as white as a sheet. Although she proclaimed she was not in fear, it was evident to me that she was, and I thought the dogs could feel that energy of fear. There was a big black dog, several smaller, viciously growling ones, and a large pit bull. They became more aggressive in their barking and stalking of us than I had ever experienced in the twelve years I'd lived here. Even after she left, this continued for several more months. Every time I'd take a walk, I'd have to mentally and sometimes verbally speak to the dogs, letting them know everything was OK. Finally, they stopped bothering to come out, let alone bark.

My friend Katy, who also had MCS, came for a visit and let me know she was extremely fearful of kissing bugs, which have been known to cause those with chemical sensitivity to have adrenal exhaustion and more intense reactions to everything. Kissing bugs are flat, cone-nosed black insects that are pretty stealthy. You can't feel the bite, but it leaves a two-pronged mark and itches intensely after. She was coming in March, and the kissing bugs had never appeared before May or June. However, once again, I watched someone's fear (worry or concern can also do this, as it focuses on the object with negative attention) draw the very thing they were afraid of right to them. Three kissing bugs showed up in her bed during the two weeks she was here. If I hadn't been there myself to witness these and other events, I would not believe it. It was amazing to watch it happen repeatedly, and it is something I will never forget.

The power we all have is incredible. I feel those events came as a gift to me so that I could witness firsthand just how powerful people's thoughts and emotions are. It wasn't just me having good or bad luck. I saw others creating their own virtual hell right in front of me.

The major theme that comes up repeatedly when people who are sick and suffering ask me how I achieved wellness is that of the mind's role in helping to create and facilitate illness or wellness. It is, in my opinion, the most crucial part of achieving and maintaining a state of being that is in harmony with everything. Happiness, joy, peace, and gratitude are the foundation for a life of health and well-being on all levels. How do we reach these feelings then? Many people say, "I will be happy or joyful or feel gratitude when everything is going perfectly or my way. I will be happy when the outer circumstances of my life match what I think they should look like or what I want them to be."

It is just the opposite. Feelings of happiness and misery come from within. It is your choice as to which you wish to experience and create for yourself. It honestly is. No use getting angry about it, as then you put up a defense against that which you truly wish to have in your existence. It is seemingly a paradox, but we create these feelings by deciding what we allow into our minds and therefore our consciousness. This is a universal law that many of us want to ignore. "Really?" we say, not wanting to believe, preferring instead to remain fully ensconced in the role of the victim—the role where everything is done to you and happens to you. I was there for most of my life. It is a place of nonresponsibility that keeps you unempowered. How much better life becomes once you decide to step fully into your power by admitting to yourself that you have a part to play in changing your inner world. It has an amazing effect on your outer world and how you view it.

This is how one steps *out* of the role of the victim and *into* full consciousness and responsibility for one's life. It is freeing to practice this in all situations. When you do this, your spiritual growth proceeds exponentially. It may seem too hard, impossible, or a fearful and burdensome responsibility. In truth, it's much easier to point the finger outward at everything and everyone else, but it won't get you the results you so desperately want. Don't take that road. This is your time to pave a new path for yourself and your world. What you do for yourself, especially in this regard, you will do for all those around you, as they will get to see you and learn by example.

We can only heal by looking at what is within ourselves. We cannot heal until we take this step and take it seriously. Be willing to do the deep soul-diving work. Find out what is really inside of you, just waiting for some acknowledgment from you. This can feel very scary at first, and yes, it takes immense courage and a willingness to become very honest with yourself. It will be the most self-loving thing many will ever do for themselves. A good way to begin is to meditate. It may be hard for many to meditate, as it often brings up issues you weren't willing to look at before. Another great way to do this is to journal about your thoughts and feelings and where you think they originate from. If this doesn't help you, a good therapist or an energy healer who knows how to help with emotional issues might be helpful. There are many out there.

It takes being willing to look at yourself any time something bothers or disturbs you, even if you think the cause is someone else or a situation in your life. Become reflective and look within to gain a deeper understanding of why it is creating such an issue or disturbance for you. I guarantee you it is always about you. This is a fabulous step in empowering yourself, so that your life is led from within your strong, centered self. You will never find yourself at the world's or anyone's mercy again.

I have to say I was stunned when I started to become consciously aware of the direness and negative quality of my thoughts. It was a real eye-opener. These thoughts had become so automatic and based on my outer circumstances I was unaware or unconscious of the fact that I was even having them. This unawareness will make you incapable of changing your situation or your internal environment. One of the darkest thoughts I had while ill was that I was probably going to die because of the supposedly progressive nature of my illness. It was not a thought based in acceptance but in fear and despair.

I had stopped watching the news years before, as I was aware of how impactful the fearful things being spoken about affected my sleep and overall feelings of wellness. I distinctly remember watching all the broadcasts about Hurricane Katrina back in 2005 and feeling very sad about all the devastation. I went to bed and lay there awake half of the night, thinking about it and crying. If you think this helps people in their moments of great difficulty, it really doesn't and actually makes their situation worse, as you add your negative, lower-vibrational feelings to it. Thoughts are energy; they go out into the ethers and have a definite effect. This is why prayer works. You pray for and think about what you *do* want to manifest. If other people spouting negativity could affect my health, immune system, and peace, why on earth couldn't my own internal negative thoughts do the same? I understood I needed to focus on my internal landscape more than anything else and that it is here that my true power and connection with Source is derived.

It was about then that I began to have a dream that I could get well, and I started to put all my focus, intentions, and energy on that. The universe started to show me the very things that would help me achieve that and brought me to situations, people, and places that were exactly what I needed at the time. I realized how much I needed to change my thought patterning, and little by little, it started to happen. For instance, once I made that intention to do whatever it took to improve my health, aside from just eliminating toxins and bad foods, the ball was set in motion.

Just a week later, I was talking to my friend Elyse, and she said she'd heard of a protocol called the Marshall protocol. The second she said it, I knew it was something I should check out; it was a gut feeling. I did find out more about it, and I knew I needed to try it. My gut feeling was not wrong. It was this very protocol that helped eradicate the Lyme, even though I was never diagnosed with it until after I'd done the protocol and it helped me so much. Others doing the protocol urged me to get tested, as they knew it helped Lymies so much. All I knew was it was good for autoimmune diseases of all types but helped those with Lyme the most.

Over time, I had to let people go from my life who continued to focus their thoughts and energy on the negative—that friend who's always complaining about their life. Or the one who calls you to dump their issues but never listens to you. No one wants to be around someone who is always voicing negativity and pointing out what is wrong. That pulls others down. It is the last thing someone who is sick and trying to recover should be doing—being a sounding board for someone who is intent on dumping or complaining and never taking responsibility for themselves. This creates a huge energy drain and burden on you. Pay attention to how you feel and your energy level after spending time with a person like that.

I know. I was one of those people. It is hard not to complain when you are overwhelmed and feel horrid most all the time. But it doesn't feel good emotionally to the listener. How can you blame them for that? You want to feel better physically, and they want to continue feeling good emotionally. It doesn't mean they are in denial about your condition or how terrible things are in the world; it just means they want to remain on an even keel, which supports a higher quality life. So, consider journaling about your feelings, getting a therapist, or, best of all, retraining your brain to hold uplifting and positive thoughts.

Yes, I know it seems as though it would feel good if everyone empathized with your illness, listened to everything you're going through, and bent over backward to change their lives to be supportive of you. I am telling you, the best support you will ever find is within yourself, changing your thoughts. You can no longer hold anyone else responsible or accountable for you feeling better. It does not work that way. When I changed my thinking to more positive thoughts and gratitude, I was often pleasantly surprised how people responded to me in the ways I always wished they would. So many people suddenly wanted to bend over backward to help make my environment more conducive to feeling well.

The way you choose to think actually changes your vibration, which people respond to in kind. You create your world with your thoughts. Therefore, it pays huge dividends to become conscious of your ability to control your thoughts. If your thoughts can change how others respond to you, think of how it eventually changes all the cells in your body. I know you have heard of people who have cured themselves of cancer by visualizing it away. I truly believe they focused so positively and so much on being cancer-free that they helped to create that new state of well-being in their physical vessels.

Let me explain. Say you are chronically ill, and much of your time is spent feeling miserable, and because of this, your mind spirals into constant negative thought patterns. For those with chemical sensitivity, it may look something like this: "I can never go out in public because all the perfumes, cigarette smoke, and pesticides being used will make me sick. My body is just a lemon. Why do I have this problem and others don't? I will never get better. I am told this is a progressive disease, so that means I will never recover. It's not possible." It can also expand to include other people. For example, "I feel I have no one who understands my illness or cares at all that I have been sick for so long and suffering so terribly."

The truth is that none of this really matters, although at the time it seems as if it matters a lot. What does matter is that what we are doing is harming *ourselves* by getting trapped in a self-defeating and energy-draining way of thinking that spirals down. All of those thoughts are about things, people, and circumstances outside ourselves, none of which we have any control over. I have learned to *let go* with love and compassion. Forgive it all—forgive the people involved, forgive the ignorance of society at large, forgive even the companies making the chemicals.

Why? Because if you don't, you are hanging onto negative, hurtful, low-vibrational energy within your being, and it takes away from your body's ability to heal itself. You can choose to remain there, but you're only hurting yourself, and the negative energy you create will change nothing in your outer world. In fact, it will make it more negative. All of those people who don't understand what's happening with you are where they are at, and no amount of your negative energy is going to change that or help you in any way. It is nonproductive and a huge waste of your time and precious energy. *You need all of your energy for you, and you alone, to come back into a state of health and balance. It's really about learning how to set and keep good energetic boundaries for yourself, realizing that your energy is a precious commodity and crucial to your recovery. I highly urge you to do whatever it takes. Really take some alone time and be a fearless warrior for yourself. Leave no stone unturned until you figure out how to do this for yourself in the most soul-searching way you possibly can.*

Stop yourself and notice during the day what your thoughts are and which direction they are taking you. Notice whether they are positive or negative, happy or sad, loving or fearful. Notice the feelings that result after you think these thoughts. Sometimes it seems as though we don't have a choice about what we are feeling, because we are not in control of everything happening outside ourselves. But when we think this way and make our thoughts and our happiness dependent on external circumstances, we make ourselves victims of the world at large. In actuality, it is all happening inside. We are helping to create our reality every minute of the day. To create a better reality is work and takes discipline and stepping into your power. Most with MCS are perhaps closer to being able to do this than many others with other illnesses, because most of us fall into the trap of blaming the world for our woes and symptoms. It's easy to do, because the rest of the world is using many toxic chemicals, and it looks like that is how the illness originated.

Many of us from a young age have had a spiritual disconnect, and this is truly the place where it all starts, regardless of physical appearances. Mine happened at the age of four. Because of this disconnect, I was not operating in true authenticity with myself. As a result of my disconnect, I became a huge people pleaser, meaning I neglected my own needs quite often so that others would be happy. That is a form of being disconnected from yourself. I will explain more about this later.

Once you begin to realize this and start to address the issue from this angle, you can begin your healing process on an even deeper level. To recognize and fully understand this is to step into your power in a huge way. It will allow you to accept that, yes, the world is using many harmful chemicals, and terrible things happen every day to many, many people, but swimming in fear and negativity and bitter, angry thoughts will be of no help whatsoever to you or anyone if you wish to move in a positive healing direction. It's a seeming paradox that changing your thinking or your internal environment, regardless of all outer appearances and realities, is crucial to changing your health and life. But it's a paradox that holds great truth.

Notice what you are talking to others about, even what you allow yourself to watch on TV and in movies and what you read in the newspaper. I also refuse to watch news media programming, as that is what it is, programming your brain to think about and generate much fear over meaningless issues in the overall scheme of your personal life. And that couldn't be more true, especially now in the year 2020. How many of you have realized how often the news pushes COVID-19, masks, and social distancing down our throats? It's become constant. There is a reason they do that, if you're ready to awaken to it. Once you're awake to that, no one can control you ever again through your consciousness or thought processes. This is empowering.

Why do you think spiritual gurus and alternative health experts encourage us to stop watching the news, as well as reading things and watching movies that induce a state of fear, worry, or anxiety? All of this, what you are taking in and putting out, has a profound impact on your mind and psyche and thus your body, where it eventually or rapidly filters down to. Negative emotions have a direct effect on the body at the microscopic cellular level, and the same is true for the positive emotions. According to *The Science of Emotions* by Fahad Basheer (2015), anger and lower emotions cause cellular contraction. Joy and happiness cause your cells to expand. In which state do you think your body operates at optimal levels? Negativity shuts off flow, while positivity opens the gateways to flow. Your body responds accordingly in the most precise of manners.

Once you have taken the time to become aware of and actually write down as many of your repetitive negative thoughts as you can think of, you might be shocked at what you have allowed into your mind. Our thoughts can be like healthy, fertile soil or a landfill piling up and choking out the tender green plants we are trying to grow. When we understand what our minds are capable of creating, we see they are nothing short of awesome. It is amazing what powerful beings we are. Watching what you allow yourself to think and beginning to change it requires a desire for positive change and a lot of discipline. It is all about learning and watching to see the results. It can become like a game when you realize there is truly no need to beat yourself up or judge yourself for infractions. It is all part of the learning process. It does take time, but you will get better and better and begin to see positive changes and reap rewards you weren't previously aware of being able to, based on your own power. This is where we as humans are evolving to.

The brain is operating the body; therefore, our thoughts have the power to create what our bodies are experiencing, although this is a process that takes time to hone and will not happen overnight, so patience is required. We need to be very careful what messages we allow to take up residence in our brain, because we want to be the pilots of this vehicle. We must stop blaming anyone or anything outside ourselves and turn the focus *within* ourselves, to our inner thought processes. Every time you say, "Well, x happened, and I had no control over it, and therefore, I am suffering," you reinforce the message you are sending to your body that outside circumstances are in control of how you feel, and it will happen again and again. Your potential to stay trapped in a vicious never-ending cycle of progressively becoming sicker and sicker is greater. In other words, our thoughts are the number one toxin, or alternatively, when changed to positive thoughts, they can become the top detoxifying and cleansing agent in our lives. You have the choice to instead say to yourself, "I feel bad, and this bad thing happened, so that surely seems to be the cause of my suffering. However, I am tired of this endless cycle I seem to be a victim to, and I want to change it right now. I am going to open myself to the idea right now that I am sick and feeling miserable and frightened for another reason." That reason could be a spiritual disconnect. Perhaps at some point in your life, you were traumatized enough that you shut a vital part of yourself off, and when you did, you felt you had no power. It began to seem that all in life happened with or without your input.

When we feel powerless, we begin to act like victims of our situation, and after a while, maybe a long while, the world begins to give us back exactly what we are putting out there energetically. So the next time you notice yourself falling down the rabbit hole of negative self- talk, please stop. Do yourself a favor and resolve to change it however you can. You can make the intention to take your power back. It seems easier to take on the victim role, because in the role of being empowered we accept greater responsibility. It is far easier to do what we've always done and find someone or something else to blame for the predicaments we find ourselves in. But if we truly want to see profound change occur, we need to step away from the victim mentality, "Everything happens outside of me or to me," to the role of total empowerment, "It is all happening within me. I am a microcosm of the universe, and I help create it all right here from within myself." Yes, it is work not to point the finger at someone or something else and instead focus on the inner, but it is work that creates the deepest kind of transformation and is undeniably rewarding, in addition to helping create a better world and life for all.

No amount of blaming (even accurately) anything outside of myself does anything positive to begin my healing. Yes, it is good to know the outer physical causative factors, but once it's happened, one of the ways to heal is rarely talked about or acknowledged. And that is to look within: confront your inner demons, your thoughts, and intend to heal those as one of your top priorities. This concept is one that can help you progress in every area of your life, not just your health but your relationships and your work. I, for one, would rather take on that responsibility to create a life of beauty, health, ease, abundance, joy, bliss, and creativity.

Anytime we fall prey to the desire to have someone outside ourselves to blame, or want someone to change, we are simply avoiding what could be looked at and changed within ourselves. Most of the time, we do this out of fear that what we find will be extremely painful and difficult to accept about our past or ourselves. In truth, it can be difficult and even quite shocking. But I promise that you will not die from doing it; it may feel as if you're going to, but that is your ego dying more than anything. And you will have freed yourself from your past and any negative or false ways of thinking you've been holding onto. All dark or negative paradigms or thoughts you have about anything, including yourself, are simply untrue. Truth always encompasses the highest vibrational feelings and thoughts possible, as this is where your spirit resides. Your body is temporary and here for a finite period to learn lessons through this particular vehicle, while your spirit is eternal. Part of the reason for the body is to learn or relearn love and that all is love while in the physical form. This is a path for those ready to take the next step out of suffering. It is not given to us on a silver platter; it is a path that must be chosen and then walked with every bit of awareness and discipline you can muster. It's not easy, but it is vastly rewarding, and you are brought fully home to yourself.

As mentioned, I once tried a brain retraining protocol. One of the first assignments was to write down all of my worst fears and thoughts. I stunned myself with what I wrote. It wasn't until then that I became aware of just how much fear I was living in, and some of those fears were magnified by some of the horrifying things that I had endured. However, I can now see that they originated from a very early age and continued to grow as I magnetized fearful events to myself more and more over time. Many, including myself at that time, would say they are not in fear. This is a fallacy. We don't feel fear when we've become accustomed to living with such an enormous amount of it over a lifetime, as it is all we really know, and we become desensitized to the level of fear we actually are in a good part of the time.

When I wrote down my negative thoughts and could see how I was thinking, it became clear to me that I was having those thoughts with a high level of fear. One of the sentences I wrote was "I am so sick I can't understand why I am not dead yet. I probably will be very soon." If that is not an attention grabber full of fear and lack of hope, I don't know what is. However, this is a thought that occurred to me with increasing regularity. I was living my life in fear that I would die almost by the hour. And yet I was still denying that I was in fear. Seeing that thought written down was stunning for me. I encourage you to do the same with writing down all of your worst, most negative thoughts. It is crucial if you want to begin to change them, which changes everything eventually. It is the same with positive thoughts; the more you focus on them, the more often they come or take up space in your mind, and the more accustomed you become to having them. It is a form of discipline or programming in the opposite direction of what we've been taught to do.

Sticking with the pattern of assigning blame outside ourselves only creates a negative, helpless, victim state. After twenty years of being sick, I finally realized that was not the path I wanted for myself. So I woke up, stood up, and began to walk the other path. I am grateful that I did. I am so much happier. I gained so much control over my life when I took responsibility for creating my circumstances. These days, I make a practice of asking myself, "Let's see, do I choose to think happy, positive thoughts today regardless of any outer circumstances? Yes, yes, yes! I do!" Try this, and you will slowly discover that we have the ability to shape our lives far beyond what we've thought and been taught. It is incredible to realize what power our minds have. If more of us understood this on the deepest level, we would make every effort to shift our focus immediately. We would desire consciousness of every thought and control of *those*, more than control of our environment or the people in our lives. This is a major spiritual premise that leads to huge spiritual growth and, hence, emotional and physical ease and wellness.

The moment we let go of thinking that we need to obtain information, or that it will all be OK if we just lay out a plan and follow it to the letter, we begin to help make our brains more elastic and flexible, the way they are supposed to be. This practice of letting go of entrenched ways of seeing limited possibilities or ways of things happening is what will change your world. This is the way brain retraining works. It opens our minds and thought processes to many more possibilities, and then we get to choose. It opens up greater channels of flow coming to you.

1. For starters, you can simply set the intention to be more open-minded and accept that there are many ways of looking at things in the world.
2. Begin a gratitude journal or make it your daily practice to be in gratitude for everything as much as possible.
3. Write down as many of your thoughts as possible, especially the ones you have the most often.
4. Decide if those are thoughts you want to keep having. If they are negative or fear based, most likely you don't, especially if you have a vested interest in changing your inner world and outer circumstances.
5. Then you get to decide exactly what thoughts you do want to have, based on what you want to see created or manifested in your life. Write down the new positive replacement thoughts.

6. Make it a point to have a visual associated with the thought and also a positive emotion. Picture yourself in the new world or circumstances that your thought is about.

7. Feel how good that feels. Enjoy the uplifting feelings. Drink them in. There is hardly anything you can do that is more beneficial for your health and life.

So often with a devastating illness like MCS, we get stuck in one way of thinking that spirals downward into a negative state. When I was very sick for a long time, I would often wish I could just have one day in which I could be well and not have any thoughts of MCS or the vast number of things I had to do just to stay safe and somewhat OK. Well, this is precisely what has happened in my brain after retraining it, thinking positive thoughts, and experiencing a shamanic healing. My brain actually has a hard time with or can no longer hold thoughts of illness or MCS in current or future time, as it knows on a spiritual level that this is not truth. It certainly is no longer my truth.

The joy this has brought me is almost unfathomable. It is as if my brain has been released from a prison of its own making. Because my mind can no longer think about my body being sick or affected by outer things, my body no longer is sick or affected by outer things. It seems like magic, and medical science has yet to understand how this works. All I know is that it does indeed hold a huge key to our physical well-being. The world had a part in how my brain was functioning and the state of fear it kept me in, but ultimately, I was responsible for changing that pattern.

The best way I can say this is that whatever you focus on (or let yourself think about repetitively) will most assuredly be drawn to you and into your life. This is why protocols that focus on retraining the brain work as well as they do. They work to stop the vicious cycle of repetitive negative thoughts, making room for thoughts about what you *do* want to see in your life, and therefore the ability to create your life anew.

I was going to visit my mom years ago, and she had an oil-based heater. I had severe muscle pain from the petrochemical fumes it put into the air of her house. Before going, I retrained my brain to believe I tolerated petrochemical fumes perfectly, well with my muscles being perfectly at ease. And that is just what happened. At this point, I had a significant amount of detox work under my belt.

With brain retraining, I began to focus my thoughts on positive things, such as spending time at the beach, which I love. I would change a thought about what I was going to endure from some unknown exposure in the future (causing anxiety and worry) to a thought of being at the beach, lying in the warm sand, feeling the sun, feeling the ocean breeze over my skin, smelling the salty air, listening to the lull of the ocean waves crashing against the shore. It became my personal cyber experience in my brain. This actually led to me thinking more and more about what I enjoyed doing and then making it possible to do those things in my life. Dance and learning astrology were just a couple of those things. It was life affirming to think about happy, positive, and creative things—and life destroying to do the opposite. I had exponentially more energy to do the things that brought me joy and happiness. You simply must try it. It's incredibly powerful.

I know it seems far-fetched to think one can heal from a devastating illness in this manner, and if I had not personally experienced this, I would be inclined to doubt it. However, it has been shown to work in many cases. Of course, one should always strive to live in as healthy a manner as possible, eating organically and drinking the purest water, and not filling one's life with toxic chemicals. However, these things just focus on the physical, which is what medicine typically does. There is *so* much more to our healing, and when you allow space for this truth in your life, you may begin to recover fully.

We become ill from a disconnection with spirit, and this creates emotional trauma, which subsequently causes fear, anger, rage, resentment, hatred, and negativity. When we are disconnected on the spiritual level, we feel alone in the world, and it seems to be a rather frightening place. We end up feeling quite fearful and other negative lower emotions. The fear is so ingrained in us from such a young age that we grow up not even aware of the level of fear we carry. Faulty mental constructs begin taking up space in our minds.

An example I'm sure most can relate to follows: *if we don't perform adequately in school and go to college, we will not have enough money to survive well when older.* Here we get into fear of our very survival being at stake. Never mind any truth in it, it's a terrible way to motivate people, especially young people. It can take the joy out of learning for the sake of learning. The young person feels they have to live up to some performance standards set by society in order to have a roof over their heads and food to eat when they're grown-up.

This is mass indoctrination, brainwashing of the highest order. It seems true because that's the way our world has operated for eons. Is it really truth? You have to go deep in your soul to find the answer to that. Using only logic or the mind will tell you it is true and to remain operating from this state of soul numbness and your intellect. That is the ego, and it's there simply to keep you alive. It doesn't care about your soul's purpose or individuality or sovereignty or authenticity—not one iota.

Yet people can survive amazing things through the strength of their spirit. Not only are we taught by society, and possibly our parents, that life is full of hardship and things to be feared, but the negative emotions we experience help to reinforce and create further negative mind constructs. Physical illness can result from the body listening to the mind. The opposite is also true; a strong spiritual connection is soothing and peaceful to the soul. The emotions are then calmed, and the mind can begin to work for us instead of against us.

Let's take a closer look at how fear impacts the body. When you are fearful, even on a subconscious level, the many muscles in the body get clenched tightly. When the muscles and cells are clenched like this, they are in a state of contraction and the body cannot release toxins or function as effectively. Every cell in your body responds accordingly, holding on tightly and blocking the natural flow and process of all forms of energy and life. We've all had that gut-tightening effect when in a state of fear, even minor fear.

While in a state of fear, and this includes minor anxiety and worry, your sympathetic nervous system is triggered from a sudden release of hormones. That stimulates your adrenals, causing them to release catecholamines such as adrenaline and noradrenaline. This affects your heart rate, breathing rate, and blood pressure. Your brain is less able to think clearly, causing you to have poorer decision-making skills and forget crucial things. It has a profound effect most of us don't really understand on every system and cell of our bodies. Ongoing processes such as this can end up damaging your blood vessels and increasing the risk of heart attacks and strokes. There may also be anxiety, mood changes, bowel issues, weight gain, headaches, and insomnia, among other unhealthy states.

This is a massive factor in how we become so ill and toxic. Imagine being overloaded with toxins in this state. It becomes exceedingly difficult for your body to eliminate these toxins at the microscopic level. It can only operate at the minimal life-sustaining levels. You know how difficult it can be to effectively eliminate your bowels if you are or have been stressed and hence contracted? It's the same principle. Every biological system and process in your body is affected. How can it not be? It makes even more sense to keep your mind and thoughts operating from the highest vibrational state possible.

The infiltration of negativity and fear is not life building; it is health and life destroying. Fear and all negative emotions are quite destructive. They take energy *from* you, as opposed to adding anything, energy or otherwise, to your life. Think of the saying *love makes the world go round.* It is true on levels we have perhaps not previously understood. Love and positive emotions, such as gratitude and joy, help us to realize all things are possible. They draw good things and good energy to us and make us feel appreciative of life and all it has to offer. This is the way in which we create our existence.

It is your choice. Which do you want? Do you choose positive or negative things happening in your life? I know I am making this sound simplistic, but in reality, it is much simpler than our minds or egos would have us believe. Have you ever noticed how someone who is cheerful and optimistic seems to have more good things happening to them? And how someone who focuses on what is wrong in every situation never has a shortage of things to complain about?

It is true that what you focus on persists, but it is also true that what you resist also persists. This is why nonattachment, learning to feel at peace with whatever happens, knowing it is all outside of you and nothing can really affect the truth of who you are at the deepest level, is the foundation of Buddhism and many spiritual paths. Who you really are, at the core of your being, is love, joy, peace, and ecstasy. When you know this, the rest is simply a matter of disciplining your mind to think the thoughts that bring peace and joy to you whenever possible.

I do not mean to ignore when you have feelings arise for healing or to be transmuted. What I am speaking of are the many situations we are presented with where we have a choice in how we react with our emotions. A certain amount of introspection needs to occur to determine which is which. This can often be determined from being the witness to our own drama and asking crucial questions about why we are feeling what we are feeling. Ask yourself, "Is it based on a faulty thought I've carried with me all my life? Or is it coming from an actual trauma that needs healing?" Once you know it is from a false thought or construct, you can choose whether you want to keep that or not. But this is only possible once we face the truth of how rigidly we may be holding onto some very outdated ideas.

We have been given free will. It's just that most of us use it from an unconscious place to experience the negative side of duality and haven't yet remembered we can do the opposite. It seems too hard because we have been taught that we must use our minds to keep ourselves safe and alive. This is the ego, telling us all manner of fearful thoughts that create separation and anxiety instead of the absolute love and unity that spirit is and knows. Going back to this way of spirit led being creates some of the most dramatic changes in our lives, ones we never dreamt were possible, until we did it. Change from the inside out is essential to recovery and unification of body, mind, and spirit.

The perspective I have gained allows me to respond to chemical reactions with curiosity. I can now say to myself, "What is it in *me* that is making me feel sick from chemical exposure? There is something in me that is making this really hard on me. Is this the path I want to continue on, or do I want things to change for me?" I had far better luck gaining my health back by changing myself from an internal level than trying to force the world to change or even understand the need for change, from a place of being sick.

I realized this after years of trying to do everything right not only for myself but also in situations happening in my life, yet nothing was changing, not on a personal, community, or global level. No matter how many chemicals I removed from my life, how much I isolated myself, how safely I built my MCS safe home, how active I was in attempting to have policies changed that would better protect society, or how vigilant I was about never allowing anyone to enter my home who wasn't the most chemically inert person, I was still unable to function normally and participate in the normal life that others take for granted.

I knew something inside me had to change. What I didn't realize at that time was how centering and grounding this whole process would be for me and how much I desperately needed that. It is a huge piece of what brings your focus to the internal as opposed to the outer. And this is what you need to access your natural intuitive state.

I started by just lying in bed each morning after waking up and noticing the thoughts running through my mind. Most often, they were quite negative and had me starting my day in a state of worry or fear. It seemed I would never get ahead and get well. The best way I found to calm these was to simply say to myself the opposite of what I had just thought that wasn't so pretty or nice. I forced myself to do this, and as if a genie had waved a magic wand, it often changed the course of my day as well as my mindset and subsequently my emotions.

I all too often used to awaken with a stabbing headache. I recall having the simple thought, *I feel so awful. My head hurts so bad*. So, I began to change the thought to *I feel wonderful. My head feels fabulous*. Now, of course it did not feel fabulous at all when I woke up, as I said. But this simple change from a negative thought to a positive one told my body that I was in charge of it. And that simple act helped me to have the energy to get up and begin my day. Miraculously, from the very first time, the headache would rapidly diminish or altogether vanish within about twenty minutes. Most of my previous headaches lasted anywhere from a few hours to twenty-four hours or longer.

I began experiencing emotions on the far more positive end of the spectrum, and I found this to be healing in and of itself. It started to seem as if my problems were not so insurmountable after all. Because of this, the universe started to naturally open its bounty to me. My intuition became accessible, and ideas and answers started to pour in almost daily. The universe I knew seemed to no longer hold back what it had to offer me. As a result, the world I knew began to look different little by little.

Forget for just a moment what medical science is telling you. There is another very powerful realm, more powerful than any of us can understand, that is at play here. Medicine says we have genetic mutations, because they don't really know how else to explain it. They are leaving out everything but the science, and even that is not all known! I believe we are coming into a time where we will understand more and more about how you can create anything you want with your mind. Even if we were born with genetic mutations or faulty detox pathways, I believe we can change that if we choose. We have the power to program our bodies with our very powerful minds.

I experimented with this early on, as I was told I had something wrong with something called the P-450 enzyme pathway. So one day when I was feeling really ill, I focused very intently on my P-450 pathways being fully functional and clearing whatever was making me feel so sick. Within a few hours, I felt as if I'd been in a detox chamber, as clear and clean as a newborn babe. It was a fabulous discovery. I believe, as many others, that the day is coming when people will be able to grow new limbs, eyes, and teeth.

Whenever you're detoxing and feeling really bad, that is when it is hardest to have positive thoughts about being well and recovering. Just remind yourself of this and give yourself permission to be down, but still try to monitor your thoughts so you are aware of just what a negative spiral can occur. The more aware you are, the less you will allow yourself to go there.

Though it really is as simple as making a choice, it also takes discipline to retrain the habitual pathways in our minds. Many of us need help in the form of a program or a regular practice that will help us take control of our runaway thoughts and begin to change the false constructs of the mind and ego. I highly recommend a brain retraining program, but you may be drawn to another path, such as neurolinguistic programming, which is a behavioral technology related to your thoughts and language, or shamanic healing, which involves a shaman experienced in working with the spirit world and the elements of the earth. Seek out help in whatever way you feel most directed to.

I started to see firsthand the power of my mind to create things in my world through an incident with a neighbor. Neighbors had bought the twenty-acre parcel next to ours and were planning to build a home on it. One of my worst reactions when I was ill had been to formaldehyde, which is commonly found in building materials, such as particleboard or pressboard. I became so sensitive to formaldehyde that I became very sick from it, even if it was as far away as two city blocks! It presented an extremely intense issue for me, especially since my previous reaction had been severe enough to cause such a migraine I could feel my brain pressing on the roof of my mouth and passed out.

This was a major reason we had moved out to a rural area. Most of our neighbors were living in mobile homes built before being delivered to their properties, so there was no phase during which exposed pressboard or particleboard would be outgassing into the air. At first, my husband and I were both somewhat terror stricken, knowing this could potentially make me ill enough to have to leave our home while the house was under construction. It seemed I had little to no control over what happened outside me. I knew that the best or maybe only thing I had going for me was where I chose to put my focus. So I decided that I wanted to stop focusing on what the neighbors may or may not do on their property. I told my husband I no longer wished to discuss that possibility or anything having to do with it. I asked him if he'd be willing to do the same, to stop any focus on it whatsoever, and he agreed to.

No more mention was made of it in our household, and I was able to stop thinking and worrying about it. I understood that any kind of worry about something that was not happening in the present was pointless and actually harmful to my health and state of well-being. About a month later, we received an email from the neighbors, completely unsolicited, informing us that, miraculously, they had decided not to build on the property after all. We had not even asked them to keep us informed, nor were we very close to this couple. They simply chose to let us know. I was being shown there are other forces at work.

Thoughts and their subsequent emotions carry and project a phenomenal amount of energy. This is universal law, as real as the law of gravity. Maybe you have heard it said that emotion is "e-motion" or *energy in motion*. "If you want to find the secrets of the universe, think in terms of energy, frequency, and vibration," Nikola Tesla said. Thoughts precipitate emotions. Be very mindful of your thoughts. It is one of the most crucial steps in regaining your health and wholeness, creating prosperity, and attracting love and the many other things we want to show up in our lives.

Do you know how you can feel the mood in a room, or just feel when someone's mood is negative without them saying anything at all? That is because that emotion is the *energy* being projected. That is what Jesus was trying to teach us. He was full of love energy, thoughts of love, positivity, and healing, which changed everything around him because of their energy. We are all sparks of God's creation. We all have this ability. Just make the decision that you will love yourself enough to do the myriad things needed to get well—not only to think well but to eat well, drink plenty of water, get enough sunlight, learn grounding and energy-clearing techniques, exercise, detox, and avoid toxins. You will set into motion the love energy or Christ consciousness.

You can find grounding and energy-clearing techniques easily on YouTube. A great energy-cleansing tool when you're ill is to take a lukewarm bath with a cup of sea salt and a cup of baking soda. This is also very relaxing as well as slightly detoxifying.

I wrote the following when I was working with my intention to manifest abundance and all I need on every level of my life: "The ocean of life is lavish with its abundance. All that I need and desire comes to me in the perfect time and space. My good comes from everywhere, everyone, and everything. I thank you, helping spirits, today and always, for helping to create in me a clear channel for this continuous abundance to flow. I am blessed beyond my wildest dreams. My intention is to live in limitless love, light, and joy. My intention is to release all resentment, anger, and fear in my life and from every cell in my being."

Other intentions I set for myself include the following:

- to shift out of all limiting patterns, karma, conditioning, and history
- to open to the path of my heart and transcend the lessons of duality (Pain and suffering versus joy and peace are examples of duality.)
- to bring forth and directly confront the root causes behind feelings of unrest or sadness
- to regenerate all the cells of my body daily

You can write your own. This is how we create our reality, our existence. It may not happen right away, but it will happen in the timing that is perfect for you. The more you can detach from the need to have anything be a certain way, the more you can let go and trust, and the easier your entire life will be. The universe can work in its unique synchronicity to bring you exactly what you have put your focus on. Use your powerful abilities, your faith and responsibility, to create wisely for yourself.

It is very much like building an empire of sorts, from a starting point of demolition. It's not an easy task, but neither is it impossible. Never allow yourself to believe otherwise. Even after you have achieved this, there are others who will still be in great fear and disbelief that we have any power over our bodies and lives. You may need to learn boundary setting with some so that you are not pulled back down into the quagmire of their makings. After all, you didn't work this hard to easily give away your valuable God-given gifts.

Boundary setting can show a great appreciation for these gifts. You are saying that you will reserve your energy you've created for yourself, and this is right to do. It is not selfish, especially when you are sharing the fruits and knowledge of your new bounty with others. Learn to be healthfully self-serving. It is the highest form of self-love. This takes a lot of practice for many of us, but it is well worth the effort.

I have enjoyed learning about the Buddhist concept of nonattachment and the way of the Tao, because I understand now that attachment to suffering and pain is a huge part of what holds us back in healing. As humans, we are unwittingly quite attached to the pain of heartache, sorrow, and suffering. As long as we attach any importance to them, focus on them, and allow ourselves to suffer over things happening outside ourselves (which we have no real control over), we will be attached to these feelings.

Even physical things happening in your body are not your true self. These are happening as a result of a disconnect from your true self, your spirit, your soul. Without this attachment, there is no real suffering. I think on the deeper level, we become attached to this pain because we think that without the pain, we wouldn't know pure joy and the ecstatic state. And we are attached to it because we desire so desperately to experience the opposite. That is the old way, the way of duality. A couple of great articles are "Attachment: Understanding the Origin of Human Suffering" on UrbanMonk.Net and "What Is Oneness?" by Roger Gabriel at chopra.com.

Resisting the dark or anything negative only perpetuates it. When you stop resisting and let everything be as it is, you detach from any outcomes. You don't need to forget about duality or stop experiencing it if you choose. This peace results from a supreme mode of nonattachment, meaning you observe all that is happening with no attachment to the outcome, trusting that the highest good will come of every circumstance, regardless of how it appears or what your conditioned judgment may want you to believe about it. This is the state one hopefully achieves from meditation, which is extremely beneficial to the mind, body, spirit, emotions, and whole being. It is healing beyond what you can imagine or believe. It brings flow. The universal flow of energy is now allowed, unimpeded, into your entire being on all levels. It is life changing.

All emotions carry their own vibrational frequency. Ones like gratitude and joy carry a high frequency, while others like anger and disgust carry a low frequency. You really don't want to be hanging out in the lower zone too often, if at all, as these emotions are so low on the vibratory level that they are not healing for your body, your being, or others around you.

I still have days when I could easily choose to go down a rabbit hole, but now I realize I have a choice. Remaining unattached to the outcome or the need to feel physically 100 percent perfect is crucial to making the most of my circumstances and therefore feeling happy, content, and joyful. It is a spiritual practice and the foundation for improving the quality of your life. The mind and the body can be transcended through you spiritually.

At one point, I had a number of things go wrong with my house, my car, and my social life. I stopped and thought, *What on earth is Spirit trying to tell me?* I realized I had let my thoughts drift more toward the negative with each subsequent thing that happened or that I helped to create. I sat down and wrote out a long list of affirmations and began to repeat them several times a day. My mood lifted significantly, and over the next couple of weeks, things began to change in my outer world, and all the difficult things stopped happening. It seemed miraculous, but I had learned from experience how well it works. Once you truly integrate this knowledge and understanding into your being, you have the keys to transform your outer existence in a way you may not be able to fathom until you begin to put some of these concepts into action. Knowing how to do this and being aware of when it is necessary will help you begin to create space to move forward with more ease.

Lightening the Load for the Ascent

Healing may not be so much about getting better, as about letting go of everything that isn't you—all of the expectations, all of the beliefs—and becoming who you are.
—Rachel Naomi Remen

When you are physically ill, it is crucial to figure out what needs balance within the body. The healthier your body becomes, the easier it is to then focus on the spiritual, emotional, and mental. One of the most important concepts I have come across in regaining my health, well-being, and energy is that of removing toxins from my physical being. I think we are all aware of the many toxins in today's world infiltrating our beings on many levels. A body that is as clear as possible is one that is capable of so many more things and enjoying life to the fullest. When our physical vessel is cleared of toxins, then on the spiritual level, we are open to understanding more and connecting more easily, even regaining a level of connection that has been lost to us.

This affects us on the emotional level in a very real way, helping us to feel more safe and secure and free from harm. These emotions are crucial in creating a solid foundation for a life that seems worthwhile, pleasurable, and full of joy. On the energetic level, we become stronger and more capable of shining our light into the world, creating what it is we came here to create, bringing inspiration and positive energy to all those we come into contact with, and creating a remarkably uplifting energy for ourselves in our own space and lives, wherever we are. In essence, it is all connected.

When I decided to start focusing on physical detoxification, I did it based on guidance I felt I was receiving from my intuition. Everything I did was based on whether I intuitively felt it was right for me at the time. Many alternative health professionals had told me physical detox was the only way to recover from MCS. However, their suggestions had always been far too much for my weakened and highly sensitive body to reasonably handle. As I previously stated, I intuitively felt it was right for me to embark on a raw food diet during part of my healing phase. And later, I was guided, first through a friend's suggestion (spirit works in many ways and often through others) and then through my own discernment, to have a series of colonics.

One suggestion was to take numerous supplements with a vast amount of ingredients, with seemingly no thought given to the claims I had repeatedly made about having serious and disabling reactions to many herbs and vitamins. To this day, I am unable to ingest many supposedly helpful supplements due to ingredients that aren't compatible with my body. I rarely take anything with more than three active ingredients. Consuming more than one new ingredient at a time makes it very difficult to detox safely and with knowledge of what is causing what.

So, yes, it does make the going very slow at first for those who are the most sensitive or sick. But it is a crucial thing to know and to act upon for yourself and your own safety and knowledge. One ingredient I simply cannot tolerate is quercetin. It's supposed to be so helpful, and hardly anyone has an issue with it. However, it causes me a severe migraine. Many health care professionals have no idea of the vast differences of each individual person's ability to detoxify, let alone how to do it with a higher degree of safety.

Because of their misguided advice, I incorrectly assumed that detoxification was not the answer, as it only made me feel far worse. Some things are easier for some of us. Acupuncture was one of the more difficult forms of detox for my body to tolerate with ease. I recall once leaving an acupuncturist's office bent over, as I could not stand up straight due to the feeling of having been punched in the gut. It also severely impacted my energy level, and it took me four to six weeks to recover from what felt like an assault.

I have no idea why acupuncture can be so intense for me, but I have since learned that if I'm going to have it done, it must be by someone who understands my need for as few needles as possible to be placed and for them to be removed after just a few minutes. Slowly, I figured out that while there was no easy way for me to detox my body, it could be done without having to make trips to the ER or getting into an even weaker state that I could not recover from for weeks.

However, soon after I finally figured out how to detox in a gentler, more gradual way, I would tell myself, "Oh, look at that. My body is detoxifying. Isn't it interesting that the symptoms from that are so similar to the symptoms caused by an exposure to a toxic chemical." I'm telling you exactly what was going on in my mind because I know how frightening it is to think you are making yourself worse when you experience exactly the same symptoms trying to get better as you do when you are getting sick from exposures.

Unfortunately, detox can not only make you feel worse just from the detox alone; it makes one more sensitive to many things while it is going on. It must be done as slowly and gently as possible and with medical supervision, most likely from an alternative health practitioner, such as a naturopath, who understands not only detoxification but your specific diagnosis.

This is very important if you don't have a medical background or don't feel confident as far as knowing your body and intuitive faculties yet. I realized during this learning process that my body was speaking to me, wanting me to know there were things in it that shouldn't be, whether they were coming in or leaving. The good news is that you can always stop or slow down the detox, and this helps you to deal with it on a mental level. I gave myself many well-earned breaks along the way.

The breaks are fundamental for your mental health, and they help you see how far you've come and your progress toward better well-being. An inspiring thought occurred to me before I began my journey; I reasoned that if I was going to feel bad from all the toxic exposures I'd get out in the world, with control over that happening not always possible, why not feel bad while detoxifying? This thought was my way of dealing with still feeling bad, because when you are very ill, you are most likely not going to be able to breeze through detoxifying without feeling how you might on a pretty bad day—especially at the beginning of any new step you take in detoxing. It does become easier over time. At least when detoxifying, I had a choice and some control over when I did it, and I was being proactive in achieving a higher level of health.

Those were the thoughts I chose to think in order to get through some of the really bad days, weeks, and months of intensive detoxifying, especially at first. I would simply say to myself, "It's true, I feel horrible, but it's no worse than if I had a significant exposure, and I haven't. I've only been detoxifying my body, so at least I'm moving in the right direction and helping myself to improve instead of getting sicker." It helped keep me out of a state of fear, which is not at all conducive to healing on any level. Anything you can do to maintain a state of peace, love, and calm is healing for your body, mind, and soul. This is why things like meditation and yoga (my favorite is kundalini yoga) are so beneficial.

It is such a paradox to think that focusing on all the toxic chemicals and the harm they are causing you will help you to achieve a better state of well-being. Of course it is prudent to stop using these things. But if you think your focus on that is what is needed to stay alive and become healthy, I will tell you, it is just the opposite. If it brings up a state of fear, anxiety, discomfort, or any other negative feelings, this is not where you want your focus or your thoughts to be. This is why spiritual gurus preach meditation and peace, as they know that clearing the mind and coming into a calm, loving heart space is what heals us on every level.

So, learn to keep your focus on how you're going to regain your health and the positive steps you will take to help your body get into better working order. Think consistently in terms of what you need to do and what will help you to improve. Do not think about what is causing it to break down. Focus with intent on the positive. I don't mean to expose yourself unnecessarily to toxins. By all means, be as prudent as possible and keep your lifestyle as clean as possible. While it may be different for each person, it is truly best to eliminate as many toxic chemicals as possible from your world. There are always alternatives available, which are generally a simple Google search away. We all need to start using natural products that are in alignment or harmony with the earth God designed and nature.

Remove your focus from incessant fear and worry around what is happening outside of you or what might happen in the future. You basically put blinders on and begin the work of moving back into a healthful state. You do have to decide to let nothing stop you. No excuses. Find ways to work around anything that appears to be an obstacle. First, you set your intention to create a positive state of being on all levels. You get to word these statements in whatever way you choose. It can be fun creating these intention statements. Just be sure it's positive and uplifting for you to create this for yourself, and thinking of it brings about joy, happiness, security, and peace.

In the past, many have turned their noses up at the increased cost of living a cleaner, safer life. We are at a point where we can no longer do that. It is just a mindset, because by paying more to help your body's health, you end up saving money in other areas, such as increased doctor and hospital visits as you age. It pays big dividends to do this and to think critically.

There can be a negative attitude and mindset that detox alone can create. Get to know what your body feels like when you're doing a healthy detox. Never let it go beyond you being able to function, if possible. In the very beginning stages, that may not always work out, but it is a goal worth striving for. When I take something my body doesn't tolerate or cannot process, I've found it makes me feel weird and not in a good way. It's somewhat different from a detox. Try to learn what a normal detox response feels like for you.

Detoxing can unfortunately make you more chemically sensitive as you release massive amounts of toxins and dead microbes. It is helpful to keep in mind that this is temporary, and if it is too much to deal with, then back off on your detox. Maybe even give yourself a complete break until you feel better. Seeing how this cycle works will give you confidence to keep trying. You will be able to see how it gets easier over time. Make a promise to yourself to go slowly enough so that your body can handle the detox as easily as possible.

Normal levels of detox should not make you feel anything more than tired and sluggish, with headaches, minor bowel changes, lack of appetite, a minor rash, and possibly anxiety, minor depression, or irritability. Taking days off is crucial and totally acceptable. If you are practicing a cleaner, nontoxic, and nonstressful lifestyle, you won't be accruing much in the way of new toxins, so you can relax, knowing you are not getting worse while giving your body a much-needed rest. There is no rush, even though you want to feel better yesterday.

Oftentimes, the increase in chemical sensitivity is a pain to deal with. However, with many years of doing detox, I've found that this is one of the things you have to deal with at times in order to improve. How do you keep from going into a state of fear over your decline in health—and trust that you will improve? First, you have paid attention to your inner knowing about what you need to do regarding your health. Why would you have been directed this way if it was bad for you? Tell yourself repeatedly that you have done the best thing you know to do for yourself, with the help of spirit and the divine, and you are getting *better* all the time.

I decided to start detoxing on my own when I realized I was feeling pretty terrible all the time anyway, with no hope of recovering if I continued doing the same things I had been doing, which mostly consisted of pure avoidance of many foods, chemicals, airborne allergens, and the world at large. This was not the life I signed on for—or was it? It certainly allowed me many days, months, and years of thorough self-examination and time to excavate every trauma I'd ever incurred in this life (and others I'm sure). I had endless time to feel every feeling and analyze it to death from many angles.

I do finally understand, with the help of all I've been through and astrology as a fabulous tool, how much of my life was preordained to happen in just the way it has happened. In other words, there are no accidents, and you can see the meaning in all of it once you accept that it is all for your learning and growth, and all is in divine order. If you can, I highly recommend having sessions with a spiritual counselor or soul path or other type of astrologer, as this can help you understand how you came in to learn many lessons in a precise way.

Make it your intention every day to accept what is and to flourish under those circumstances, asking for help from God, your angels, your spirit guides, and your higher power. Accept that there is something greater than yourself and surrender, trusting that you are not in control of the universe. This letting go and trusting in the universes and God's plan for you is crucial to your recovery and serenity.

This premise is based on the twelve-step philosophy used for recovery from alcoholism and many other addictive and dysfunctional disorders. MCS and other illnesses can also be seen and treated as dysfunctional and addictive disorders. They are all an unfortunate consequence of dysfunction of the spirit as a result of a major disconnection, which our society encourages in a huge way, and they are all perpetuated by the resulting negative thought patterns that become instinctual and addictive.

With that said, I finally realized I was not going to get better unless I did a lot of detox. Avoidance alone had not proven to be the answer for me. And, God knows, I did the best job possible of that. Yes, it kept me from getting worse. But the body simply cannot recover while laden with poisons held in the liver, brain, kidneys, colon, and other organs, and they are not released by the avoidance alone, especially if some of the genes for your detox pathways have become mutated. You're going to have to help your body out.

When I finally began a detox program in early 2006, I followed my intuition, doing only what I received through muscle testing or pendulum swinging. I discovered I am my own pendulum. By breathing in deeply and releasing my breath, my body shivers on the outbreath for "yes," and there is no movement whatsoever for "no." Many of you may notice a similar type of ability. Even then, many times I'd do a fraction of what I got was an OK dose for my body. I realized I was going to feel bad and maybe worse some days, but I had already felt bad for many years, almost sixteen years at that point.

In that time, I had not improved much. So, going on that reasoning, I finally stopped being afraid of doing what I needed to do to get well. I changed the thoughts I was having and stopped running away from the things that were making me feel bad. I began to face what was inside myself, instead of running away from what was outside of me.

For years after beginning to embark upon a lot of detoxification, I would still feel some of that burning acid-like pain in my shoulders at times. Detoxification is one of the things you must do to heal, but it can be a double-edged sword, especially at the beginning. *You must go slowly*—as slowly as necessary for you to still function at your normal level. Know that each little step you take, as painful and difficult as it is, is a step in the right direction of healing, as long as you don't overdo it.

You will know when you have overdone. it You will know how much is enough for you. You cannot go slowly enough in the beginning. You need to get a handle on exactly what your body can tolerate. It is best if you don't make yourself feel worse than you already do on a moderately bad day. Of course, when you do finally decide enough is enough and start healing by detoxifying, you can feel as if you are going backward, as your reactions can feel more severe than when you are not detoxifying. When this happens, you should stop completely. Take a break or as long as you need to get back into a stable place.

You won't have lost ground. You will simply be able to see that your body reacclimates and goes back to the former level of reactivity, gradually lessening each time. I felt emotionally lighter, having made this decision, as I knew I was feeling bad from the toxins leaving my body, just the same as one does from the toxins entering and not being able to leave. One way, you are getting progressively worse with a greater toxin load, and the other progressively better with fewer toxins and hence a better functioning body and more rewarding life.

At any rate, the whole process helped me to become very in tune with my body and my intuition. After a while, some mornings I would wake up, and answers would just come to me about what I needed to do or focus on for better health. It is like beginning to use an atrophied muscle and starting to trust your judgment over anyone else's. It is a reconnecting to your spirit self. The main reason I would do this upon awakening is that this is the time of day when you are the most relaxed and open to the spirit world. You have just spent time there while you were asleep.

This is truly the biggest thing that led to my recovery. I would lie there and simply ask spirit or God, "What do I need to know or to do today to improve my health or my body?" Then I would stay in bed a few more minutes, relaxed, with my eyes closed, open to any message or visual I might get. You may not hear or see anything just then. I certainly didn't always. It may come to you later in the day in a conversation with a friend, in a song you hear, in words you read on your computer screen or in a book. Once you've asked, spirit is going to give you the answers you need. You just need to be open to receiving those answers.

And yes, if it comes to you indirectly through another source, pay attention. It's never a mistake or coincidence. You start to be aware of the signs and messages you receive yourself and through other sources. This is how spirit operates. You must start to exercise this part of yourself not from a place of fear but being centered and calm. It is the ultimate in taking care of oneself. It is stepping out of victimhood. It is stepping into your own power, owning it, and not giving your power to anyone else. No one else can be responsible for you or your health to the degree that you can.

When you understand this, you will know what it is to feel truly powerful and not anyone's victim or at anyone's mercy. It is a huge responsibility, however, as you are now at the seat of the helm. At some point, you will forgive others for poisoning you and this world. It may even cease to be something that gives you much of a rise at all. You will understand that this is a result of where others are in their consciousness, and it doesn't make it right or wrong; it just is what it is. The judgment falls away when we start to truly love ourselves. When we practice intensive self-love, we end up letting go of self-judgment.

Part of what got me here was inner child work, and another large part was learning my natal astrology. It helped so much to learn astrology and see how everyone had different planetary influences, placements, and aspects in their natal charts, which determined a lot of what they were going to be dealing with, learning, and growing from in the current life. How could I possibly judge what any other person was doing or how they were handling matters in their lives when I had no idea what they were here to learn, what level of evolution their being was at, or the influences they came in under?

I could not do it any longer. It was a new level of awareness. Releasing anger, resentment, and holding anyone else responsible for anything going on with you is a major part of detoxifying your body. It is also another crucial step in healing. After I let go of some of these negative feelings, I was able to see that whenever I had judged someone, it was often because I held a certain hardness against myself for the very thing I was judging them for. So, once I forgave myself for being so hard on myself and accepting myself as I was, all judgment dissipated for others—like a miracle.

Look where you are nonaccepting of others, and then look within to see where that is really coming from. Leave no stone unturned until you know. That takes a lot of honesty and willingness to feel your pain and judgment regarding yourself. For example, when I was with Aragon, I would sometimes notice what I perceived as a character flaw, his ego or harshness in speaking. And suddenly one day, I had a moment of knowing I also had those in my character. I do not even recall what made me understand this, but it was a huge revelatory moment that caught me so off guard I had the feeling of wanting to run away screaming from my own self! I will never forget it, because it taught me so well that whenever you are judging someone, you are doing so because you are afraid to look at the same flaws within yourself.

And you do have them. It's been hard for me to judge anyone since, for I know that if I do, I am being unloving to that person and to myself. It is so much more healing to accept that part of yourself with love, for that is how you truly begin to heal it. You can begin to do this introspective healing work by journaling about your feelings when something outside you seems to be the cause of your negative feelings. Also, it can be done by self-inquiry, which is the practice of having an internal conversation with yourself and inquiring into your true nature. Ask, "Why is this upsetting me to this degree? What is it in me causing my discomfort? What am I afraid of seeing in myself? What am I unable to accept that I may have within my own nature? Why do I have this seeming flaw? Can I accept it so that I can integrate it, love it, and heal it?" That is the only way you will heal on this level.

It helps you to cultivate self-awareness, which helps you move into your own power and responsibility, for it is from here you can be truly proactive in your health and healing. It helps you develop your discernment and learn to trust your inner knowing. It's brought me more peace than anything else and is worth more than gold. Your peace is so worth it. Also, much spiritual evolution can occur from learning to go within for your answers, in addition to releasing this judgment and resulting negative feelings for others.

Before I decided to embark on detoxifying my body, I made the decision based on my intuition (without having been diagnosed with Lyme disease) to go on the Marshall protocol, which is designed in part for killing Lyme spirochetes and what is called cell wall–deficient (CWD) bacteria, and it was quite difficult to accomplish. It uses very low doses of pulsed antibiotics, meaning you take a fraction of pill once every few days. This kills off a phenomenal amount of CWD bacteria, far more effective than a full course of antibiotics. I don't think I had more than what amounts to two rounds total of antibiotics in the one and a half years I was on this protocol. When you've had undiagnosed Lyme for two decades, you have a lot of CWD bacteria hiding out in the immune cells. While I won't highly recommend it to anyone, because of the level of difficulty and severe limitations, it did help me achieve a new level of well-being, so much so that I was now encouraged to follow my inner guidance more than ever. There are other, more natural protocols one can do to address Lyme disease, such as Dr. Lee Cowden's, Dr. Stephen Buhner's, or Dr. Dietrich Klinghardt's protocols.

One of the difficulties inherent in doing the MP was the need to take high doses of an antihypertensive drug (found to reduce the herxheimer response), which kept my blood pressure so low it was hard to stand up at times, and it drastically reduced my level of energy. Another difficulty was the required blacking out of all the windows in one's home environment. That is because with the amount of die-off created from killing the cell wall–deficient bacteria, one could have intense reactions to too much sunlight exposure, even to the eyes. So, I had to wear the darkest noIR sunglasses to keep out all infrared light during the protocol; otherwise the light hitting my amygdala from my retinas could have caused wild responses. For me, these had mostly to do with fight-or-flight or a very stressed out response in my body.

I realize now I stood up and stepped into my power when I decided to act on my intuition instead of being a victim of the world, doctors, and so on. Now, it did take some time, but the world started to respond accordingly, and the more time that passed, the more speed this freight train picked up. It was as if the world said to me, "OK, so now you're finally going to take *full* responsibility for what's happened in your life (not to you), and so the rewards will become immense. Are you ready?" It was one of the most empowering decisions I've made in my life.

When I was on this protocol, the die-off overloaded my body, since the minute amount of antibiotics goes for all the cell wall–deficient bacteria that hide out in the very immune cells that are supposed to kill them. The problem with taking full-strength antibiotics repeatedly is they cause morphing of bacteria into cell wall–deficient bacteria and end up helping to cause autoimmune diseases. This is one reason you feel better taking full-potency antibiotics, but meanwhile, they do significant damage you end up having to deal with later. While I was taking the high doses of antihypertensive medication that helped control the inflammatory response from the die-off, such as severe body aches, inflamed organs, and headaches, the toxins from the die-off that could not be discharged quickly enough from my body eventually caused me to go into that dreaded medical state of porphyria.

The Mayo Clinic explains, "Porphyria refers to a group of disorders that result from a buildup of natural chemicals that produce porphyrin in your body. Porphyrins are essential for the function of hemoglobin—a protein in your red blood cells that links to porphyrin, binds iron, and carries oxygen to your organs and tissues." I believe porphyria is in part caused by too many toxins being released at once, too much for an overwhelmed system to cope with. I don't believe medical science knows much about this. It can manifest in a myriad of ways. Most often it affects the skin or digestive tract, or neurologically, affecting mental health. Most commonly, porphyria affects the digestive tract or skin with side effects of constipation, nausea, vomiting, skin rashes, blistering, and extreme sensitivity to sunlight.

For me, the porphyria manifested as the most bizarre feeling in all my muscles. It almost drove me insane. I would go for entire nights with no sleep, as I was so wildly uncomfortable. It felt like I was on a ride spinning around at the fair, and the centrifugal force was pulling all my muscles away from the bones. I wouldn't have called it cramping, and it wasn't painful exactly, just unbelievably uncomfortable, disconcerting, and miserable, and the only thing I could do to deal with it was get up and pace nonstop. If not for my intuition and subsequently using the treatment (basically glucose) prescribed for porphyria, which helped dramatically, I would not have known what it was.

In all the medical literature, this is not one of the mentioned ways that porphyria presents. I was so thankful I had some ability to intuit what was going on in my body. This was just one more reminder for me that we are all different and to trust my gut knowing and intuition above what anyone else tries to tell me. My medically intuitive state had grown great enough by 2006 that I was able to diagnose this on my own and treat it accordingly. I got that it happens primarily from the toxic load being too great for the liver and red blood cells to adequately handle, which allopathic medical science still doesn't understand.

At the hospital, they would have given me IV saline with glucose, so I thought, *Why not try dextrose powder*, the sugar most similar to glucose, which can be obtained at most health food stores. A tablespoon was all it took to put me out of my misery and help me sleep the rest of the night, which was a true Godsend. I took it directly, without mixing it with water, and it worked superbly for calming down my nervous system and my symptoms of detox. Many think this is high-fructose corn sugar. It is from corn, so not everyone would be OK with using it, but it does not spike the blood sugar in the same way and is released much more slowly into your system. It was of supreme help to me many times when the detox would have become too difficult to continue. I am fairly certain whatever form of sugar you can tolerate can help calm a detox that is over the top. Just use it as sparingly as you can, as medicine for when you truly need it. You definitely don't want to use it indiscriminately, because sugar lowers your immune function and can increase your candida levels if overused.

I encourage you to remain out of fear about that when you are trying to successfully manage a crisis. The process of recovering will be two steps forward and one back at times. The fact that sometimes the going will be slower than others must not stop you from trying to heal and continuing. That is one of the best tricks I know for stopping or reducing some of the unbearable detox symptoms. Of course, there are other herbs such as manayupa or Nutramedix Burbur, which are helpful in getting detox or herx symptoms under better control.

One of my daughters was addicted to heroin for a while (she is now thankfully recovered), and what I watched with her trying to detox from it a couple times was quite akin to what a person with MCS goes through when they are either detoxing to get better or when they've received an exposure that their body cannot adequately eliminate. This is actually what is causing your symptoms in most cases, not an allergy or sensitivity.

Why does it feel so severe when it's happening? Because it is. Your body knows this and is trying to tell you, but the only way out is to go through the detox. Of course, you never want to take it to that point where it is too severe, which means if you are unable to function at all. It does get easier the longer you've been doing it. After the first one or two years, I didn't have very severe symptoms from detox. And the best news is that MCS, Lyme, and many other immune illnesses are not progressive the way medical science and doctors think and tell you. Sure, they're progressive if you keep living your life the same way, out of alignment with God and nature. All illness can be healed and, if not entirely cured, at least drastically improved. I'm trying to help you do it more safely and with greater hope and inspiration for a better life.

After a year and a half on the Marshall protocol for Lyme, I decided to stop. Not only was it extremely difficult having almost zero energy and living in the dark all the time, there was simply too much detox going on in my body, and there seemed to be no professional medical knowledge of this side effect I spoke of above, called porphyria, or how to properly handle it. I embarked on a program I designed for myself to mop up the toxins that were swimming around unabated in my system.

Many who are severely debilitated, especially those with MCS, must be exceedingly careful when detoxifying. I can't stress this enough. If too many toxins are released into the system at once, your body may not be capable of handling it adequately, and you could end up suffering more for a time or making a fragile state even more delicate. It's very important to take it as slowly as possible and always trust your inner guidance first and foremost, or find a medical intuitive or someone who does muscle testing to help guide you toward what your body can handle with ease.

After all the detox, there were many supplements my body seemed able to tolerate that I had not been able to tolerate before. I began taking B$_{12}$ drops as well as homeopathic glutathione patches and doing coffee enemas almost daily. I could also now tolerate

NAC and vitamin C. Before, when I had tried those, I always felt worse. Glutathione, in particular, made my legs hurt so bad it was intolerable. I was only using supplements that helped me to feel better, instead of using those that would pull more toxins out of my cells without any mechanism to make the process easier. Therefore, I avoided the herxheimer effect and raised my energy and well-being.

You must learn to employ muscle or pendulum testing before you try anything. I cannot stress enough how important it is to ask your guidance or find someone in the alternative health care professions, such as a chiropractor who does kinesiology, before trying anything new. Often energy healers have this ability. If you feel you are reacting or intolerant of something you are already taking, it's a good idea to use muscle testing or guidance.

Most all of us carry a load of heavy metals in our bodies; it is inescapable in the world we live in. These are so dense and heavy they have the capacity to interfere with many of the body's physical functions and our emotional state. Therefore, it becomes exceedingly beneficial to eliminate as many of these as possible from our physical being. This is much easier said than done, however, and an extensive protocol for doing so is beyond the scope of this book. I do not recommend it as a first step, except perhaps in the case that it is life threatening, and only then under a doctor's very close supervision. It can be very difficult, dangerous, and frightening to eliminate or chelate heavy metals.

My particular horror story is that I took the chelator known as DMPS at one point, given to me by a naturopath, just to determine how high my heavy metal load was. This trial test was far too much for my weakened body to handle safely at the time, as the dose pulled out enough heavy metals at once to cause me to have every symptom in the book of a heart attack. I really thought I was done here. I had nausea, sweating, shortness of breath, faintness, and severe squeezing pain all over my chest and down my left arm. However, cardiac testing afterward showed I did not have a heart attack. I was in a very weakened state for several weeks while I recovered. I have heard of at least two autistic children dying from this particular chelator.

The reason is it releases far too much heavy metal into the system at once from where it gets stored in the organs, and it redistributes to other organs where it can cause irreversible harm. I wish more doctors were aware of how dangerous it is. I do *not* recommend taking DMPS even to be tested for your levels. Later, I tried doing a heavy metal detox protocol for autistics and severely sensitive people. Even this protocol had me up nights, feeling in a state between life and death. It's a terrifying feeling to have heavy metals swimming around in your system, trying to get out of your body. I never care to experience it again.

Speaking of heavy metals, I guess that was the universe's way of waking me up to the fact that I hadn't done a tremendous amount of chelating heavy metals. Chelation is the process of removing heavy metals from the blood by forming a chelate with them. Whenever I attempted this, it was always too much for my body to handle with any degree of ease. And I am a proponent of going slowly when it comes to detoxifying, especially when one has been ill with multiple chemical sensitivity. As I've said, it is less that we are sensitive or having reactions and more that our bodies have become extremely toxic, and any exposure is just over the top for us, making our bodies have to work very hard to detoxify the minutest of exposures. The body does this to try to keep us at a level of some homeostasis; if it didn't, we might more readily succumb to the level of toxicity our bodies are carrying.

So, in essence, each exposure creates a certain amount of detox in and of itself, causing us to feel terrible, or at least worse than we already felt. When the body is carrying this degree of toxicity, it is crucial to go slowly and not make yourself feel any worse than you already do when you have an exposure. That is the litmus test. If it makes you feel worse than a typical exposure, you need to back off. You don't want to push your body any harder than that.

This is a fairly hard place to get to mentally, where you decide that in order to get better, you are going to have to feel as bad as when you have an exposure for a while. The upside is that gradually you will feel less and less bad while detoxing and having exposures. That is when you know you're ready to up your detox game a wee bit at a time. My trip there was a long road. I hope yours doesn't have to be. I was made very sick numerous times trying to detox in a way that was just too much and too fast for my weakened body to handle.

This was often at the advice of professionals, some of them naturopaths, who I mistakenly assumed would know more than I, or at least all the ins and outs around detoxifying in a safe manner. Many practitioners, even naturopaths, do not understand the extreme state of fragility many with MCS (and other autoimmune diseases, such as CFS and Lyme disease) are in. Many bodily functions can go awry much more easily with this disease. Because of that and my firsthand understanding, I caution you to go as slowly as possible and be as careful as possible with your body. I hope I have driven that point home successfully.

One simply cannot know until one has experienced firsthand how toxic a person can become and how close to death one can get when attempting a detox that is designed for someone having only mild issues. This is not to put you into a further state of fear. Being so highly sensitive is in some regards a blessing. You will not need as high a dosage in your supplements to make drastic improvements. You may be able to make vast improvements even with a tiny fraction of the dosage or length of time your ND or MD may prescribe for you. Although it is my feeling that once you learn how fast your body can go and what it can tolerate and needs as far as recovering your health, it should become a lifelong program for you. No sense in slacking off, as I have discovered the hard way. And there is absolutely no benefit to getting on the pity pot about it either.

I began my first detox program in 2006. Here it is, 2020, and I still work a program. I feel it is now just a lifestyle, as MCS became, only this is a lifestyle I am consciously choosing. It behooves me to continue on. I change it up as needed, and over time, I am more and more able to detox the way a person can who has never been sick. That is so encouraging, even though it has taken me years to get to this point. I can see it also took years to get as sick as I was. The following is basically how I live and the tools I've used to help me succeed in rebuilding my mind, body, and spirit for the best possible health and well-being.

Every morning upon awakening, like I said, I lie in bed silently and as mindlessly as possible, allowing whatever spirit wants to whisper to me to flow in. This is my time of aligning myself with the flow of whichever direction the divine is asking my attention to move in for this day. I am just letting spirit know I am on task, paying attention, and available for the work. Often, I don't get anything in that moment, but I am always paying attention, as I've learned that spirit communicates to us in many ways that sometimes seem to be coincidences. Pay attention to those. There are no coincidences. Whatever is happening is happening for a reason, though we may not know it until later.

There is always meaning, regardless of whether you understand what the meaning is at the time. After paying attention for many years, I am better able to decipher the meaning, and it is quite stunning how the universe works in this way. It is called serendipity or synchronicity. The more aligned and in the flow and open you are, the more you will notice this type of thing happening in your life. Really start to pay attention to everything in your daily life—right down to what types of animals cross your path. There is spiritual meaning in this alone. Every animal carries its own spiritual meaning, and if you look it up, you will often find it's very fitting for what is going on at that moment in your life. Knowing the meaning can encourage you or give you guidance.

One of the most crucial tools is the coffee enema. I currently do and probably will continue to do two coffee enemas per day (I prefer coffee but have also used green tea, spring water, or reverse osmosis water at times) with a two-quart silicon enema bag. This may seem a lot, but many longtime coffee enema supporters have done just this with very good results. It is similar to being on dialysis when your kidneys are malfunctioning. If your detox pathways are not functioning as well as they should, or you can't tolerate glutathione, you may want to consider these.

When I started doing coffee enemas (CE), I noticed that I could easily eliminate a bad headache or migraine, as well as feeling sick or too drained from detoxifying. There is nothing that works as well for me to increase my energy, clarity, and well-being. It does feel like dialysis for my liver, and it is simply amazing that there is something like this that can vastly improve how well your liver functions while rapidly removing highly toxic matter from your body. For these reasons, I cannot recommend the CE highly enough. It is similar to removing toxins by sweating them out in a sauna. If you are debilitated or have lost your body's normal thermostat functioning, as I had, raising the body heat and being unable to sweat adequately is more damaging than helpful, even life threatening.

However, most people with MCS I've spoken to have not had this issue. It is crucial to be able to remove toxins as fast and efficiently as possible, as they are being released, without putting your health into a greater state of fragility. Safety first.

And coffee enemas are something anyone can learn to do on their own, at home, quite affordably. There are online companies that are extremely knowledgeable about the coffee enemas, and they sell top-of-the-line coffees processed to remove all mold and be gentle for the intestinal tract. My favorite one is Optimal Health Network.

Next, I have my morning lemon water and green juice and then a smoothie made with raw organic fruits and vegetables. I also add varying superfoods or herbs to the smoothie. I began eating this way when I realized I couldn't tolerate synthetic vitamins or minerals and wondered how I was going to get an adequate intake of vitamins and minerals. It turns out nature's vitamins and minerals are much easier to assimilate for me. I had no idea how much my intestines and body were rebelling from different supplements. I feel so much calmer and less inflamed when I eat this way.

It can be hard to make the change to eating this way. I started with breakfast and gradually had lunch be a salad every day. It took about a year before I finally made my dinners be raw veggie too. I still have some steamed vegetables, root vegetables, or vegetarian soups when I need something heavier or warm. Eating this way has proven to be one of the best ways to keep my body supplied with vitamins and nutrients, as well as a quite slow and gentle way to detoxify. You may notice right away that you feel better and lighter and more clear from eating in a similar fashion.

I then usually do some gentle kundalini yoga or go for a long walk, or often, I meditate. Then I take my supplements, usually herbal tinctures for the most part. Like I said, my body is much happier with only natural, whole superfoods and herbs going in. Ayurvedic herbs are traditional Hindu herbs whose main goal is to promote good health as opposed to fight disease. They seem gentler on my system than many other herbs. It changes over time which ones I take, and I don't think it's a good idea to take many of them on a permanent basis.

You must have a binder that you can tolerate, such as activated charcoal, bentonite, or zeolite, and take them one to three times per day when you are detoxifying, with at least a couple hours between the binders and the other supplements you take. Binders absorb the toxins you are releasing from your liver and cells. This will keep them from being reabsorbed into your body and keep you feeling as well as possible during the whole process. Always remember to take the binders when you're not feeling well. They are important to have to bind to the toxins and keep you from feeling worse while toxins are on the way out.

Also, you need to replenish your system with electrolytes and minerals regularly when you are using binders and coffee enemas. I know there are tri-salts, but I prefer coconut water with a pinch or two of sea salt. It is a crucial part of recovery, as you are doing your body no favors if you release toxins only to reabsorb them before they can be expelled. Also, you need to make sure to have a two-hour window around taking any of your other supplements or medications, as the binder will bind those as well to remove from your system. Here are some binders you can try: nano zeolite or ACZ, activated charcoal, bentonite, modifilan, or algin. Be quite careful with the clays, starting off with a tiny amount, much less than the dosage on the container. This is because they will pull toxins out of the cells as well as binding up the loose ones.

I do not recommend pharmaceutical prescription binders, such as cholestyramine, as I've found them to be entirely too much for people with MCS. They tend to pull too many toxins at once, and as a result, many who take it end up constipated. You may feel good at first because of its ability to clear toxins, but over time, I have found (and others have told me from their experience) it's too much. However, in all honesty, it may be just the thing for some people. So, check in with your inner knowing, muscle testing, pendulum swinging, or higher self. Having at least two to three binders to take is an integral step in recovery. These, along with coffee or green tea enemas, have been my saving grace whenever I've felt horribly sick from die-off or the herxheimer effect. These two methods have helped me more than almost anything to move along my path of healing with a great deal more ease and quality of life.

Many health care professionals treat detox as if it is a simple process that anyone should be able to do with ease. That might be true, unless you're saturated with toxins or have one or more faulty genetic detoxification genes. Once I got into a state of releasing too much into my blood at once, it could be hard to get back to how I felt before. It's never a good idea to move too quickly on the road to health when you are just beginning—another reason to make sure you use the smallest amount of any supplement or treatment that causes detoxification or kills off candida or any coinfections.

Before going any further, I want to caution you about chelating mercury. Unless you've had all your silver amalgam dental fillings removed, do not even attempt to chelate mercury. I would not do anything that claims to chelate heavy metal or mercury if you still have amalgams. Why is this? Because you will be endlessly pulling mercury from your amalgams, and it is highly probable this mercury will redeposit in your brain or other organs, where it can create havoc.

This can be far too much mercury for your body to handle safely when it's on the loose. I've known people who are put on glutathione by their seemingly knowledgeable physicians while they still have amalgams in their mouths! At first, it may seem to help, but before long, their bodies are overwhelmed by the mercury being dumped into their bloodstream and deposited wherever on the way out. This may be OK for some people who aren't as sick, but I don't agree with taking this kind of risk. Definitely check with your hopefully knowledgeable doctor, and even then, only do what feels right to you. Glutathione, ALA, and MSM are known to be mercury and heavy metal chelators. It is far better to find a biological dentist to safely remove your amalgam fillings and then begin to chelate mercury.

Unless you are having serious health issues caused specifically by heavy metal poisoning and chelating after having your amalgams removed is the only answer, leave heavy metal chelating as one of the last things you try. It may well be the granddaddy of all detoxes and is nothing to play around with or do on your own. You may need to have much of your other load reduced drastically before you are able to handle this with. I tried, of course, before having done much other detox, and the testing to determine how high my mercury load was with DMPS nearly killed me. I've heard of people who've done simple things, such as added a cup of cilantro to their smoothie, and it took them months to recover from it. It is this type of advice that is thrown out there as if it will cause no ill effects. It is another reason to develop your intuition, so you are easily guided into what is correct for you.

Having developed my intuitive skills, I do sometimes wonder about the need for some of the medical testing, especially the type of testing that puts one's health into greater danger. When you start to awaken your inner knowing and intuition, there isn't as much need for testing. You can do something as simple as muscle testing (many short YouTube videos explain this) and get your answers. That's step one. Then you do the research using online forums for your specific health issue, or a Google search using keywords, to find out what is helpful for your situation. Then you use your intuition to determine which one or two of these modalities, supplements, or methods will best support you. You can use the same method to find the right dosage level.

If it ever starts to feel like too much, you back off or stop until your body is at an equilibrium again. Or the easier but slower way is to start with one drop of something and very slowly work toward a gradually higher dose. I've even just put one drop in a quarter cup of water and taken a sip or two to start off at times.

One helpful bit of info I learned in my quest for wellness was the fact that many pollens are concomitant or cross-reactive with different foods. So, when certain things were pollinating, I felt dramatically better if I avoided all the foods that were considered to be concomitants with that particular pollen. For instance, I was very allergic to grass pollens. As it so happened, I felt far better just avoiding all grains during grass pollen season. Even rice was a problem for me.

Quinoa and buckwheat were about the only ones I could eat. I rarely eat any grains now, as I have switched over to mostly raw, whole organic foods. This has become a lifestyle for me, as opposed to a form of imprisonment. Once you start eating this way, the flavor of the fresh whole foods just becomes a pleasurable joy. Grains, wheat in particular, act as a form of glue in the intestines. It's the same with all the white foods, rice, sugar, and dairy. You do not want food acting as glue in your intestines when you are working to detoxify your body and eliminate toxins as rapidly as possible. Wheat and other grains have glyphosates sprayed on them and are genetically modified.

With all of this going on, your intestines don't stand a chance of having a healthy microbiome, let alone moving toxins through at a speedier rate. With that said, what works for one, or even for most, simply will not fit the bill in all cases. I understand that some of you may be having issues with increased bowel motility or even diarrhea and need to slow things down. In this case, grains may be helpful, but at least try to ingest organic whenever possible. Everything can be used as medicine at one time or another.

If you feel as if it would help to try a raw diet for your health, there are many good resources. I particularly like Gabriel Cousens, MD, who wrote *Rainbow Green Live-Food Cuisine* in addition to many other books. I'm also a fan of Ronnie Landis, author of *Holistic Health Mastery Program.* David Avocado Wolfe is also a very well-known raw food, superfoods, and herbs expert.

When I first tried an all-raw diet, I became quite spacey and very relaxed. At the time, this concerned me, because I didn't fully understand the dynamic behind that. What I now know is that, for one, the raw diet eliminated all my anxiety. It aligns you more fully with life the way nature and God intended it to be. When the body no longer has to work so hard to move all the processed and heavy cooked foods through, it is far more relaxed. This can leave you feeling spacey when you are used to a highly wired and anxious state. In addition, you are receiving far more nutrients from all the vitamins and minerals alive in the foods, and you are able to absorb these nutrients thanks to the action of the live enzymes, which have not been destroyed by high heat in the cooking process.

When I've talked about how eating a live raw food diet (unprocessed, whole, organic plant-based fruits, vegetables, nuts, seeds, and some oils) helped me regain my vitality and health, I have heard repeatedly from people with MCS, "I can't digest anything raw." This may be true, but if one is open to the vastness of possibilities, there is always another way or option. This is not to say that a raw diet is the best one for everybody, although there are distinct advantages if one is trying to heal. The point I am making here is that in healing, opening the mind to alternatives is crucial. Try to begin to operate from a state of mind where you allow yourself to ask, "Is there a way that could work for me? Are there possibilities I haven't considered?" instead of deciding, "That will definitely not work."

For example, if you would like to add more raw foods to your diet, but you have trouble digesting them, what about consuming a small amount of raw fruits and vegetables after they have been juiced or blenderized? Once your body gets used to the enzymes present in raw foods in these small quantities, you can slowly add more variety and quantity to your diet. Usually once you get beyond the first hurdle your mind creates by thinking something is not possible for you, the advances begin to happen more and more rapidly with each thing you thought you couldn't possibly get beyond. Rigidity of the mind with narrow thinking can be a major barrier to getting well. This is something you would do well to stop; ask yourself if it is possible to move beyond a barrier your mind may be creating for you. The mind has a way of making us think there are no options, but the truth is that there are always options and alternatives.

Raw, organic whole foods are huge not only in creating health but evolving your consciousness. It is crucial for those trying to heal to begin ingesting only the highest-quality foods. Raw foods contain not only concentrated nutrients but also live enzymes, which are crucial for digestion and many other bodily functions. The living enzymes also help you to absorb nutrients more efficiently. When I am eating mostly or all raw, I feel calmer, lighter, more vibrant, and even more luminous, which means I am capable of carrying more light energy, which aids my health, well-being, and ability to function. Everything functions better. It has been a major precursor in my kundalini awakening, which is the life force energy everyone has available to them. It runs unimpeded through all the chakras, meridians, and energy channels of the body and aura. Kundalini is a Sanskrit word from India that describes the spiritual energy and consciousness that is the source of the life force, prana or chi, in human beings. It is an extremely potent and healing energy.

Once I put my efforts into listening to my inner guidance, I started to eat 100 percent raw. It was after I came off the Marshall protocol in 2008. This came after many years of trying almost every diet known, including the rotation diet, caveman diet, macrobiotic diet, and Eat Right for Your Type diet. When you are willing to listen to your inner guidance, you will make amazing contacts with others who steer you in the right direction. And of course, it must resonate with you. Once I began to eat raw foods, I met others who were also raw foodists, and they encouraged me to try colonics. A colonic cleanses and hydrates the entire length of the large intestine, enabling the liver to more easily dump its toxins. The coffee enema only cleanses the lower part of the colon, approximately one foot. It does help the liver to produce its own glutathione, though, and therefore also has significant liver-detoxifying effects.

The other raw foodists told me eating raw would facilitate a lot of detox in my body. The colon hydrotherapist I went to talked me into doing as many as I possibly could. She described to me how the colon becomes like the bottom of a dried-up mud pond, and successive colonics help to soften and then remove the dried-up fecal material that accumulates over the years. I thought she was trying to get my money but also decided there was no harm in trying it for one week. I made the decision to have five colonics done in one week. That was all I needed to convince me of this modality's potent healing ability. At the end of the week, my energy jumped to a level I hadn't known in years. My skin looked, well … glowing. My twenty-one-year-old daughter asked me what I'd been doing because she thought I looked fabulous and much younger.

I had been doing coffee enemas for a few years at this point, so the hydrotherapist said I released a lot more than most people do when first starting colonics. I'm sure the raw foods were also a factor. If you feel guided to do this and find it is helpful for you but don't feel you have the funds, I encourage you to focus on manifesting the funds in a positive way, knowing and believing that you can indeed find a way to manifest money or whatever it is you really want in your life. It may take time, so be patient and keep your thoughts positive, regardless of what happens. They were instrumental in helping me to remove many years of toxic matter and parasites from my intestinal tract.

During my first one, the colon hydrotherapist let me know she thought I would benefit from having a colonic done as often as I possibly could afford. She even suggested a regime that would be five days a week, Monday through Friday. This was one of the better investments I made in my health, not only physically but also emotionally and spiritually. Having that many colonics seems absurd and possibly unachievable to many, but it is a profound way to open yourself to greater healing on all levels. As you dump physical toxic matter, you also dump old, toxic, emotional, stuck garbage. It's amazing how that happens. And in that process of clearing yourself physically and emotionally, the door is opened wider for your spiritual evolution and growth. It's akin to removing darkness to let in the light. It was a profound game changer for me.

As I previously mentioned, I had lost my ability to sweat or detox through saunas after having had heat stroke—or coming very close to it. Therefore, colonics became the way for me to get the toxins out of my body. Not many naturopaths or environmental docs will recommend it. Perhaps they know folks are reticent to partake in a modality of this nature, not just due to the physical nature but also the emotional discomfort or possible embarrassing nature. It can be dangerous for some—for example, if you have a thinned intestinal wall from Crohn's or other intestinal dis-eases.

Some of you may be able to accomplish the same thing by sauna detox or intense exercise. When I began, I was not able to exercise intensely or sweat, so those things made me quite sick. Since regaining my health from treating myself inadvertently for Lyme disease, then with colonics and raw foods, I gained back my ability to break a good sweat, so I added dancing to my list of fun things to do. I remember a dance teacher asking us all to say how we were feeling at the end of a class, and as we went around the room, most were saying things like *joyful, peaceful,* and *vibrant.* I said, "I'm happy because I'm so sweaty." Little did anyone know just how happy I truly was.

Helping our bodies to detoxify is a primary factor in being able to more easily tolerate harsh chemicals, pollens, molds, and foods. In addition, when done consistently over time, it can lead to regaining our health to a degree that many doctors have told us is not possible. Using colon hydrotherapy to remove toxic matter from my colon proved to be a crucial component in regaining my health. It is nothing short of miraculous, especially having been affected by a toxic buildup in my body for over twenty years.

Assimilation and elimination are two basic functions of the body. When the colon or the liver is not functioning properly, the entire body becomes quite toxic, unable to efficiently rid itself of its own waste. As a result, waste that has not been eliminated begins to putrefy and become toxic, then is reabsorbed into the bloodstream, settling in the weakest organs and tissues. Colon hydrotherapy (CHT) has proven to be the best one as far as removing toxins and other debris of die-off from my system. The intestines are one of the body's largest organs for removal of toxins and poisons. And it stands to reason, as the liver is the primary organ that detoxifies the body of the many chemicals and poisons that we encounter or ingest.

With CHT, the toxins are removed through the bowels. If the large intestine is cleaned out, you are simply going to feel better. Since the blood from the large intestine travels throughout the entire body, you now have a more purified bloodstream flowing through you. Toxins leaving the body through the large intestine, so it makes wonderful sense to have this part of your body as cleansed and pure as possible, especially while attempting any sort of detox or cleanse. Also, when the colon is cleaned out regularly, it allows the liver to dump its toxins much more efficiently, since the pressure of a backed-up colon is now removed from the liver's emptying points.

I have seen this in action time and again, myself. You may believe that your colon is clear if you have a bowel movement every day, but this is not at all the case. Most everyone has fecal matter that has become hardened and impacted on the walls of the colon over a lifetime of improper diet, elimination, faulty detox pathways, and stress of many types. Also, the colon is full of pouches and pockets in which this material can become impacted. It is true that one can still eliminate daily with this condition. So, just think, if the walls of your intestine are clogged, how well are you able to absorb the food you are ingesting and the nutrients in it? You may be constantly ravenous due to this, or you may have little to no appetite due to the liver being too backed up.

Colon hydrotherapy accelerates detoxification of built-up waste products and toxins held in the intestines. Signs that the bowel is toxic are many, including gas, bloating, abdominal distension, poor digestion and absorption of nutrients, body odor, brain fog, fatigue, bad breath, lower back aches, poor elimination, irritable bowel syndrome, spastic colon, colitis, hemorrhoids, diverticulosis, parasitic and yeast infection, and constipation, among others. All of these are clues that our bodies need extra help detoxifying. Those who have become very toxic have much more trouble tolerating any additional exposure to toxins. Colon hydrotherapy is one of the gentlest and safest forms of detox for those who have become so sensitized, because it doesn't pull additional toxins out of the cells; it basically just removes what toxins have been released and are in the gut, unable to be completely released.

Colon hydrotherapy can help flush out parasites and fungal infections as well as remove die-off from these types of parasite or fungal cleanses. It can also be used in place of a barium enema for sigmoidoscopy or colonoscopy or prior to surgery. If you are worried about creating an imbalance of the physiological flora of the large intestine, this does not occur with colonics that are done even up to once a week. One can always supplement with probiotics to counteract this. It has been my experience that the benefits of toxin removal through this route far outweigh any perceived risks.

Colon hydrotherapy includes a gentle infusion of water into the colon, which is the last five to six feet of our digestive tract. It gently soaks and softens hardened fecal material that may have been in the colon for years. If you are worried about contamination of any sort, make sure you go to a colon hydrotherapist using a closed system, which is entirely enclosed, and that brand-new, disposable speculums and tubing are used each time. The new tubing and speculums are standard, but not everyone uses a closed system. In this way, any offensive odors are avoided, and the utmost sanitation is maintained. Any good colon hydrotherapist will be skilled around maintaining an individual's privacy and dignity.

In case you are worried about the risk of losing your gut microbiome, most colon hydrotherapists will do probiotic implants if you request them. If you search, you'll get a really good one who understands how to hold space for you as you release toxic matter from your gut, as sometimes this will also cause a lot of old emotional trauma and mental constructs to be released. By holding space, I mean to be available for to talk without passing judgment and practicing empathy and compassion. I happened to get one of the best, and this experience helped me to decide to become a colon hydrotherapist myself.

Colonics can quickly result in dramatically increased energy levels, better bowel function, weight loss, better nutrient absorption, and clearer, more focused thinking. I know some of you may find the thought of colonics disgusting or even frightening, but the results may be well worth your moving past these feelings. Many times, I was able to see old, black, hardened matter, parasites, and fungal balls leaving my bowel through the observation tube, which you can watch if you are the type to want to do so. For me, this was very encouraging, to say the least, since I now had toxic matter being removed at an accelerated rate from my body.

Purification creates health and integration on very deep levels, so it is the foundation for a life worth living. It allows room for the light or spirit to come into your being. I plan to keep up with it for the rest of my life for not only this reason but because my detox pathways need it, and the world is not the purest place to live as of yet.

I'm going to go into some real detail as to what I do as far as detox goes. This is for those interested in that and to learn how one can achieve a better state of health and well-being. If you are seriously ill and cannot start at this level I am describing here without possibly incurring serious harm to yourself, then I encourage you to do some of the very simple steps only, those you can tolerate well. I will list some of these first.

Some easy things to do to start off slowly purifying your body are breathing, gentle stretching in bed, short and slow walks, gentle massage of your face and neck, reflexology, acupressure points, dry skin brushing, hot and cold showers, and lukewarm bathtub soaks with sea salt and baking soda. Even things like singing and talking help to reset your vagus nerve, which can help you to feel better, think more clearly, and have greater emotional stability. Always make sure your diet is all organic, whole foods (nothing premade, processed, or in a box or can) and as alkaline as possible. While it's best to do this in the most natural possible ways, using diet, when you're having real trouble staying alkaline, I do recommend using half a teaspoon of baking soda in four to eight ounces of water once or twice a day to keep your body more alkaline. Staying more alkaline as opposed to acidic is a good way to keep dis-ease and degenerative processes subdued.

Before embarking on a detox program, make sure your gut health is as optimal as possible. Without this healing first, you will have more trouble absorbing nutrients from foods and supplements. I highly recommend following a good gut-healing protocol, which can be obtained by the steps listed in the following paragraphs.

For starters, it's best to avoid foods such as gluten-containing grains and high-lectin foods, which can be quite inflammatory. If you must consume some high-lectin foods, it is better to take the supplement Lectin Protect just before eating them, if you know you have this issue. This will protect your system from increased inflammation from these types of foods. Foods that are highest in lectins include kidney beans, legumes, grains, soy, potatoes, eggplant, tomatoes, and peanuts. Peanuts are also high in aspergillus mold, making them quite toxic.

If you are at a point where you have virtually no beneficial intestinal flora from too many antibiotics, you will need to limit or not have any fermented foods for a while, until you can get some beneficial flora reinstated with a high-quality probiotic. The reason for this is that without any good flora, if you eat a fermented food that is slightly tainted with a bad bacteria, it can overcome your system, causing a systemic infection. It is best to have a stool culture done by your doctor or naturopath before starting to consume fermented foods. It's a really good idea to make sure you have some good flora left first before consuming anything fermented.

Of course you'll want to avoid sugar, cane sugar especially. Some sweeteners such as honey, maple syrup, and date sugar are OK. Try to use primarily stevia, however. The only sweeteners I consume are manuka honey, coconut sugar, maple syrup, or stevia. No dairy, eggs, soy, grains, white foods (empty calories and are horrifyingly bad for your health), corn, beans, nightshades, coffee, alcohol, peanuts, meat, or chicken. Most of these foods are very high in lectins, a highly inflammatory agent, and it makes no sense to add anything inflammatory to a struggling body. You have to find what's right for you, however.

Some of the best supplements I found for rebuilding my intestinal wall lining were aloe vera, collagen, immunoglobulins, spore-based probiotics, digestive enzymes, L-glutamine, licorice root, N-acetyl glucosamine, marshmallow root, and slippery elm bark. Dr. Josh Axe is well known for his wonderful advice on this issue.

Once you feel you're strong enough to begin a more involved detoxification protocol, it's best to make sure you are getting enough minerals, amino acids, and electrolytes to support your body in the process. I really like magnesium glycinate and ReMag, which is liquid magnesium chloride. It tastes terrible, however, so mix it with juice or even water with stevia in it. I feel zinc, selenium, and manganese are pretty important ones. Sea veggies are high in minerals if you have trouble tolerating minerals. I know they've been easier for me. The nori sheets make great snacks.

For electrolytes, I like Pure Planet Sports Salts, or sometimes I just add sea salt and lemon juice to my drinking water. I tend to stay away from tri-salts, as I don't do well with excess calcium.

Anyone with any arthritis will do better keeping calcium intake lower, as the excess tends to deposit in the joints. Everyone is different, so you must find and do what is right for you.

Next, I feel it's important to make sure your bowels are working efficiently so as to help in the process of eliminating toxins in a timely way. I use the ayurvedic herb called Triphala, which is a combination of three herbs that are very cleansing to the digestive tract. It is probably the most gentle laxative there is, and it is also antiparasitic and anticancer. I also use Cape Aloe, as it's more gentle on my stomach than other aloes. I also use aloe vera juice in smoothies. Essiac tonic or tea, in addition to being a great cleanser, also has turkey rhubarb in it, which is great for moving the bowels. I tend to stay away from the harsher laxatives, such as senna and psyllium. I've also used Oxypowder, which is magnesium oxide, at times.

Also, it is very important to have enough antioxidants, such as vitamin C. I like Ester C or camu camu powder, which is a fruit from shrubs in the Amazon rain forest and high in vitamin C. I'm a fan of bilberry as an antioxidant. You may also want to take vitamins E and A. There are many herbs that are high in antioxidants as well. Rhodiola is one of my favorites, as it's also an adaptogen and helps with muscle recovery after exercise.

Adaptogens are helpful in counteracting the effects of stress and are very supportive to your immune, endocrine, and neurological systems. These are found in many herbs, roots, and fungi. They can be a stimulant, so it's best to take in the morning. However, they are adaptogens, so if you have trouble sleeping, they may help you fall asleep more easily, even when taken earlier in the day. In addition to rhodiola, I also like ashwagandha, schisandra, and eleuthero.

Amino acids are pretty crucial to have in the detoxification process and are essential for all metabolic processes in the body.

If you're not allergic to dairy, then whey protein powder is great. If so, you can get an amino acid supplement at your health food store or make your own vegan protein powder by grinding up any combination of seeds like hemp, chia, pumpkin, flax, and pea protein powder. These are all high in amino acids. Also, camu camu powder and maca powder, which is one of the most nutrient-dense superfoods, have amino acids.

If you think you have to take antibiotics at the first sign of an infection, you usually do not—even when it's strep throat. There is something called Rife frequencies, which you can listen to on YouTube for free, that can treat or cure almost any malady. All conditions have a certain frequency, and an impulse of the same frequency is used to kill or disable diseased cells, just by listening to them with headphones or earbuds. I've used them quite a few times, usually when I feel a sore throat coming on, as I've had strep in the past and don't wish to take antibiotics ever again if I don't need to.

Every single time, when I catch it right away, the sore throat has been cured with two sessions within a twelve-hour period of listening to the Rife frequencies. These have been more potent and faster acting than antibiotics ever were for me, with zero side effects. I urge you to try listening to these, as opposed to running to the antibiotics. At the very least, there are many herbals with antimicrobial properties.

Once you've gotten your gut health in order, it would be good to start doing an antimicrobial and antiviral. I never found pharmaceutical antifungals helpful. I do agree with the medical mediums' views on candida. The reason why is that in all the years I was sick before discovering I had Lyme disease, antifungals did almost nothing to improve my health in any way. Nor did limiting my fruit intake. I no longer believe fruit to be a culprit in fungal overgrowth. Pure sugar and starchy, nutrient-devoid foods, yes. Fruit is actually one of the best foods, as it is very high in vitamins. Pharmaceutical antifungals always made me worse, if anything. I had horrible side effects and was weaker overall after a course.

What cured my yeast infection was addressing my bacterial overload. I cannot explain that scientifically, but I know for me it was true. It may have to do with the symbiotic effect of coinfections. I found my overload of yeast was taken care of after I addressed bacterial infections. I was so shocked that any symptoms having to do with yeast were gone after treating Lyme and other cell wall–deficient bacteria. It may be that many more with MCS have actually been infected with Lyme or other viruses, such as EBV, at some point. I would encourage anyone who questions it to get themselves tested.

For a Lyme test, however, you cannot rely on how just anyone interprets the results. You really need to have it interpreted by a Lyme-literate doctor. To find one, simply Google "Lyme-literate doctors." Part of the issue is that with the antibiotic overuse, bacteria have become smart, stronger, and cell wall–deficient, which means they can hide out in the immune cells that are designed to be killing them off. This, unfortunately, is the reason for a lot of autoimmune diseases, heart disease, diabetes, and many others. Many will not be able to improve without addressing underlying bacterial and viral infections. I cannot stress to you how crucial doing this is. We have been largely misled to believe that our issues with chemicals are unique to us and that we are allergic or otherwise having an odd response.

This so-called odd response, cancer, or other autoimmune diseases without any seemingly good reason will eventually happen to anyone who ends up with a toxic slew overloading their bodies with chemicals, untreated viral and bacterial infections, too many emotional or mental stressors, and things like toxic vaccines and radiation. As all these toxins have increased, more and more people are having serious health issues. The only reason everyone doesn't become chemically sensitive is that we're all different, and this toxic mess affects each one of us in different ways. It eventually could affect almost everyone. We live in precarious times, but I sense those times are on the verge of changing drastically for the better as more people awaken to the truth.

There are many natural products that eliminate these infections. One of my favorites is berberine, which is in Oregon grape root and goldenseal. I feel it is actually more potent by itself. The one I like best is Thorne Berberine-500. Not only does it have anti-inflammatory properties, it's a super antioxidant they claim rivals turmeric. It has dramatic health benefits in almost every category. It helps blood sugar balance, energy, brain power, heart health, blood pressure, digestion, and GI microbial balance and protects the liver, pancreas, and kidneys. I also like Lauricidin, as it is one of the most potent antivirals and has monolaurin in it. Lysine is a favorite antiviral. I drink pau d'arco and rooibos teas, as they both have antimicrobial as well as anticandida properties.

I like Chloroxygen in particular. It reduces inflammation and improves the quality of your red blood cells. I know my blood cells had reduced oxygen-carrying capacity when I was sick, as my oxygen level hovered around eighty-eight, and below ninety is too low. It is so much easier to take Chloroxygen than to breathe oxygen from a tank regularly. It also has anticancer and detoxifying effects and helps to decrease aflatoxin biomarkers.

Now, when you are starting to detoxify in earnest and feeling some side effects from it, taking some binders can really help, as they mop up or bind the toxins in your bloodstream to be moved out. They can help you feel better while you detox. My favorites are activated charcoal, liquid bentonite clay, modifilan, zeolite, pectin, and algin. Use them whenever you feel the need, but try to use these two hours away from any other supplements and your electrolytes. You will need to replenish regularly with electrolytes while taking binders or doing coffee enemas or colonics.

My favorite technique for feeling better while detoxing is the coffee enema. There is a reason they are becoming so popular. There are even coffee enema support groups on Facebook, with thousands of members worldwide now. In addition, I sometimes take a bath in with a small amount of French green clay or desert red clay (there are so many different types). I never use more than two to four tablespoons of clay, although I know others have used up to a cup. Or, I may use a castor oil pack over my liver for about twenty to thirty minutes, with a hot water bottle on top of it. The clay is excellent at drawing out toxins and heavy metals through your skin pores, and the castor oil pulls toxins out of your liver.

Coffee enemas are hugely helpful in detoxifying the liver. The ellagic acid in the coffee causes the liver to produce extra amounts of glutathione, which is the major detoxifying antioxidant your body has. They are also thought to stimulate bile flow, which aids your digestion and helps you absorb fat-soluble vitamins in addition to providing a huge energy boost. You can also use various supplements in your enema water for your colon health or overall health. I like to use the Chloroxygen, as it contains chlorophyll, kills off intestinal bacteria, and loosens debris from the intestinal walls. I regularly add probiotics and essential oils. Optimal Health Network provides information about this and sells the oils as well as organic coffee beans for enemas.

The colon is a major detox pathway, so it's crucial to take care of it. My opinion is that one of the major keys of best health is an optimally functioning and cleaned-out colon. This is one of the ways I got to the place I'm at now, radiant health and bliss.

Detox is not always easy, and it's always different depending on what organ you're concentrating on and what is being released.

Sometimes what gets released is purely physical toxins, and other times it's emotional toxins. Sometimes the body decides to release more in this way, and the emotions that come up are the more deeply buried sort. We sometimes must go through the dark night before we reach that light at the end of the tunnel. Nothing that is worth attaining comes without a great deal of effort. Usually these emotional releases are over in a few hours to a day or two at most.

Whatever you are releasing, whether it be emotional or physical, acceptance is a good thing because it is clearing space for the light and lightness of being to enter, which brings more peace and joy into one's life. And it is this that will ultimately bring you to a state of bliss for prolonged periods.

Connecting with Bliss

The solace everyone is looking to find … is not to
be shut away from the world in some place
but to be free in the world … wherever you are.
—Ron W. Rathbun

I will now describe how I more fully awoke to the essence of my soul, my being, and hence my higher purpose. I will explain how that relates to not only my soul healing but my physical healing. Sometimes things of the spiritual nature are a deep mystery to the logical mind. So, please do not read the following with the idea of it needing to make sense to your mind. Many things can only be understood on a deeper, more intuitive soul level. Try to let go of the need for this to make logical sense or follow any linear timeline, and you will understand far more on a deeper level. I started to awaken to my inner self and intuitive knowing when I began the journey of healing. Precisely a week after I had decided I was done spending the better part of my adult life trying to get my health back, and I let go of needing anything to be other than what it was, I had my first shamanic journey session.

A shaman is a spiritual healer who is gifted in interacting with the spirit world through altered states of consciousness, such as a trance, using the four directions (north, east, south, and west) and elements (fire, earth, air, and water) for the purposes of healing themselves and their community. This ended up being the *cerise sur le gateau* (icing on the cake) for me in my healing journey.

As a result of the shamanic ceremonies I partook in, I became aware of how I came into this world to express my unique individuality and life path. In other words, it fully reconnected me to my spirit. It is hard to fathom the importance of this spiritual reconnection in your overall health and wholeness until you have achieved it. It is the most crucial component for your health and well-being. Many of our ancient and current indigenous tribes have known this and lived by it. I had been reading many spiritual books for a couple decades, partly as a way to deal with being so ill and unable to function in the world but also because I found that type of reading fascinating. I knew it was very important.

My spiritual foundation was learning about the twelve steps used in many groups where addiction is addressed. I found twelve-step programs to be crucial in healing some of the damage done from growing up in a dysfunctional, alcoholic household. Although I am not a supporter of the idea of being sick or limited in any way forever, the twelve steps are a fabulous foundation for spiritual healing and growth—that is, if you truly do the twelve steps in your everyday life. After that, my self-healing journey had a gradual beginning of simply using affirmations. I honestly couldn't tell at first whether or not they were working very well. However, some days I would wake with a crushing migraine and, having young children to take care of, I would tell myself, "I feel wonderful. My head feels fantastic and clear." And within the time it took for Tylenol to take effect, often it would be gone or significantly reduced. Even though I had been lying there in a lot of discomfort and misery and it seemed as if declaring what was obviously untrue to myself could not possibly be of any benefit, I did it anyway.

Affirmations are a beginning step in learning how to do positive self-talk. Later, as I realized the benefits and how the thoughts you let permeate your mind actually begin to create your reality as well as your entire outlook and emotional state, I started to allow *only* positive and uplifting thoughts into my mind. I reasoned if a little was that good, more must be better. And indeed it was. It got to the point where I could no longer let a TV run nonstop in my living space and eventually decided against having it on at all.

Being around people who wanted to persistently speak in a negative way felt exactly like having garbage spewed all over me. I realized it felt much the same being around people who thought that way, even when they did not give voice to it. I felt this sometimes with my husband when we were married. He would not often express negative feelings, primarily as he wasn't aware of them in himself, but he would instead use an unpleasant tone of voice or speak to me in a condescending manner of haughtiness. Or he would not be totally honest, by omission. Those sorts of behaviors are very perceptible to an empath. I feel many who are sickened by living in this world have some degree of empathic-ness.

I began realizing how energy sensitive I was and how programmed my mind had become by living in a fear-based, mind-control-based society. I started to awaken to how asleep everyone was to the energetic effects of our world and how much could change from simply becoming aware and more mindful of exactly what thoughts one allows to take up space in one's mind. One way I know to leave what I (and many others) call the matrix is to retrain your brain to think higher-vibratory and positive thoughts. You begin to think only what you want to be in your world and simply allow no other thoughts. It doesn't happen overnight, but the end result is beautiful and the motivating factor to continue.

Meditation, prayer, and shamanic journeying are some of the best ways to accomplish this reconnection. Or you may want to work with a spiritual guide, intuitive energy healer, or shaman.

When you are in alignment, your focus is more on feeling positive and hopeful and the joy in living, as opposed to things that make you feel stressed or worried or any negative feelings or drain your energy. A great article is "A Meditation to Get into Spiritual Alignment" at www.gabbybernstein.com.

I began my journey of self-healing when I had dental work go very wrong. I had lost bone in two molars, and a dentist told me they needed to be crowned to keep from losing them. He was a biological dentist, and I trusted he would do a good job. Many others with chemical sensitivity had had successful work done by him. I ended up having far too much pressure on my gums from this, which caused an out-of-control infection from the Lyme spirochetes that had hidden in my jaw.

I couldn't easily find a dentist willing to remove the crowns, even though I was in constant discomfort and knew something was quite wrong. The original dentist refused, so I went to another dentist, who also wouldn't, until I kept going back and demanding their removal. When he finally removed the crowns, he gasped in horror at what he saw and insisted I have a root canal to save one of the teeth. I told him that with my autoimmune disease, it was not a good idea. He had no understanding and, in his fear, insisted. His fear was palpable and contagious, and he let me know that as soon as the anesthetic wore off, I would be in a great deal more pain.

So, I had it done against my better judgment. Within a week, I started feeling sick, as the infection had now spread, becoming systemic from having the remains of a dead tooth, which bacteria feed off of. The infection traveled into my heart. I knew this, because I could feel it in my heart. Unbelievably, I was ignored by all health care professionals, as I didn't have a fever or any pus at the site of the root canal. No one seemed knowledgeable of the fact that when one's immune system has been under siege for years, one loses the ability to spike a fever. It didn't seem to matter that my temperature registered at 96.5. Nor did it seem to register at all that I was saying I could feel the infection in my heart! So, no one even prescribed antibiotics for me. I ended up taking every natural and herbal antibiotic I could get my hands on, around the clock. Every three hours, I had to combine three of them to keep from feeling like I was going to keel over and die. I was shaking constantly and had to lower myself to the floor repeatedly to keep from falling.

Unbelievably, two different oral surgeons refused to pull my teeth. I finally found one who would pull them. I still didn't feel normal. I began researching what to do. I was lying there very quiet one day, and I had a vision of these huge spirochete bugs crawling around in my jaw. With this vision aiding my research, I found I could hopefully be helped by having cavitation surgery, which was majorly expensive, so I arranged a trip to Mexico, where it was far more affordable, to have it done by a highly recommended dentist skilled with the procedure. I was so happy because I now was going to get help and maybe survive!

But as my husband was driving us there, we encountered a sandstorm in Yuma, Arizona, on the highway. A woman in front of us panicked with her children in the car and decided to do a U-turn in the middle of the highway to get off. My husband could not avoid hitting her after putting on the brakes and skidding on the sand. Our car was totaled. He said to me, "I guess we're not going."

My iron will rose up, even as sick as I was, and I said, "Oh, we're going. We are getting an ambulance ride or a rental car, and we *are* going." We got a rental car and continued down to Mexico for what I knew was probably the only way I had to stay alive at that point.

After the dentist performed the surgery and burred away some of my jawbone with the infection in it and had the bacteria evaluated, he said to me, "Do you realize if you'd had an autoimmune disease, this amount of infection would've killed you?" It was after this that I returned to the oral surgeon in my town, as the surgical site was not healing well, and he thought I should be checked for cancer. By this time, I was sick to death of health professionals not paying attention to me and then instilling the fear of God into me unnecessarily. I had had enough of that crap for a lifetime.

I calmed myself and left his office. I went home and forced myself to remain calm and not go into fear. As soon as I had the chance, I lay down on my bed and asked spirit what was needed for my jaw to heal. I heard telepathically that infrared laser treatment would be helpful to kill the residual bacteria impeding the healing process. I found a chiropractor who did this work and went to her, and within four four-minute sessions of cold laser therapy, it healed beautifully. There was no cancer. It's just that doctors and dentists don't fully understand many things they see, so they are taught to jump to worst-case scenario in some cases, as they don't want to be the cause of something horrible happening that escaped them.

I learned from this harrowing experience that you may have to become demanding with health care professionals, especially when you know what you need or that you are in a precarious situation. It's hardly the time when you should have to exert that kind of pressure on someone, but be ready in case you do. Also, it's very good to have done as much research as possible on your particular situation so that you can present them with the facts. You need to be very strong within yourself and know you are empowered enough to disagree with someone in a professional or authoritative position. You may need to advocate for yourself and possibly even save your own life. People, professional or otherwise, are not always able to do what needs to be done to address your specific situation properly. This is just one reason it is imperative to step into your responsibility concerning your health.

Many have asked me how I am able to tune in and know certain things, like what I described above. To receive information intuitively, I have to become still and quiet, refusing to allow fear to set in. Fear stops all flow and renders you unable to receive answers from the spiritual realm, and our spirit guides do not operate on that frequency. So, how can you expect to communicate with them while in this state? It's not likely to be successful for you. Those who have had a strong religious upbringing and feel that it is dangerous to ask for help from those in the spirit realm other than Jesus or God can always ask that they are contacted only by Jesus or spirit beings of the light. Those in the spirit realm will know this means you do not want dark, evil, or negative spirits to communicate with you. Always be mindful to ask for what you *want*, not what you don't want. You would not want to phrase your request, "I don't want the dark to connect with me." Instead, ask that only beings from God's hierarchy and legions of angels, archangels, and the light be allowed to come to you.

I knew from early 2009 that if I wanted to survive, let alone heal myself, I would need to do it on my own but with the help of my growing connection to spirit. I began daily, upon awakening, to just lie quietly in bed and ask spirit what I needed to do for my health and well-being. I was never steered wrong, not even once. I didn't always receive answers right away, but maybe later something would cross my path, and I would just know, *This is my answer*. Little by little, I began making sure that my diet contained only the highest-vibrational and densely nutrition-packed foods that I could tolerate.

This involved mostly whole, organic raw foods. I still ate a normally cooked dinner, until one day my naturopath told me to start eating more red meat, as my B vitamin levels were very low. My body immediately gagged at the thought of eating any red meat, so I took this as a sign and the next day began having a big salad for dinner instead of a cooked dinner with red meat! Within three short days, the high anxiety I'd suffered from since the beginning of the dental crisis was gone! I still made the effort to research which raw foods contained the highest amounts of B vitamins and included those daily, and I took hydroxycobolamin B_{12} sublingual drops.

In early 2010 when I was receiving all these colonics, I began to do once-a-month liver flushes, which are a way of cleansing or flushing the liver and gall bladder of accrued toxins and gallstones. I used the one by Andrea Moritz, with olive oil and grapefruit juice. I would go for a colonic the day after each one to help as many of the gallstones as possible be moved out of my system. You can feel fairly ill from leaving them in your intestines longer than necessary. And they don't all come out necessarily just with laxatives or home enemas.

By the time I did the third liver flush and went in the next day for my colonic, the entire time I was releasing, there were large gallstones coming out. For a solid forty-five minutes, the tube was filled with these garbanzo bean–sized and larger gallstones. It was incredible. The therapist was practically screaming with excitement. It was springtime, and I noticed immediate results after releasing that many gallstones at once. I no longer had the springtime allergies I had suffered with for over twenty years.

They were just gone. Completely. My energy levels soared. I could suddenly eat without esophageal reflux and hiatal hernia issues. I lost weight and a roll I'd had around my middle. All of this was mostly from hundreds of gallstones! I had no idea a person could have that much toxic stuff inside them. Gallstones are filled with all kinds of toxins, heavy metals, fungus, and parasites, which is why it is crucial to eliminate them from your body. I had no idea these were contributing so much to so many of my health issues. Life had suddenly taken a new turn for me.

My colon hydrotherapist recommended a shaman whom she held in high regard, telling me she thought I should schedule a few sessions with him. She continued to bring him up periodically and persistently. A few months later, she called a friend while I was on her table having a colonic. I had no idea why she was doing that in the middle of my appointment with her, as this was out of character, so I figured I'd give her the benefit of the doubt and assume there was a really important reason she needed to do it at that moment.

Within a few minutes, she gave me the phone, saying her friend wanted to talk to me. I took the phone, and it was the shaman I had spoken to a few months ago. This time, I submitted to fate and let him talk me into coming to see him. That turned out to be pivotal, life-changing, and one of the best decisions of my life. It was the first real step I had taken in this lifetime to start to truly know and understand myself on the spiritual level.

The truth of who I am was revealed to me in a way that was a building block for what has come since. It had the effect of turning me inside out and upside down in absolutely the best way possible for my soul and hence my entire being. It was very intense, as it ultimately caused me to have a profound spiritual awakening. I know some may not be able to handle or appreciate this kind of intensity, but as an astrologically Plutonic personality, it is my life's breath, transformation at the core. Pluto is the planet of death and rebirth, depth and transformation, and in my birth chart, Pluto sits in conjunction with Jupiter, the planet of expansion, abundance, and spirituality on my IC, or inner core angle. In addition, almost every planet in my chart is aspected to Pluto, making me a Plutonic person.

Although I had been on what I considered a spiritual path, seeking answers to everything for many years prior, I had just started being able to receive information and answers through my own connection to the divine. At one point, I bought an oracle deck of ascended masters cards. I felt more drawn to them than any others at that time (such as the archangel or goddess decks). I started drawing a daily card to help me better access my own wisdom. Many days, the message of the particular ascended master seemed right on target. I had been doing this for a few months and was also just a few months into the raw foods and the colonics. For five straight days before the shamanic ceremony, every single day, I drew the Ascended Master Aengus card from my deck, the representation of twin flames. A twin flame is considered to be a mirror soul or a very intense soul connection. I had no idea at that time what the message of the twin fame card meant. I feel the significance of it now, as I was brought into communion with my soul and spirit in a way I had never known—a merging of my divine feminine and masculine attributes.

And of course, people feel they have met their twin flame (a partner who has also merged with their spiritual self) in life, and this is said to differ from a soul mate. Soul mates are supposedly plentiful, whereas twin flames are an esoteric or new age spiritual concept, and there is only one other who is considered to be your absolute divine counterpart. I had no idea what drawing this card every day for those five days in a row meant, and I had not even been searching for, much less thinking about, finding my twin flame *or* soul mate. I was married and had been for twenty-four years. I was not totally happy in my marriage for many reasons and was not truly compatible with my husband. Nevertheless, I didn't pay too much mind to the twin flame card, except to think it was a little odd that it kept coming up.

For my first shamanic ceremony, I was told to formulate an intention for what I wished to achieve, gain, or manifest as a result of the session. I had reached a point in my healing process in which I had let go of any need to be what I deemed well, healed, or whole. Just the week before I went, I had an epiphany of sorts, in which I was exhausted from the struggle of striving intensely to heal myself. I had a moment where I suddenly and profoundly understood I may only have a couple of decades left on the earth plane. I didn't want the remainder of my life to be spent trying so hard to achieve what might not be achievable.

I also realized I had glimpsed some of the joy and wonder life held, and I didn't want to hold onto needing to be healed and well to experience as much joy and wonder as I possibly could in the time I had left here on the planet. I had a conversation with spirit or God and said silently, "OK, I get it. I get that I came into this life to experience it as a sick person. There is no rhyme or reason in that for me, but so it is. I am done with being unhappy with my plight or state of affairs, and from here on out, I am going to live my life in a state of gratitude and joy and happiness for whatever is." Of course, I still desired wellness and was committed to guiding myself along a path that would hopefully lead to this. I knew I would still be very proactive in my healing journey. But I was no longer willing to say to myself, "I will be happy and my life will be worth living *when* I get well."

Therefore, I was no longer willing to submit to being miserable because I wasn't in a state of perfect health yet and might not ever be. In essence, I surrendered to my life as it was, vowing to make the most of the cards I'd been dealt instead of wallowing in sorrow, misery, regret, victimhood, anger, bitterness, and on and on. I made the decision to be happy with what was, while at the same time continuing to work on improving my health and life. So, I found it felt inauthentic to make my intention be for the shaman to help me get well. I wasn't resigned to being sick so much as I surrendered to it. I accepted it in March 2010, finally after twenty years! I still have a hard time understanding why it took so long.

I think it was in large part because I was very invested in my mind or intellect being able to figure this thing out and healing myself that way. Science, my intellect, and medicine would surely have the answers, I reasoned. Well, guess what? It never worked that way. And it wasn't as if I was not blessed intellectually, especially in the area of medicine. I did try most of the treatments and modalities out there. It improved things for me and also for others I was in contact with at times. And now I understand why, as it is only a part of the puzzle, and it's not even the foundation or major part. But we've been trained to use our brains over all else, our minds, and we have all been, for the most part, firmly entrenched in believing this untruth that the mind, intellect, or ego will guide us correctly and safely on the best path in life. I had woken up ever so slowly to this untrue belief system.

I showed up on time on March 21, 2010, for my first shamanic ceremony and told the shaman, Aragon, that my intention was to receive from the ceremony an understanding on the spiritual level of why I had suffered physically for so many years. This ceremony was my introduction into a world that blew the cover off of most of the premises and mind constructs I'd been taught all my life. It expanded me in a way that may terrify some who are not fully surrendered and ready. The reason for this is that the ego will do almost anything to avoid discovering the truth about itself, as there is a basic human fear of the void, of nonexistence. When you have a spiritual awakening, it is, in a sense, death for the ego. It can feel like one is literally dying, although what is really dying is the old you, the parts that do not serve you any longer. I know now, beyond any shadow of doubt, I was very ready for this to take place in my life. And because of that, it was anything but terrifying. It felt exciting and so expansive to know there was something beyond what I had thought to be my reality.

Shamans work with the elements water, earth, wind, fire, and ethers and the four directions, in addition to the spirit world. Aragon called in the four directions, east, south, west, and north, as well as above and below, each representing the elements of air, earth, water, fire, and ether. He also called in all of the spiritual helpers and animal spirits that would be assisting. He cleared me and the room with burning sage and began drumming rhythmically and loudly and rattling over me. Aragon was quite the dramatic and showy shaman, speaking and proclaiming authoritatively and forcefully in his deeply resonant French-accented voice. He was very tall and magnetic, with an air of mystery. He extremely good-looking, with dark shoulder-length hair and wearing all white, as he had asked me to wear for the ceremonies. He put on quite the show, and it was not a facade. He turned out to be the most gifted and powerful of all healers I have ever known.

He guided me through breathing in and up through all my chakras, having me visualize the colors associated with each chakra and the energy flowing into and out of each chakra. Then he demonstrated how and guided me through about an hour of what is known as breath of fire (a rapid panting breath with the mouth wide open and tongue hanging out). I was determined to do it for as long as he wanted me to, as I was in a place of surrender and trust, not having any attachment to the outcome. In the middle of it, he placed some intense pressure on my solar plexus, which was somewhat uncomfortable (but never too much to handle), and he encouraged me to scream as loudly as I felt like screaming during this. This was to help me release pent-up emotions like anger and rage from past traumas.

There were other things that occurred during the ceremony that I still don't have total recall of, due to the trance I was in. Aragon also did some physical work with my feet and ankles, most likely to ground me back into my body toward the end, as I recall. I had no fear of being harmed and just trusted and acted. I was very energized by the oxygen coursing through me, although it did cause numbness (for a short time) not just in my hands and feet but my arms and legs and even lower torso.

Did I care? Not at all. I had been sick for so long and had come close to what felt like death multiple times. And perhaps due to some of the brain retraining work and affirmations, I didn't have a lot of fear left around death. I figured when it was my time to transition, it was my time. My reconnection with spirit must have begun happening before doing the breath of fire, in the trance mode, because at that point in the session, I was no longer fearful about anything. My limbs and part of my torso becoming numb was not dangerous as long as I was capable of breathing that intensely for so long, and it wore off fairly quickly once I stopped. This surrendering allows all manner of miracles to flow into your being. I didn't feel as if I was in an altered state at the time, as I was conscious and completely aware, but I have looked back in retrospect and absolutely know I was in an altered state. This altered state is essential for being open to surrendering and receiving whatever it is possible to receive in this state, as well as to put what is received together in a way that may have been previously unfathomable to you.

The altered trance state feels similar to how you might feel after a deep meditation or hypnosis. Aragon guided me in a visual journey and had me visualize people and describe to him the animals that appeared to me. He had me ask them if they had any wisdom to offer me. I don't remember it now, but I do know it was pertinent information at that time. A very short time after being in this trancelike mode, perhaps only ten minutes in, he asked me what my relationship with my mother had been like. It struck me as a bit like therapy, only I was lying down on a comfy mat on the floor, fully relaxed and trusting and open.

In this state, I was able to have a clear vision of sitting at the kitchen table with my mother when I was four years old, and she with her head on the table, crying. I was very sad not only because she was so sad, but I saw myself reasoning very naively from my four-year-old mind that I was the cause of her sadness. I wanted her to be happy with me but felt she wasn't. Remember, I knew I had been born with a level of sensitivity that did not seem to please my mother or make her life easy. I saw that she had a lot of trouble either identifying with my extreme sensitivity or accepting that about me.

I knew my mother was unhappy, and I recalled very vividly in this trance state, as a four-year-old, deciding to be who she wanted me to be, to make her happy. I felt so awful and sad and wanted so much for her to be happy. Why? Because I loved her and also so that she could be a better mother for me. I decided to try my best to be the person she wanted me to be. And in that moment, I realized I had most definitively decided not to be who I came here to be. People don't think children that young can make such decisions, but I saw myself in the trance state at that age, and I know damn well that is exactly what happened.

The second I said these words, "My mother wasn't happy with who I was, so I decided to be who she wanted me to be," out loud to Aragon, my body, which had been lying peacefully, sat bolt upright seemingly by itself, and I screamed, "Oh my God, oh my God, oh my God!" It was as if I had woken from a bad dream and been removed from the illusion I had been playing a part in my entire life. I knew in that moment how that decision had affected my life. I also knew in my heart and soul that it was I as that four-year-old child who had made that decision and carried it out.

I was gifted at the same time with the knowledge that on the deepest level possible, that decision had left me feeling alone in this world and separated, at the age of four, from who I was, my spirit—my connection to Source. I knew that in that state of perceived aloneness, this world was a very scary place. Because I was *alone*. When you are connected to Spirit, to Source, to Who

You Are, you are never alone. You always have help and guidance for the asking. This brings peace, serenity, love, joy, and healing, and it is why we are always encouraged to meditate by spiritual gurus who understand this premise. It is why many of us are here, to return to this beautiful remembrance. It is the remembrance of unity and oneness on a personal level.

It took many years of living in this constant state of disconnect, and the underlying fear was so pervasive I didn't even recognize it as fear, and I didn't know how much of it I had carried with me constantly, until the day after this first ceremony. I think my body went bolt upright in the moment my spirit reconnected with my being because it actually moved in through my crown chakra and gave me downloads of a lot of information at once, which I would have been conscious of for many years, had I been connected, but I was just now allowing it in and to happen. I had given my spirit permission to come back and reside in me.

You cannot imagine how different I felt after that took place. The spirit is what gives the body life force energy and keeps it alive. You need your spirit connected to be whole and vibrantly healthy. I was finally at peace, calm in a way I didn't ever remember feeling in my life. I was also quite stunned, in a daze of new understanding about many, many things. It felt miraculous, and I am still certain that it was one of the biggest miracles I will probably experience in this life.

I lay back down after sitting bolt upright, and Aragon continued the ceremony. Finally, he closed the four directions and thanked all the spiritual helpers who had come to assist, then completed the ceremony. I then had the chance to sit up, use the bathroom, have a drink of water, and sit quietly for a few minutes. Then he returned and asked, "So, how are you feeling?"

I was in a daze, and what spilled out of my gut I could not have predicted. I said, "I know I need to leave my husband." The moment that came out, I felt shocked. It was almost as if I had heard someone else say it, and at the same time, I knew I was expressing my deepest truth in that moment. Subconsciously, I had known I had needed to do it for a very long time, as we were incompatible.

I had no clue at the time how much going against my spirit had contributed to my illness. I do not blame my husband. In fact, it is the opposite. The responsibility was mine. I had been so disconnected from my soul that I was incapable of making decisions based on my heart, my soul and spirit. Instead, I had been in the habit of making decisions for myself based on my intellect, mind, or ego. This was all about to change and put me into a very different place, a place that came from my core power. That place of power is the only place one can be in when connected to their spirit source. You cannot behave with anything other than true alignment with your spirit when in direct and conscious connection with it—your I Am, your oneness with all that is.

It is this that gives you your true power and provides all the guidance, safety, security, love, and joy you will ever need. It is what is meant by the universe being within. You do have everything you will ever need inside you. I began to understand that was what drawing that twin flame card from the ascended masters deck was about—the internal integration of my divine feminine and masculine. This is what the true twin flame relationship is about, your connection to yourself at the deepest level and your connection to all that is.

I went home, and when I awoke the next day, I felt very different. Something profound had shifted inside me, and I had yet to discover what it was. It was such deep inner work. I could have gotten up and gone about my day as usual, but all I really wanted to do was lie there in this state of divine grace and sweetness, letting my body and my being integrate whatever changes had happened. I found myself looking around as if I were a newborn babe, examining all I saw and thought with a totally fresh and vibrant new perspective. I cannot begin to adequately describe how luscious it was. The memory of that feeling has stayed with me to this day, ten years later. A miracle had occurred for me, one that I sincerely wish upon every being on this planet. I know it is possible, and as I write that, I smile with the deepest knowing.

I did get up the day after that and decided without any real thought or hesitation to go to several places in town, just because they sounded like fun things I really wanted to do. This may not sound terribly impressive, until you recall that for about fifteen years before this, I had not really gone anywhere other than the grocery store or the doctor's office in my efforts to avoid inhaling and absorbing potent toxic chemicals that I would later detox much like a heroin addict detoxes heroin. It was far too nightmarishly uncomfortable to endure repeatedly. That day was different, however, and it wasn't until I arrived back home that I realized what I had done. I was floored. At first, I could not fathom what had possessed me to do what I had done. As I said, no thought had gone into what I was doing. It was as if my body was being directed by this new soul connection, making it feel as if I was on autopilot.

However, I soon realized all the years of being directed by my mind were the times of true autopilot. This other way is so much more meaningful, bringing synchronicity and a true connection with the possibility of all that is. I thought, *Why on earth did I do all these things, go to all these places that I haven't allowed myself to go to in fifteen years?* The only answer I could come up with was they were things my spirit really wanted to do. I went to a fabric store because I wanted to get some art supplies, and then I went to the library to check out some books and videos. It felt good, like I was partaking of what life had to offer, even if only in a small way. However, one with MCS realizes these are actually huge steps back into wellness.

I realized that I had had no thought whatsoever of being sick or not being able to do exactly what I wished. It was as if any concept or thought of illness or disability or limitation had left my brain. It was like an amnesia of sorts, and although I could recall having been desperately sick, it was with a detachment I found incredible, almost as if it had happened to someone else, but I had a front-row seat to what it had been like. And I now understood more fully that what had happened resulted initially from a disconnect with my spirit, so total that it left my body and psyche physiologically unable to maintain a healthy equilibrium. I began to understand that without Spirit here with me, operating through me and propelling me forward in life, I had been open to attack or invasion on many levels.

As the days following this shamanic ceremony went by, I became increasingly aware that my thought processes and the way I saw life itself had been quite altered in the best of ways. I was *unable* to focus on worrisome thoughts or anything that brought forth any amount of fear. These things now seemed irrelevant. What struck me as relevant was just *being*, enjoying the state of bliss that I now found myself in almost constantly. It turned out that without all the fear-based thoughts I had been trained all my life to maintain, everything became peace, bliss, and ecstasy—or one might say love. It helped me understand how much fear is the opposing force of love.

I knew on a profound level that this is the way it is supposed to be. This is what Creator Source intended for us. I knew that God is a benevolent being wanting only the best for us, like we do for our children. He knows we will have to go through some suffering as part of our learning process, but He also knows that when we are ready, we will choose to be in alignment, to surrender to the greater plan or will, and in essence choose nonsuffering. All is happening just as it is supposed to happen according to the divine plan. Just because we have not understood or remembered that on this planet for eons doesn't mean there isn't a divine plan and that we can't choose to allow it to run the show.

And then we will look around and say, "Oh, so it was that easy?" It was there for the choosing all along. When you are ready, it will always be there just for you. It seems so much harder from the outside looking in. When you do finally choose, you will be stunned how simple it is. You don't run the show, and your ego/mind does not, as much as it wants to think it does. It never did. Twelve-step programs know all about it; they call it *let go and let God*. Many fear this will be a fate worse than death, and the ego/mind definitely wants you to believe this. It does seem that most people do it only when they have no place else to go and are down for the count. I don't know. Maybe this is the only way.

I prefer to think it's easier for some. It's not a horrible thing at all; it's the opposite, in fact. All striving, suffering, and struggling ends because you decide to let it go and trust that Spirit will reach out and catch you the moment you decide you no longer want to hold on with your last bit of strength. It will be there every time for every person, to reach up and cushion you as you fall in your surrender. It is just a decision you make, when you are too tired to go on in the same way you have been. It must be a universal law that there is something, some energy, that is greater and understands more than the left sides of our brains. That's the old three-dimensional way; the new way uses both sides of our brains. That is what begins to catapult our entire planet into a higher vibration.

The best reason to let go and surrender, which means to step away from your ego, is you will find yourself feeling much happier, peaceful, and joyful. Once you do this loving thing for yourself, it begins to ripple out and affect all you are in contact with. Some of the best ways to accomplish this are practices of gratitude, meditation, forgiveness, honesty, openness, prayer, and letting go of the need to control outcomes. We have been under the illusion that we can and should try to control as many outcomes as possible. That is an illusion. It's so much better to give the control to a higher power or God. Lack is another faulty construct we've been taught from early on. Learn to have faith and trust that this is a universe of abundance that always wants the highest good for you.

I proceeded to initiate my divorce and knew my husband would be better off with someone who could really love him in the way he deserved and that was more suited for him. Also, after living with someone who was as sick as I was all those years, he had a difficult time with the changes that happened almost overnight in me. It is hard to go from one paradigm to another in such a short time, harder for some than others.

A few months after my initial meeting and ceremonies with Aragon, I had a chance encounter with him at a spiritual gathering. I believe I had some knowing at this point about an attraction and karmic past lives with him, although it hadn't entirely bubbled to the surface at that point.

I was shocked to see him, and he asked me how I'd been since the ceremonies. I had realized that ever since the first session, whatever my being was feeling or intuiting just seemed to pop out of my mouth with no thought. I said, "I finally understand what Rumi meant when he wrote, 'My heart is on fire.'" I sat there trying to think what that meant, as I had no thought about saying this; it was one of those things that just popped out. I think I was referring to the kundalini energy having risen up to my heart chakra and beyond, and it felt as if I was completely in touch with my heart and the passion it felt for life and for my beingness. It was such an incredible feeling. When I looked back at him, I felt suddenly struck, as if by lightning, when my eyes met his. I was overwhelmed with an intensity coming from him, it seemed, that I'd never felt in my life. I truly saw a blinding golden light pouring out of his eyes when our eyes met. I believe now he was a mirror for me, and I was seeing my own radiance mirrored back to me and witnessing it for the first time ever.

Shocked, I looked to the side and down, not understanding why I felt something so magnetically overpowering when I looked at him. I'd been attracted to men before, even incredibly attracted, but this was different. It was a force of nature that dropped right into my lap with no warning, no thought. I cannot describe the strength of it accurately; maybe there just aren't words. If I could, I would say it was perhaps like seeing the most beautiful sight you've ever seen for the first time ever, having been completely blind before this moment. What popped out of my mouth next was "Oh my God, you're so magnetic." I was instantly floored and mortified that I had said that, with no real understanding of why I did. But there it was, laid out, bare and naked. Then he said to me, "You are too."

I gasped and said, "No, I'm not," as I had never thought of myself that way. I had been incredibly unaware of myself for years. I was immediately sorry I'd said this, as I knew that what he said was true, and not just to him. He said he felt we'd been together in previous lives as healers, one in Atlantis. I had already been told by a psychic that I had been a healer in Atlantis in a past life. I am clairaudient, meaning I hear the voice of Spirit or the divine speaking to me, especially when I really need some help or specific knowledge. I heard Spirit say to me that it was a divinely orchestrated meeting at this point and to know and trust that all was in divine order. We are all individuals, and we must learn to listen to and trust that inner voice, the voice of Spirit, to guide us.

If I'd used my mind in that situation, it would have said, "What are you thinking? This is ludicrous." To the thinking mind, that can certainly appear to be true. The rational mind wants to keep us safe at all times, constantly trying to keep us in a box, which feels like safety. Spirit knows different. It understands things our rational thought process cannot begin to fathom.

A few days later, after I'd heard from Spirit, I contacted Aragon and asked to meet again. When we met again, after greeting warmly and clearing any negative energies with sage and sweetgrass, we began with the tantric kiss, and we stayed in this kiss and seated embrace (my legs over his) for about fifteen minutes. It was very beautiful and not like anything I'd experienced before. Then we almost flew into bed together and proceeded to engage in the most beautiful tantric lovemaking for several hours. It was as if we knew each other's bodies intimately already and had been made for each other.

Tantra is a Sanskrit word that means "woven together." Tantra is not only a sexual practice; it is a spiritual science for self-inquiry and evolution, as well as a path for liberation from karma, reincarnation, and the Maya or matrix. Hindu and Buddhist meditation practitioners use sexual union as a metaphor for weaving together the physical and the spiritual: weaving man to woman and humanity to the divine. The purpose is to experience oneness with God. The Western form of this sacred sexuality, called Tantra, teaches slow, nonorgasmic, meditative sexual intercourse (www.besthealthmag.ca.), as removed as it can possibly be from the Western culture of pornographic sex. It changed my life immeasurably. For those who have no previous experience or knowledge of tantra, when used in the sexual realm, it combines yogic principles, meditation, and breathwork with sex.

This all works together to create a state of profound relaxation and bliss in the body and being. It is a modality used to intertwine sex with spirituality, which brings the act of making love and your entire being to a new level. I can definitely attest to the fact that it did this for me, and it became a crucial part of my healing. I can't say for sure why. It is a known way to help the traumas of sexual abuse, although I had no sexual abuse in my background. It just seemed to be exactly what I needed, an incorporation of my being on *all* levels—not just one level of being, but the spiritual, physical, sexual, and emotional, more fully awakening my kundalini life force energy.

As I got up from the bed, I realized I was completely distracted by a feeling I was having internally. It was a vibrating or shaking going all the way up my spine. Since I'd never had this feeling in my life, I was trying to identify what it was. I started questioning myself, asking if I felt nervous, as it felt sort of like a nervous shakiness. I checked in and realized, *No, I am not nervous. I am very relaxed instead.* Then I asked myself if I was cold, as it could've been a shaking from being cold to the core. I was not cold either. I tried then to ignore it since I couldn't put my finger on what it was, although I knew I'd not previously experienced a sensation quite like it.

Within a week's time after this encounter, I began waking every morning at three o'clock, writhing all over in a state of bliss and ecstasy. That was the beginning of my kundalini awakening or rising. To this day, I cannot fully explain why my kundalini woke up and happened the way it did, but I do have some nuggets of information on it. The first factor is that my gut was cleaned out from the months of raw food and colonics. The intestinal tract is in the exact location of the sacral chakra and very close to where the kundalini lies sleeping at the root chakra. I had been seriously working on detoxifying for close to two years at that point.

The second factor is that I had done years of counseling and twelve-step work to clear myself emotionally from early childhood trauma as well as emotional trauma that was happening within my marriage. And, finally, when I did an astrological synastry chart (comparison of aspects between astrological charts to determine relationship compatibility) that put our two charts together, I discovered that Aragon's Lilith, the asteroid of sex, was conjunct my Mars, the planet of male sexual energy, action, and desire. Further research into this aspect uncovered that it is a known recipe for a kundalini awakening. Later on, another astrologer told me that it was in my natal chart for me to have a kundalini wake-up in midlife. Again, they say it happens when it is time for that person to awaken.

Kundalini is life force and the same energy that a Reiki practitioner will use when they do energy healing work. Now I had a connection to my own supply twenty-four seven! It was unfathomably healing and superbly energizing. I know that I was directed by my higher self to do exactly what I did. I feel certain that Aragon and I were fated to reconnect with each other in this lifetime. I do not know for certain whether he and I are twin flames. However, I'll expand a little more on the subject of twin flames, as that is exactly what I believed was happening at the time.

A few weeks later, I suddenly recalled that I had drawn the twin flame card five days in a row just before meeting him, including the day I met him. When I did more research on twin flames, I found that often they will meet in the most unusual of circumstances and have instantaneous past-life recall and phenomenal, off-the-charts attraction to each other. I also found they will often meet on numerological dates that are significant in the world of numerology, such as a 1/1/1, 2/2/2, or 3/3/3 date. We had met first on March 21, 2010 (numerologically, a 3/3/3 month, day, and year). When I was in his presence, I could physically feel a magnetic push and pull between us. It was as if we could not physically move apart or come closer at times. The energy was electrifying. It also had woken up a psychic connection. I became unusually perceptive, even more so than I'd already been, of many things and also felt a psychic tie to him that was sometimes a bit overwhelming.

I didn't understand a lot of this at first. Thankfully, the state of near samadhi that I was in for several months after my kundalini rose kept me from seeing it all as cause for concern. I mostly had trouble understanding why everyone else was so worried about everything, as it seemed I had lost the capacity for worry or fear about most anything. I just knew, being on the high spiritual plane I found myself on, that I was being cared for, as we all are, and that all would turn out exactly as it was supposed to, regardless of whether I frittered my time away worrying (and making my body sick) or sat there in that state of absolute bliss doing nothing but being (and healing a vast amount).

When I started to awaken at three every morning, writhing somewhat violently all over my bed, it didn't scare me at all; it was a pleasurable sensation. It felt as though all my life force energy was flooding my body upon awakening, and the pathways were so open, and there was so much energy coming in that it physically shook me and twisted me with an incredible force. If it sounds a bit like receiving an electrical shock, it was. I know this feeling too, as I was somewhat violently shocked as a teenager with a force that knocked me back against a wall. It did no serious long-term damage other than precipitate premonitory dreams and a couple of out-of-body experiences that helped me to understand more fully how the spirit lives on after the body dies.

This new sensation included no pain. I experienced only pleasure, in addition to becoming seriously sleep deprived, although the lack of sleep didn't seem to be an issue at all. My body was being sustained by this new and higher-frequency light energy that was flooding it all day long. This shaking continued to happen for twelve straight hours daily, from 3:00 a.m. until 3:00 p.m., for four straight months. I would have some breaks for a few minutes at a time, several times an hour, but other than that, it was pretty much nonstop. I did have rest from it the other twelve hours of each day, and it was not as exhausting as it sounds. It was actually quite energizing and healing on multiple levels.

It was energizing because it was life force energy running unimpeded through me constantly. I was in connection with this vast flow of universal life force, which I know now is everyone's birthright. It was healing, as the energy was akin to Reiki energy being directed through my body from a healer's hands, only multiplied as if I had one hundred healers working on me at all times. It seemed to know exactly where to go, leaving no area untouched, healing my mind, consciousness, and etheric and auric bodies. I had all the commonly known experiences of light, bliss, extreme feelings of oneness and connectedness with all in the universe, and fears completely vanished.

The fear of death was no longer with me. It connected me with a oneness consciousness, and I realized we are fundamentally infinite light, energy, and consciousness that never dies and only transforms. Realizing that has the power to change how you view life, and once that is changed, the possibilities for you are limitless. I feel brain retraining programs can have the same effect but possibly take much longer. I had no need to continue with any brain retraining after my kundalini awakening.

I began looking this up on the internet, as I didn't understand what was happening to me. What I found out shocked me. What I came to discover was that I was experiencing spontaneous and full body orgasmic activity. Oh, that did help to explain why it was so pleasurable and why I was constantly in a state of high arousal, which was not entirely the typical sexual arousal located in the root and sacral chakras but a complete body, mind, spirit melding of ecstasy. I began to understand how connected this life force energy is to our sexual energy. It is all the energy of creation, and it is powerful beyond measure.

I knew at once why our churches and religions have tried to suppress sexuality. Once you are fully in touch with this energy, you become very aware of your own power as a human being and the power of this energy to heal and create almost anything. Religion and authority in power for eons do not want to lose their control over humans; they want us kept and looked after like a herd of sheep, easy to direct and control and dominate. But when you are aware of this unending supply of energy flowing through and around you at all times, you start to become aware that there is much more to everything than we have been taught.

Little secrets from the universe began to flow into my being as if riding in on the waves of energy. This is why it is called a kundalini *awakening*. It is as if you have woken from a deep sleep in which you knew nothing, now highly awake and conscious on a great new level. I had a volcanic kundalini awakening. It was so intense. Like I said, I was in a state of near samadhi for four months, experiencing all the common feelings of being totally expanded and filled with light and bliss and oneness with everything and everyone. I had extreme trouble functioning in linear time.

This may seem terribly important to someone who is functioning fully from their ego state, but it seemed unimportant in the overall scheme of things to me. I really had to force myself to think in terms of time and how I was going to get someplace at a specific time. I've never since felt any need to wear a watch since I cosmically understood there was no time, and all would happen as it was supposed to, regardless of our human-made clocks and schedules. I know many of us think time is terribly important, and if not for timetables, nothing would happen and the world would stop. This is simply not true. Many things that we think should happen do not without the aid of time, but the things that are truly important and ordained by Spirit happen with or without it.

I was in such a state of bliss and new awareness that it was heavenly beyond any experience I've had here in my earthly existence. All I could do was surrender to full body orgasmic bliss, laughing and sitting there in wonder and awe. I could not even remember to eat with any regularity. I experienced very few hunger pains, as my body was constantly fed by this stream of light and love energy coursing through it. At the same time, this energy was burning off as much as it could, any traumas, old beliefs, and toxins that remained in the path of my healing. This is what unimpeded life force energy running through one's body does.

Many become afraid of this energy when they have not come face-to-face with their shadows and inner demons and accepted, healed, and loved those parts of themselves. Much of what may come up could look frightening, especially when these parts of you have been denied or kept hidden from yourself. That has not been my life path as a Plutonic individual with sun and moon in water signs. And even though my entire life has been spent feeling things very deeply, I still had quite a bit of my shadow side come up to be healed and released. This process took years longer, even after the awakening.

Visualize the kundalini serpent, lying coiled at the base of the spine, sleeping until it is awakened. It consists of the *ida* and *pingala*, or male and female energies, which can rise, when awoken, in a spiral from the base of the spine to the top of the crown. Each energy, male and female, crosses over the other through the center of each chakra. I've heard it described as a spigot being turned on and the water running full force through the hose it's attached to. The hose goes suddenly from coiled and contracted to straight and expanded. This helped me understand why I was having all the kriyas, the spastic and sudden rigidity and writhing happening in my body from the energy rising up repeatedly. It felt as if something was being turned on or amped way up at lightning speed inside me, dozens of times daily.

I was told that after a year of this, it would most likely settle down, and I would probably experience a massive depression. The person who told me this clearly didn't understand that mine was a supremely intense volcanic awakening. I have no idea why it was this way for me, and many others have much more sedate awakenings. I think it is different for every individual. At first, I truly thought this had happened to everyone else on the planet and that I had just been missing out or not privy to these special delights, having been so ill for so long. I went about in utter naivete and delight, asking people about their kundalini awakening. I was in dismay that almost no one seemed to have experienced their awakening to the same degree I had.

It does appear now, ten years later, that more people are beginning to experience noticeable awakenings. I have seen this happening on social media platforms where actual groups have formed for people who are undergoing a kundalini awakening or going through the process known as ascension with their physical bodies. It took two and a half years for the energy to settle down, and then it was another year later that I went through depression, a result of being high as a kite for so long and then thudded unceremoniously back down to earth to complete my mission here.

I've heard others who have had near-death experiences describe this awful depression when coming back into their bodies to continue existing here on the earth plane. It is so heavy and dense and hard here compared to the spiritual realm, which is so beautiful, light, blissful, joyful, and peaceful. I can now thankfully say I did not succumb to the depression, and it did not last terribly long, although it was very deep and hard. It happened at the same time as my second Saturn return. Saturn just had to make sure that I was going to ground it here.

I don't believe one needs to have a full-blown kundalini awakening in order to recover from an illness, although it certainly didn't hinder it in my case. It is just what happened in my body at that time. I was not even trying to awaken my kundalini. I don't think I was fully aware of what it entailed. I've heard of people trying for years to wake their kundalini energy through meditation or yoga, and it still doesn't always happen. I believe it happens when it is supposed to and not when we decide with our minds or egos that we are ready for it to happen.

If this is what you are desiring, please be open and as relaxed as you can, letting Spirit guide you as far as your life choices, what you put into your body, who and what you surround yourself with, and how you spend your time. Try to make sure it is all of the highest essence and vibration of pure love and light that you can imagine. I do not think you can achieve this state without a lot of discomfort unless you have been willing to face yourself as honestly and forthrightly as possible and have been a courageous warrior for your own healing (emotional and physical) and transformation. Courage does not mean being fearless; it means facing your darkness in spite of your fear that you are not a good person or your fear that the pain will never end. You will find your true strength and passion and reason for being here once you've really done your deep soul-diving work.

My whole awakening was an all-inclusive event, encompassing physical, mental, emotional, and spiritual healing. I do think that years of a very clean physical lifestyle; all the work I did around healing and releasing negative emotions from childhood; and the serious detoxification I did with raw foods, supplements, and colonics were all precursors to making space to allow the kundalini to rise up from my root chakra, through all the other chakras, to my crown.

I had been on a spiritual seeker's path since about 1987, the time of the Harmonic Convergence. I had had a deep curiosity as well as an inner knowing about many things once I saw, read, or discovered them for the first time (in this life anyway). I think having developed this fairly extensive knowledge of metaphysics and the spiritual realm really helped me to move through the difficulties and limitations in my life with a much greater ease and fortitude than I otherwise would've been able to. Understanding universal law and how it works helped lay some of the foundation for my recovery.

Heaven knows organized religion offered me very little in this regard. This gave me great strength and hope, both of which went a very long way in living a life of much higher quality and meaning than I would have been able to otherwise, considering I had been stripped of so much of what one considers to be normal in life—the ability to work, to be surrounded by many friends and family, the ability to partake in life in general, and having material items that most consider normal or standard.

My personal relationship with Aragon had nothing to do with my divorce, aside from the fact that the shamanic healing work I did with him enabled me to connect to myself and admit that was the direction my life needed to take. That being said, we did begin an unconventional relationship of sorts, and it just so happened it was of the very intense, passionate, and volatile variety. We saw each other sporadically. Yet I cannot begin to convey how much this sporadic relationship continually brought up all that was still unhealed in me for my continued healing and transformation.

I also empathically felt some of his unhealed wounds, and he never really expressed or took ownership of this, so the dichotomy between what I could sense and what was being communicated to me verbally was too much for my sensitive being. It was difficult to spend long amounts of time in his presence with comfort and ease. As much as I loved and adored him, I had to send him on his way each time he came to visit after just a few days. It blew my mind that I could feel so much love for someone and have trouble being in their presence for an extended period of time.

After a very tumultuous summer and fall of 2011, I saw him off to the airport to his home country, following a romantic and sweet rendezvous. He was gone for five months. In some ways, it was almost unbearable to me. In others, I was so blessed to be in the aftermath of the blissful kundalini awakening that anything painful was barely noticeable to me. I was under some sort of illusion that we might have a normal relationship, whatever I thought that was for twin flames. Obviously, we did not have anything close to a standard type of relationship, nor would we ever, even though my feelings of love for him ran deeper than what I had ever known before. At the same time, my paradigm on relationships had completely shifted, and my need for freedom and independence was stronger than ever.

Within two or three weeks of my awakening, I had an amazing dream in which I found myself in the Akashic Records room, a real place on the etheric realm that holds all the records of every being from beginning to end. Edgar Cayce, the famous "sleeping prophet," speaks of this room and his many visits there, where he was able to obtain helpful and at times life-saving information and medical protocols for his clients. I saw myself in this room, pulling records on stone tablets out of a wall. First I got to look at mine, and then I saw myself pulling out Aragon's record tablet. It said I had crossed his path at this time to help him learn to express his emotions. I pushed his tablet back into its space in the wall and then woke up, but just before I awoke, I heard the Akashic Records attendants say to me, "Only if he is willing."

I knew from the second I woke up that it was *not* just a dream. It was as real as anything here in the three-dimensional realm. I was incredulous because I felt this was a fated meeting from the beginning and not just for my own healing. I knew I had what it took to help someone express themselves on an emotional level. I also knew that was possible only if someone was truly willing. I had no idea at the time just how much I would need those words, "Only if he is willing," in the future. Those were the very words that let me know when it was time to give up, and they knew how much I would need to know this, as they probably knew I would die trying, and I think I would have. That was how profound my feelings for this man were.

A few weeks later, in May 2010, I went to see a psychic friend. I found her help with all I had just experienced in my life to be far above conventional counseling. Who else was going to understand what I was going through and all that was happening in my life? Having a kundalini awakening seemed, at that time, to be unknown to most people. I have since heard of some being committed to mental wards when a spiritual awakening has happened. I needed someone with an understanding of the spiritual realms.

I was no longer operating completely on this third-dimensional plane of existence; therefore I needed a support system of people who could guide me in the new world I found myself in. I had asked her a couple of questions not only about my life and impending divorce but also about my healing experience with Aragon, and she got curious and asked me for his birth data. A couple weeks later when I saw her again, she had done a composite and synastry astrological reading between me and him. When I got there, she said to me, "I believe from these two chart readings that this man is indeed your twin flame. One of your major roles in his life would be to help him with expressing his feelings." My eyes bugged out, and I almost screamed out loud from the validation she'd just unknowingly provided me.

Twin flames come together as they have a mission to help humanity in some way, and the mission can be fulfilled more profoundly and easily together rather than separately. They are supposed to be role models for the rest of humanity, showing us what truly unconditional love looks like. A relationship with your twin flame is most definitely not your conventional relationship, although there are some who try to make it fit into the shapes they have previously known in the past. These are not easy relationships and can be filled with a lot of drama unless both people are highly evolved and emotionally healed from most past traumas and faulty thought paradigms. It is common when twin flames come together for both to trigger many unhealed issues and want to project this onto the other. It's quite hard to look at yourself and see your shadow side when you're in judgment of it. Hence, what we end up doing is judging anyone with that particular characteristic we possess that we don't want to see in ourselves. That's what judgment is about really—a projection onto others of what we are refusing to look at and heal within. If you get really honest and courageous with an inward look, you'll see what I mean.

It is also common to idolize the twin flame above all reason, not realizing that they are *you*. Often what happens is that you idolize certain traits in them without recognizing that you contain the exact same traits, because you haven't stepped fully into your power as an individual yet. It is a power your twin has—to be a mirror for you, to show you your hidden or unacknowledged talents and shadows. Once twin flames have met, it is most important to spend considerable amounts of time apart, as this is the way each has time to integrate all that has been brought up in them. It is also a time to learn and grow more fully and completely into a healed and whole human being.

Aragon and I had the planet Pluto conjunct the IC angle in our composite chart together. Pluto in this position represents a shared sense of power, which can add strength and resiliency in a relationship and bring a family-type bond to a couple (Jewel Mayberry, astrologer). It was unfathomably difficult for me to be in his presence for longer than three days at a time, as the transformation that would begin to take place was so profound and deep. I really needed space to integrate what had been brought up in me. I now think, *You have got to be kidding me. I was supposed to help him learn to express his feelings?* I could not even begin to deal with all that was brought up in me, let alone help someone else. I could see later how just being in the presence of your twin, you don't have to do or say anything in particular. It happens as if by magic, an alchemical transformation. It helped me to begin to imagine the power that can be unleashed and generated when two fully healed and whole human beings come together for the work they are here to do.

I felt very strongly at the time that Aragon was my twin flame. I also knew in my soul early on that I was aligned to be doing similar work to what he was doing, not exactly the same but possibly in conjunction. I could see the potential for a coalescing of two potent human energies coming together to cocreate and channel huge amounts of healing energy together. With the energy between him and me, the work seemed almost more important and compelling than the actual relationship, if that was possible. I say this with a degree of incredulousness, because my feelings for him were unlike anything I've ever experienced in this lifetime. Never had I been so completely drawn to someone on so many levels.

Very shortly, I began referring others I had known or heard from with MCS, CFS, and Lyme disease to him. Anyone who knows these illnesses is familiar with the vast support network we begin to form through the internet and world publications. One woman I had referred to him was very ill with liver cancer and was extremely frightened and asked if I could be there in her sessions with him. I spoke to him about this, and he agreed. I could see it was very needed in her case, and I've been told by many that I have a very calming and supportive presence. This enabled him to more easily perform the work he needed to do with her.

I started working in the ceremonial space with him at times, and I heard from more than one person that together we radiated an extremely powerful presence. Apparently it was evident enough for people to comment on. One woman we worked with had some psychic abilities, and she told me that she'd seen us as a married couple in a past life. She shared that we'd been incredibly in love with each other in that past life but that we'd had problems relating to each other and had come back together in this life to try to work through those problems! That blew my mind, as I had not imparted any information about our personal relationship; all she knew was that we were working together on her behalf.

At any rate, my whole world and perspective on life changed immeasurably from my kundalini awakening and healing. I saw things in a different way, no longer restricted by ways of being that had seemed set in stone at one time, from my indoctrination into this world. This is called flow, and moving with the flow of life and Spirit opens one up to much more possibility and is mind expanding. Some find this frightening, as they are conditioned to believe that all will be OK in life only if things are done the way they have been taught (not always correctly) from a very young age.

When you let go and trust in Spirit—this innate life force that we are all connected to that always knows what's best for us and moves in amazing and synchronistic ways—it just happens, instead of trying to force things to happen and driving yourself crazy in the process, trying so hard to control outcomes. Oh, it will drive you crazy when you resist this flow. Think of it this way: you begin to save your energy for healing yourself instead of throwing it away or frittering away your time and effort worrying and forcing.

I now saw that, for me, a committed relationship did not need to involve marriage. I saw that I could grow and learn vast amounts, even in a relationship that was intense in its depth, without committing in the traditional sense to being with only that one person forever. I saw that I did not even need to be in a relationship at all for my growth, happiness, and well-being. Perhaps I was not designed to fit into that box, just like it is not correct for everyone to have children in the course of their lifetime. It's quite possible that much of what is spiritually right for you is not going to appear to be OK, normal, or even acceptable in the eyes of societal standards and conventions.

As an example, our society is quite focused on making money. After my awakening, I could no longer even think about working a job just to pay bills. In fact, my focus was hardly on making money at all. It was more on just being and on what it was that brought me joy and purpose. That may seem very foolhardy to many who have never examined their belief systems around money. I rarely did anything anymore with the sole purpose of making money. It was not in alignment with my spirit so did not come up in my thoughts. And, amazingly, I was supplied for in this way.

You find, when connected to your spirit, that all of your needs are met. This thing around money has been a very rigid paradigm that almost everyone in our world has held onto quite tightly. The more you hold onto a belief or paradigm like this, one that brings no joy, pleasure, or purpose (just slaving away for someone else), the harder it becomes for you. Because your focus is on it being a certain way, it now becomes that way in your life. This is precisely how you create with your thoughts and focus. So, focus on what brings joy and purpose, and then you will get just that.

Being reconnected and awakened makes you unafraid and not disturbed at all by what others may think. You become free to do what you're here to do, to express the essence of *your being* fully. You know you have your own connection fully supporting you to do exactly what you are here to do—to be who you are. I fully believe we all choose the life we are living; it brings us full circle to our original intention before we incarnated here on earth. It is this belief system that puts the responsibility for our lives back on us, and that puts us back into the seat of power in our own lives. If we are responsible for our own lives, we tend to be operating from a place of power as opposed to a place of victimhood and blaming others for what goes wrong in our lives.

I met a woman while living in northern Arizona in 2014, Paola, a past-life regressionist, in a serendipitous way. I met her at an outdoor drumming circle on a mountain plateau. I was sitting on a long rock ledge, and she walked over and sat down next to me. We hit it off and became instant friends. One evening, we went to an outdoor concert in a neighboring small town. We ended up being pretty bored with it, so we took a walk and ended up sitting on a bench on the main street of this small town, and while we were sitting there, she asked me if I'd like to try a past-life regression with her. I said, "Here?"

She said, "Yes, it can be done almost anywhere."

I agreed, and so we started. She expertly and quickly guided me into a trance mode. I could hear vehicles on the street, but soon they seemed very far away. She asked me about Aragon, as I had told her some about him, and she found this story fascinating. She could see I was still reeling somewhat from the whole experience, although it had ended two years prior in 2012. In this regression, I saw that he and I had indeed been married in a previous life, probably near the beginning of the nineteenth century. He had been a Native American Indian woman, and I was a white man in the military. We were very much in love with each other, and there came a time when I had to leave her because our lives were under some sort of threat.

I didn't quite understand why, but I got the feeling that I was leaving because I wanted strongly to make things safe for her. I left and promised her I would return as soon as I could. I did return, but it was at least a couple of years later. When I returned, she was devastated and could not get past her anger and hurt for some reason, and so it wasn't the same. I also saw myself in another past life with him. We were in Atlantis, and we were married and loved each other deeply. We were the same genders we are in this lifetime. I was a very powerful high priestess, and he was threatened by my power in this life, and as a result, we fought a lot, as in *War of the Roses* style.

It wasn't until about a week after this regression that I recalled something that happened the first time we met. As soon as I sat down across from him for my first shamanic ceremony, he said to me in a sharp, almost angry voice, "What took you so long to come to me?" I was floored by his remark. I had no idea what he meant. I said, "I don't know. I just came when I was ready." The second I remembered him saying that, it made so much more sense in light of the past-life scenario I had just been privy to learning about. It seemed possible he had held onto that hurt deep within his cells.

It also helped me to understand why we seemed to be fiery and competitive with each other and easily angered by each other. Of course, all of this made for intense fire and passion in the sexual arena, but it was energy that needed careful channeling, and we seemed unable to accomplish this together. It was hard to be in his presence for too long without one or both of us being triggered terribly, especially me, from what I could tell. I remember more than once, the tone he used with me when he was upset about something felt like a dagger in my heart.

And, of course, this type of feeling or response usually gave me the opportunity to examine what it was in me that needed healing and integration, in order to stand more fully in my own power as opposed to giving another the power to wound me so deeply. This particular feeling went back to my early childhood when I was the family scapegoat and made to feel responsible for anything that went wrong—and therefore guilty and subsequently unloved or not good enough to be loved or accepted fully for who I was. It was the conditional love we are all, for the most part, raised with.

Now, granted, he was triggered enough by his own wounding to speak to me harshly. That does not mean that I am unworthy or at fault in any way. That was about him and my reaction to it, about me. Being able to be triggered in so many ways by one person makes for a lot of excitement and volatility, a huge potential for transformation, and a new understanding of who one truly is as well as becoming empowered in one's true strength. It was a real life-shaking merging that taught me more about love for self and others on the deepest of levels, to the core of my being.

Just as an example, to show how the body can react physically to buried or repressed emotions, one day in 2014, Paola and I decided to do a ceremony to release all anger toward men from past lives. We both sensed there was a lot we held onto deep in the cells of our beings. We planned to hike to the top of the strongest male energy vortex spot in that area to do this. The day came for doing this ceremony together, and I felt quite sick and told Paola I couldn't complete the mission. She was leaving the following day on a trip, and she was insistent. This was a woman with five planets in Scorpio, so anyone familiar with astrology knows that I am serious when I say that you cannot refuse someone like this. It's simply not allowable. So we went. She had already hiked up previously and made an altar for the ceremony.

We hiked, and I kept complaining about how bad I felt. We didn't make it to the top, as I had to stop about two-thirds of the way up and heave my guts up. I still didn't feel right even after that.

Paola finally agreed to do the ceremony on the spot instead of making the full trek. We did this beautiful release ceremony, and it felt like loads of ancestral anger and resentment just left me. Afterward, I felt totally fine, as if I hadn't been sick at all that day. I am certain my body had been starting to feel all that garbage coming up from just the intention of planning to release eons of stored rage, and it was nauseating how much there was. It is a somewhat common phenomenon to vomit repressed rage or anger once you've intended or begun to release it.

This may seem like an exciting diversion from the real nuts and bolts of how I got well, but this part of my healing, the kundalini awakening, changed a lot for me, and I want to be in honesty and integrity about not only what happened but how I think it happened. I also believe it happened because I had let go of the need to get well, which I had held onto for many years. What a relief this was. It is what so many of the spiritual gurus teach us. One I love is Mooji. He has many videos, all of which are so calming and freeing to the soul. You can hear him at Mooji. org. I became much more in touch with this whole other part of life, the spiritual side, which we often ignore completely. And this helped me open my inner knowing, intuition, and psychic abilities. It opened me up to so many new ideas and made me aware that life is not always what we think it is. There is so much more that lies beneath the surface if you are brave enough to expand yourself into it and look more deeply.

Helpful Tools for the Ascent

The practice of forgiveness is our most important
contribution to the healing of the world.
—Marianne Williamson

Healing for many who've been sick for a prolonged period is not
ordinarily an overnight miracle that is going to happen without a
lot of work going into it. It's seriously hard work, but it's also hard
as hell being sick all the time too—right? In addition to not being
fun, it causes your thoughts to spiral out of control downward.
Which do you choose for yourself? You have to be willing to do
the work and take the responsibility for yourself. It's difficult, as
all hard work is, and it doesn't stop, but it becomes a lot easier the
longer you have worked at it.

Once you truly take on this challenge and accept that the
work is yours to do and no one can do it for you, you will begin
to feel your power. It is one of the better parts. You get to stand in
and own your power. No one can ever take that from you. Some
days, the results will feel like a miracle has happened, but it will
have been nothing other than your hard work and commitment,
with a lot of the universe's help to back you up.

If you have trouble feeling the will to even begin, or just feel
overwhelmed with it all, simply state and write down an honest

intention. You can state out loud and write in a journal or on a piece of paper that you see daily, "It is my intention to begin a true healing path for myself." Word it however feels best for you. It is a universal law that whatever is needed for you to begin this process will start showing up in your life. Be ready to pay attention to the signs and messages.

After setting this sort of intention, you may come across something you're reading or hear something a friend says to you, and it makes a particularly strong impression on you. Or you may be walking down the street and see a sign that has meaning for you in particular. This is your intuition and Spirit working together, and it happens this way so that you are open to the signs and messages and can interpret them properly as being meant just for you and your process. Be open to receiving what is so rightfully yours.

One thing many who are very ill do when first beginning to detox is scare themselves silly, thinking they have made themselves terribly worse, and I certainly fell victim to this thinking and subsequent emotion of fear. Usually this is not true; it is just a sign to slow down and take the time needed to move the toxins out of your body. This is what is causing you to feel so bad, too many toxins in your bloodstream not being released quickly enough. And it is why you must take it as slow as possible until you really know and understand your body's limits. Many have said to me, "But I don't want to feel worse." That's your choice, and you get to make it.

I made the choice to, as I reasoned that I felt pretty dreadful most of the time anyway (after twenty years of being sick) and I was progressively getting worse during that time, regardless of everything I was avoiding and living in the middle of nowhere in the desert with very clean air. I reasoned that it made no difference to me, detoxing and feeling bad from that. It did help tremendously on the psychological level to know that I was making the effort to move in the right direction toward improving my health, and as it turned out, I definitely was right about that.

There are many healing modalities and supplements I can list for you that have helped me on my healing journey in ways both small and tremendous. I will not recommend them to you, necessarily, or tell you how much to take, because each person is so different and must follow their own inner wisdom. Some of them may not work for you, and you may discover different ways to deal with your own recovery. The more ill you are, the slower you should go in the first few years.

Most people with MCS or Lyme have some idea of how ill they are, based on the intensity of their symptoms, how long it takes them to recover, lab results from bloodwork, and a good doctor. Those with milder MCS may have a reaction response that lasts a few minutes to hours. When you become more severe, it may take days or weeks to eliminate the offensive agent and its effects on your system. Take care to introduce new supplements or treatments one at a time until you get a feel for how your body is tolerating each one.

I would like to preface this part by saying I tried so hard for years to figure this out from my intellect or mind. It bothered me terribly, being so sick and not knowing what to do to make things better for myself, especially since none of the professionals I had been to had much to offer me, including hope. I could see the moment I healed that I absolutely had not healed by figuring out what to do from my intellect. It actually happened from *not* listening to what was going on in my mind, as the mind can be so irrational and contain thoughts based in fear and illogical concepts. This is where something like meditation can be helpful. Healing is not a thing that happens from your mind, as we have been led to believe by science.

Operating from the intellect alone will not heal you. When I say this, I mean from the logical mind. Generally speaking, it will not even lead you in the best direction for you. You stand a better chance of healing from the mind after you have done a thorough brain retraining program or some other type of spiritual healing. Brain retraining helps to change your subconscious programming, which does not have a lot to do with the operation of your intellectual mind, as you are programming your mind with thoughts not based on the reality you see in front of you. The logical mind or intellect operates based on what is seen in your reality. The most profound healing often happens from your connection to your intuition or your heart. This is why people meditate, in order to stop listening and giving so much importance to the mind. Learning to detach from the mind is a form of surrender into your heart space. You begin to make decisions for your life based on your heart instead of your intellect. Learning to live from this space is *the* most healing thing you will ever learn to do.

Why doesn't medical science know this yet? I believe factions of it are beginning to know. But mostly, I believe they don't entertain it, as it is a left brain / mind and science-based profession. Your mind doesn't have access to universal wisdom and your own innate wisdom like your heart. Even your body knows more than your mind. Pay attention to it. Let your spirit take up residence in it by tuning in regularly through practices such as meditation, sitting quietly and doing deep breathing, yoga, gentle stretching exercises, or dance. Also, spending as much time as possible in nature will benefit your body, mind, spirit connection like nothing else.

There is a form of dance called journey dance that helps one to go within, getting out of the mind and into the body while dancing. This will inform you and guide you like nothing else. And in the process, it will help you to become more embodied and to relax, open, and flow. Trust. The universe has your back. Always. Once you remember this and know the magic of how the universe works, you will have left a piece of yourself behind, the ego. It's a beautiful way to live life, so light and carefree and joyful and free—as the spirit-led life is meant to be. You trust there is a greater plan at work that your mind can't necessarily figure out and doesn't need to.

How many of you have been very sick and frightened that there was no real help for you from any health care professional you sought out? I was at that point many years ago, 1992–1996, suffering from (among many other things) severe insomnia. At times, I did not sleep more than an hour or two for days in a row. Nothing seemed to help, and many of the supplements and physical exercises I tried only made it worse. I got to the point of being so loopy I was at times bordering on being psychotic from lack of sleep. Finally, in desperation, I tried a method recommended by the well-known psychic Sylvia Browne.

The following is one of her recommended meditations. I started to visualize that I was in a room with three walls and one open side, at the ocean, so that I could see, hear, and smell the ocean on the open side. I would visualize myself lying on a table in the middle of the room, with tables along the walls filled with the most beautiful flowers, candles, and gorgeous arrangements of fruits, vegetables, and cakes. Then I would invite all of my spirit guides, teachers, counselors, angels, goddesses, and ascended masters to come there and help me with the incorrigible issue I was having. I sadly only asked for this help once I realized it was the only thing I had not tried. Having been an RN, trained in the ways of allopathic medicine, I used to be a believer in the science of pills and thought that just exhausting myself physically with exercise, or anything that treated the physical aspect of the problem I was having, should work.

When this did not turn out to be the case, I knew I would need all the help I could get, and this was when I finally became desperate enough to begin asking my spiritual guides and helpers. Amazingly, it worked every single time without fail, and I would fall asleep while they were working on me in the spirit realm. I became so filled with gratitude for this unseen help I was receiving that I started to thank them profusely for all the help they had given me in the past, being there for me currently, and for all the help I knew they would continue to give me in the future every single time I invoked them. I have a feeling this helped make the work they were doing with me that much more profound. It never failed to put me right to sleep for many rejuvenating hours.

When you first begin to try to meditate or calm your mind, it can feel close to impossible, especially if your mind has been on an endless hamster wheel trying desperately to get somewhere different from where you are. It can be an endless, unresolvable battle on that wheel. I suggest trying to meditate for only two minutes a day at first and gradually increasing to five minutes. Once you've shown yourself you can do five minutes, then keep adding a minute or two every few days. You can find many guided meditation videos on YouTube that are calming and uplifting.

When you notice thoughts come up, give them little to no significance, like you are simply watching the thoughts drift by as if you were a detached bystander. Later, when not in meditation, as you are becoming more aware of your thoughts and what exactly is running through your mind, you can ask yourself if these thoughts are really true, and if so, what makes them so? Where did the thought originate? Something you were taught as a young child? Something you think you need to create safety and security in your life? Ask yourself, if that is true, do you need what you think you need to be safe in your life? Really? Usually these thoughts are based on false paradigms we've been taught throughout our lives. This is a big thing that gets us into so much trouble.

We make our thoughts out to be very significant and all-powerful and earth-shattering, which then affects how we feel and our emotions. Usually these fear based thoughts have us spiraling down in a sea of negative emotions. This creates the opposite of healing within the body. Our thoughts create an energy that emanates from us out into the world and universe. There is a saying in homeopathy that "like cures like." It has been proven repeatedly. Like also attracts like. So, it is true to an extent at least, what many new agers have said, that we create our world.

Fearful, anxiety-producing thoughts attract fearful, anxiety-producing things to our lives. And likewise, uplifting, happy, and joyous thoughts put out a certain blueprint energy that attracts more of just that, like a magnet. It's hard to believe this when you are so down in an abyss of despair, and it's harder yet to begin to change these thoughts. It is a discipline. It is one you must embark on to truly heal. So, the mind is important, and you are in charge of programming the mind. We get to decide what is allowed in there and what must go.

There is a hierarchy. It is 1) spirit, 2) mind, 3) emotion, 4) physical. Your evolution, happiness, health, and vibration will change dramatically when you realize that spirit is of supreme importance. This is not what most of us are taught. And it is why I say to let Spirit take up residence in your being. Never ignore it again. Allow your spirit to decide what is right and fitting to take up space in your mind. Allow your spirit to create your world in this way. And it all filters down through this hierarchy accordingly.

Allow Spirit to create what thoughts you want to hold in your mind. The thoughts create the feelings and then the emotions you experience. These feelings and emotions are hopefully now ones like happiness, joy, abundance, and peace. They actually begin to create a different structure in the physical cells of your being. And since our bodies are primarily made of water, I want to remind you of Dr. Masaru Emoto and his proven experiments that revealed the effect of thoughts on the molecular structure of water.

He wrote the book *The Hidden Messages in Water* in 2004. He showed through magnetic resonance analysis technology and high-speed photographs that toxic, polluted water, "when exposed to prayer and intention can be altered and restored to beautifully formed geometric crystals found in clean, healthy water" (thewellnessenterprise.com). We think of it as miraculous, but it is really part of science and metaphysics that is not completely understood yet. It is the meeting of science with Spirit or the unseen.

What changed things drastically in my life was letting go of anything needing to be any certain way for me to be able to access my place of personal joy and happiness. Because I did it, I know it can be done and that it is a choice, but it seems to maybe be a choice that only comes after a long, hard battle your mind thinks it can win. It discovers in the long run it cannot and will not win, and it has depleted your energy more than anything and taken years from your life. I decided to squeeze as much joy, peace, and happiness out of each moment that I possibly could and to be blessed. It simply involves a change in perspective.

I do believe part of the reason I was able to change this perspective was that I realized I had a limited amount of time left to live and I had wasted numerous years not feeling so blessed and abundant and happy. I just did not wish to live out the rest of the time I had in this manner. I no longer thought it would increase my internal happiness to have any of the circumstances of my life be any different from what they were. I could begin to experience my own brand of heaven on earth.

Life becomes vastly easier when you do this. The struggle and resistance to what is brings you into a state of feeling you're in hell and abysmal unhappiness on earth. The second I decided I was beyond exhausted to resist or fight any longer, things began to miraculously shift. I stopped focusing on all that was wrong and really started to savor and focus on any good feelings I had about anything. It was a conjuring of sort, just as when you're not happy and you smile, it begins to shift your internal terrain and uplift you. Once I started to place my focus on the goodness I noticed in life, life seemed to bring me more in the same vein.

My entire focus became on what was going on inside. I realized nothing outside me could make me feel any certain way, unless I allowed it to—even illness and unpleasant sensations in my body, as the body is not the spirit. And the spirit trumps everything. It really does. It has dominion over your mind, hence your emotional state and body. We've all just been so cut off from our spirits for so long; it's hard to remember how to slow down and really connect and remember the true beauty, ethereal quality, and extremely blessed comfort this connection can bring. Once you come back to remembering and knowing this connection, you won't want to give it up for anything. Many of you may have had a first-time epiphany about this, having just been through the worldwide situation of being in a lockdown mode.

It becomes the most important and precious commodity in your entire existence. It is the one thing you need never let go of again. Start to make yourself pay strict attention to the joy in your life, the smallest things even, and just sit and let it sink in. Luxuriate in it. This is the practice of cultivating gratitude. This lifts your vibration as well as those around you. It is from this higher-vibratory state that healing can begin and can be profound. Examine your beliefs and ask yourself if they are ideas you really want to keep. Are they bringing you joy or keeping you stuck in an outdated thought pattern that is bringing you down and contributing to not only your misery but those around you.

When I was first sick, I had to really examine where my sense of worth as a human being came from. I was too sick to work or participate in a lot of life, such as family gatherings and outings. I couldn't do things that had brought me joy and pleasure, such as art, since I couldn't find any art materials I could tolerate working with. Even gardening was not doable, as I had become so violently reactive to the mold in the dirt. I was left with myself, and that helped me to understand that my worth didn't come from anything outside myself. Nothing I did increased my worth as a human being. I simply was worthwhile, just being. That was a huge revelation. I no longer had to feel as if my worth had been stripped away or that I was guilty on any level for not being able to do the things healthy humans do, or to lose self-esteem because I couldn't do the same things. When I realized this, it caused me to focus on my internal nature, and thus began my healing on that level. If I couldn't do anything else, I could still be the best human I could possibly be. Sometimes it takes having nearly everything stripped from you to be able to have this sort of realization and understanding of how you've been programmed to believe all manner of things that hold no validity.

Those of us with some of the most challenging circumstances have a path of learning how to create and manifest better circumstances for ourselves through the power of our minds, not using the intellect in the scientifically taught ways but using the power of our thoughts, which we can change at whim. The definition of the word *whim* is a sudden desire or change of mind, especially one that is unusual or unexplained. This is one of our God-given spiritual powers. I am urging anyone reading this who is not in this habit to begin learning how to put this into action in your life. I cannot stress the life-changing benefits enough.

I was so sick that I could not work any type of job, even part-time. I did not have the energy reserves, and I was made too ill from chemical exposures that were everywhere. I ended up applying for and receiving disability benefits after a long two-year wait, way back in 1992. For this reason, I had a lot of time to devote to researching and then implementing what I learned on my own to improve my overall health.

Even if you don't have time, I highly recommend doing whatever you can find the time to do for your well-being and your ability to make a living for yourself. I was fortunate to have a husband who made a fairly good income, and I realize many are not so fortunate in this regard. I have encountered my own obstacles in healing, and it has always been extremely helpful for me to surrender these to God and ask for His help. I move myself mentally as far from feeling like a victim as I possibly can. Whether you believe in God or not, there is a greater power than you at play, and it is there for the asking.

Many other things have also helped me immensely, and they are as follows:

Time Outdoors

In addition to focusing on my spiritual connection, I make it part of my daily routine to spend time outdoors in nature, even if it is only to sit in a chair on my porch. If you cannot do this because of toxicity in your neighborhood, it's crucial to either move to a location where you will be able to, or find a place you can go to, such as a park, the beach, or a nearby mountain or lake. Rack your brain until you come up with a safe place, and make it a point to get there as often as possible and for as long as you can each time.

Sunlight, clean outdoor air, living and growing plants, earth, and animals are healing in a multitude of ways. Try to make contact with the ground by going barefoot or even lying down on a blanket or towel on the ground. Beaches and grassy parks are great. Where I live in the desert, it is more difficult, but I simply lay a blanket out and lie on that. Also, just putting my bare feet on my concrete patio seems to help a lot. It's so important, this grounding yourself. We are electrical beings, and we need to be grounded as much as possible to function well. It actually grounds the electricity running through your body and keeps your nervous system healthy. Otherwise, you can fry your circuits.

Highly sensitive beings need this even more, as we may be so sensitive in part because our nervous systems are running more energy and electricity than others. Therefore, grounding is essential and must be done regularly for good health. There are now grounding or earthing shoes you can buy, as well as different things you can get to help ground you while you sleep, are on the computer, and so on.

For times you are unable to get outdoors easily, you can take a sea salt bath, as water is another grounding element. Meditation is a great way to center and ground yourself. Exercise is another grounding tool. I like dance and yoga. Eating heavier grounding foods is also helpful. Healthy ones are root vegetables, grains, and beans. Think a hearty root vegetable stew. Also, you can do grounding visualizations, which you can also find online.

There are grounding crystals you can carry, and most of them also absorb negative energies so they can't affect you as much. Black tourmaline, obsidian, hematite, shungite, and orgonite are ones I find very helpful. They are also good for EMF shielding. High electromagnetic fields can have a very ungrounding effect. This is why it is important to limit your time on cell phones and computers and avoid cell towers and smart meters. For smart meters, to bring the EMF exposure way down, simply wrap it on the outside with heavy-duty aluminum foil and use aluminum foil tape to secure it.

Exercise

Do whatever exercise you are able to do with ease. I don't recommend heavy exercise unless you can do it without creating a state of detox that is too much for your body or setting yourself back. I think gentle is far better, without creating extra stress on a healing immune system. If you have been bedridden for any length of time, it is crucial to start off slowly to rebuild your muscle strength. Start with short walks and gentle stretches, perhaps restorative yoga. You can do a fair amount of stretching exercises while you are bedridden. My favorites are walking, gentle yoga stretches, dancing, and kundalini yoga. Kundalini yoga is a blend of bhakti yoga (devotion and chanting), raja or ashtanga yoga (practice of meditation, mental and physical control), and shakti yoga (expression of power and energy). If you choose to experiment with this, start off very slowly, doing only a few of the poses or mantras at first and in limited amounts.

I certainly wasn't able to do the recommended number of minutes for each pose—not because I wasn't capable as far as muscle strength or flexibility but because the detox they produce is too much for a very toxic body to handle with ease. So, be careful if you choose kundalini yoga. It is still my favorite yoga, as it is helpful in detoxifying the body, mind, and spirit. It has been called the yoga of awareness.

I love dancing or just moving my body to music in a way that feels freeing to me. Some of my favorite forms of dance are NIA (neuromuscular integrative action, which is nine forms of dance art, healing art, and martial art). I has helped me with some of the inadvertent brain damage that resulted from years of chemical toxicity. When I first started to do NIA, I had trouble with my brain being able to command my body to take a step backward. I would see the teacher taking steps backward, and my brain would tell my body to do likewise. I would think, *Go backward now*, but my body simply wouldn't move.

I've heard of this happening with a few others with pesticide poisoning. After doing it weekly for about a year, I began to notice I was no longer having the same difficulty. Now it is a rare occurrence. I realized NIA also has some profound brain retraining effects. Some of you may like qigong or tai chi, which both have detoxifying effects and increase your overall life force energy. I have also really enjoyed ecstatic dance and journey dance, which are both free form movement and dance.

Music

This was an essential part of keeping my spirits uplifted. Music is healing to the spirit and hence the body, especially peaceful, soothing music—as opposed to heavy, dark music, which can induce a state of anxiety. Solfeggio frequencies are highly beneficial to the body and state of mind. "The solfeggio frequencies are part of the olden six-tone scale believed to have incorporated sacred music, inclusive of the famous and beautiful Gregorian Chants" (naturehealingsociety.com). You can undo a lot of mental/psychological trauma by listening to these.

Just before my healing and awakening, I got an iPod and stayed connected to it with earbuds a good part of every day. It helped to alter my brain chemistry, although I had no idea that might even be happening and it wasn't part of any thought out plan. Any kind of music that helps facilitate a peaceful state of mind is helpful to your overall well-being. It can be anything you find uplifting and soothing. New age, shamanic music with tuning forks, crystal or Tibetan brass bowls, flutes, shamanic drumming, and guitar or didgeridoo is great for healing.

Meditation

Meditation can be as simple as lying in bed upon awakening, in the morning or middle of the night, being very still and quiet. Try placing one hand over your heart and the other over your lower abdomen. You will start to feel calmer, which enables your answers to come to you in this still, quiet space. Your meditation doesn't have to be any certain way. Once you set your brain up to think, *I have to meditate to heal*, it will automatically be harder. Your mind will automatically start to resist and wander, and then you may think, *I'm not doing it right. I can't meditate. I can't keep my mind from wandering and thinking.*

Some of this (even a lot of it) is normal. Just try to imagine yourself lying all the way at the bottom of a deep, dark ocean, resting there with the marine life. There are many meditation and visualization CDs available to help. Ask for your spirit guides to help you calm your mind. There is a method called four-eight-seven. Breathe in to the count of four, hold your breath for eight seconds, and release to the count of seven seconds. There are also countless meditation videos online, and most cities offer classes.

Energy Work or Body Work

This can be very helpful, but since it can be so powerful, I would recommend interviewing the energy worker before you allow them to do this work on you. You should ask them about their credentials or formal training, as well as how long they've been practicing. You can ask what their belief systems are and if they've ever worked successfully with someone with your exact medical issue. Make sure you resonate with them and that they fully understand your need to have the work increase your energy levels and/or address certain physical issues you're having, as well as your need to control how strong or intense your detox is.

Ask them specifically not to do any work that is very detoxifying at first, and ask that it be their intention (as well as yours) for any detox that results once you do allow for this to be mild and within your limits of being tolerable and easy to recover from. If they are a good fit for you and a good energy healer, they will know how to accomplish this. I think the best energy healer for those with MCS or who are extremely sensitive is one who has been there and truly understands the extraordinary limits and circumstances MCS creates.

Brain Retraining

There are many programs out there: EMDR, Annie Hopper's Dynamic Neural Retraining System, Ashok Gupta Program, Psychological Kinesiology (Psych-K). Psych-K reprograms the subconscious mind to hold clear thoughts on the subconscious level of the positive things you want to see happening in your life. For example, say you're very reactive to mold, pesticide, or formaldehyde. You would reprogram your subconscious to have the thought at all times that you tolerate these things with ease. All of these protocols are detoxifying, as they eliminate negative and morbid thoughts from the brain, which most with MCS get understandably entrenched in.

These thoughts are just as harmful to your well-being as are toxic chemicals. Because they are negative, they are just as toxic to your body. Whatever is going on in the subconscious filters down into your body. In Psych-K, it is taught that the subconscious mind is basically in control of the body. Brain retraining has shown great success in helping people to get better. "McMaster University Observational Study Shows Significant Changes in Health Outcomes with Dynamic Neural Retraining System" and "What Doctors Have to Say" are articles that can be found at Retrainingthebrain.com. Even EFT (emotional freedom technique) can be very helpful. There are many YouTube videos you can listen to that change your brain's subconscious to help you create new thoughts and hence a structure for your new reality.

Network Chiropractic or Chiropractic with a Kinesiologist

These forms of chiropractic do not generally use harsh, cracking manipulations of the spine. So, the chances of being injured are extremely low. Network chiropractic is more like energy medicine used to align the spine and nervous system. After a few sessions, from which you will probably notice detoxification symptoms, you should start to feel more joy, peace, and ease. This was not a quick fix for me but definitely helped me to align my body more with my spirit and release negative emotions. It also helped tremendously with the pain I had, which was ongoing and severe at times. You can usually find the network chiropractors in your area with a Google search, and hopefully you can see some good reviews too.

When dealing with the heightened sensitivity of MCS, high-vibrational energy work is much easier to tolerate than heavier, more dense therapies. Network chiropractic works with the nervous system on a gentle level, nudging your body to make its own corrections instead of using excessive force. It helped me with increased vitality, better brain function, heightened intuition, and increased quality of sleep, making it easier for me to make better decisions for my care and to be more self-loving, productive, and creative. The movement of energy practiced in network chiropractic precipitates detox, especially detox of old, rigid thought patterns and habits that are harmful to the body and psyche. This helps one to become more optimistic, which is a necessary foundation for changing the thoughts.

I also have a very good chiropractor who practices kinesiology and is able to tell exactly what organ or system is being affected, then uses the kinesiology (muscle testing) to determine which supplements would be best for my condition and tolerable for me.

Kundalini Yoga Exercises

Kundalini yoga is a healing yoga for the mind, body, and spirit. There are many books out there, and one I especially like is *Meditation as Medicine: Activate the Power of Your Natural Healing Force* by Dharma Singh Khalsa, MD. When I first started to practice kundalini yoga, I used this book as my guide. I began with only one to three of the exercises in this book at a time and only two to three times per week, as they had a fairly significant detoxifying effect for me. The first ones I tried were simply hand mudras with specific breathing and eye movements. Each exercise is designed to work on a different part of your body and your entire being. They address the root cause of illness in each part of the body, which of course is spiritual, and in turn begin healing the physical symptoms.

Most of the exercises are fairly detoxifying, so I recommend not doing the full amount of any pose, asana, pranayama or mantra to start. In fact, with MCS, I only recommend starting with a tiny fraction of anything recommended by anyone. Never go beyond your ability to do any exercise with ease. I would start with just one or two exercises and wait to see how you managed with those. All of these exercises help connect us to the primal life force energy, which not only keeps us alive but is the most innate healing force available to a human being. It is known that this particular branch of yoga is supreme in connecting us to our source energy and detoxifying whatever is in the way of this. I found a gentle kundalini yoga class that I attend regularly now, and I have noticed it keeps my life force (and thereby, my detox pathways) going quite strongly.

For me, this surpasses any other type of exercise regimen, as it is specifically designed to detox certain organs and bodies. (I am speaking of not only the physical body but the auric, pranic, etheric bodies that are all part of the human energy system). Breath of fire is often used as part of kundalini yoga poses, and this is a fabulous way to oxygenate all the cells and tissues of your body. A surplus of oxygen is energizing and regenerative to the body and all its organs and systems. Practicing breath of fire may be less troublesome than getting a prescription for oxygen and dealing with all the subsequent issues. It certainly is more empowering.

Massage Therapy

Massage therapy has always been helpful to me, as it mobilizes toxins in the tissues to be released. It's best if you can find a really good therapist, preferably a very intuitive one who knows myofascial release, very helpful in relieving intractable muscle pain. Of course, always drink a lot of water after this or any type of therapy to help move the toxins out of your system with the least amount of ill effect.

Shamanic Journeying

Journeying, with the help of visualization, power animals, spirit guides, angels (and whatever spiritual help you would like to call in for guidance) is a fabulous way to access your intuition and receive answers. There are many CDs, books, and online articles and videos to help you learn how if you are interested. Some cities have meetup groups to help people learn about shamanism.

Coffee Enemas

I lost my ability to sweat when I was sick and wasn't able to again until I detoxified my body a significant amount. I still do coffee enemas, even though I've long since regained my sweating ability. They have benefited me so much, primarily because the cafestol palmitate in the coffee causes the liver to produce its own glutathione, which is a huge detoxifying aid to the body.

The ellagic acid in the coffee is a powerful antioxidant. I had trouble tolerating any other form of glutathione, which is seemingly always recommended for people with MCS. It has been the most beneficial tool in dealing with excess toxins, the herxheimer response, and feeling well. There is almost nothing like a coffee enema to help your body feel purified, calmer, and more at peace rather quickly.

Colon Hydrotherapy

When one cannot sweat easily or much, another route of detox becomes crucial, and the bowels are a fabulous route for toxins to leave the body. After becoming a colon hydrotherapist myself, and having a number of clients who were sick with MCS or Lyme, I feel it is due (at least in part) to the client's level of toxicity. The bodies of people with MCS are more than ready to eliminate as much as possible with this type of help.

Granted, it can sometimes (especially at first) lead to feeling worse after a colonic. I think this can be evidence that the body is being helped to detoxify. The liver is now dumping extra toxins because there is not so much pressure on it from the fecal contents of the intestines. This is a good thing. It can also affect your electrolyte balance, so be sure to supplement with coconut water or whatever electrolytes you can tolerate afterward. I had this issue more often in the first year of doing colonics. I would at times feel weak and drained afterward but would usually feel fine after taking electrolytes. This is not only the body needing to have electrolytes replenished; it can be a side effect of a lot of toxins being released at once. In either case, electrolyte replenishment is key.

It is not generally recommended for someone with serious inflammatory bowel disease, intense colitis, or severe leaky gut syndrome to have colonics until the intestinal lining and wall are more healed. Other than with those sorts of issues, colonics are highly beneficial in restoring your intestinal health over time (and therefore your brain function, vitality, and energy). One colonic will not do the trick. Having one colonic is like doing a sauna once. It should be a regular thing if you can handle it, especially if you are quite sick and overloaded with toxins. For those worried about a colonic flushing out the good flora in their digestive tract, you can supplement with probiotics each time you have a colonic done, or have your colon hydrotherapist give you a probiotic implant following the procedure. There are even ways to set up your own gravity colonic system at home if you are comfortable learning about and doing it.

Liver Flushing

One of the reasons people become sick with MCS and many other diseases is because their bodies are unable to keep up with ridding the many pollutants and chemicals they have ingested either orally or through the lungs or skin. Most with MCS have genetically faulty detox pathways, either from birth or from damage to the DNA responsible for the detox pathways. See "The Relationship between Genetics and Detox (It's All about Methylation!)" at drhardick.com. Therefore, in order to get and stay well, their bodies need a little extra help. Since most toxins are processed through the liver, it can be helpful to cleanse and clear this vital organ. Of course, avoidance is a good thing, but even when avoiding every possible exposure, we can stay sick, because there is such a heavy backlog from our entire lives.

I have now done around twenty liver flushes, and there appear to be no gallstones left. This puts to rest some of the claims that the gallstones are just clumps of oil that have formed from the olive oil you drink for the flush. However, I will continue doing one per year for the rest of my life as maintenance. After I completed my third liver flush, my colon hydrotherapist estimated one thousand gallstones the size of chickpeas were released during my next colonic. I also lost a bit of a spare tire around my middle that had been adding to my level of discomfort. I always have a colonic within a day or two after doing a liver flush to help remove any stones that may be left in my intestines. If not removed from the gut, these stones can cause one to feel quite sick, as they are filled with parasites, microbes, and other toxic material.

Liver flushing may be too aggressive for some. If this is the case, there are other ways. Diet alone can really help, and there are supplements, such as Chanca piedra, that are known for breaking up stones. There is also the liver rescue diet nine-day plan by the medical medium Anthony William. I've done this several times now and find it beneficial and gentler.

Acupuncture

I would have used acupuncture too, but I found it far too stimulating for me to handle with any degree of ease. It seemed to open the meridians so fully and for such an extended period of time (and my body was so toxic, as are many with MCS) that the overload of toxins pouring into my system was too much all at once. I still need to be very careful and conservative when using acupuncture. I go to an acupuncturist who understands that I need very few needles at once and I need to have them all removed within five to fifteen minutes. You may be different. Certain things will work for me that may not be doable for you. Each of us must find our own path. However, we can take bits and pieces from another's path that may work miraculously for us.

Most people with MCS deal with fungus or candida, due to multiple factors, including overuse of antibiotics and the resulting loss of good intestinal flora. Also, failing to treat your genetic detox mutations can cause overgrowth of fungus due to excess ammonia in your system that fungus feed off of. Heavy metal toxicity is another food for candida. Having coinfections such as parasites, Lyme, Epstein-Barr virus, or a toxic body in general will make eliminating excess candida very difficult. If your blood is too acidic, this stresses the entire body, and a body under stress is more prone to candida overgrowth in addition to degenerative issues.

When the intestines and gut are not working optimally our brain and entire system suffer. Our bodies are nourished not only by what we put into them but how well those nutrients are absorbed. During the decade I ate zero fruit, sugar, or white carbohydrates, very limited amounts of grains, and numerous anticandida herbals and natural supplements, I was unable to lower my body's yeast overload to any satisfactory degree. It was only after I had done the Marshall protocol with low-dose pulsed antibiotics for one and a half years that I felt my body had been cleansed of a massive amount of this fungal plague. In that time on this protocol, I took approximately one normal dose of antibiotics.

The way low-dose pulsed antibiotics work is that they are able to eliminate what become cell wall–deficient, or CWD, bacteria that hide in the immune cells designed to eliminate them. This is a big player in many autoimmune diseases today, as well as heart disease, diabetes, MS, and numerous other diseases of unknown origin. While candida doesn't cause these diseases itself, it sure does add to the overall number of symptoms and misery you may have. You can imagine my shock when I got off the protocol and noticed I no longer had all the same "candida" issues, and the food cravings I'd known for so long were gone. I've also noticed that the more alkaline I keep my metabolism, the less inflammation I have overall. The more greens, fruits, and vegetables I have in my diet, the better I feel. If you can, try a week of just these types of foods and see if you don't notice a huge difference.

Here are some of the things I've used for controlling candida. You'll notice I don't say *killing*, as I believe we live in a state of symbiotic coexistence with all, even microorganisms that become harmful when out of balance. I use probiotics. One of my favorites is Dr. Ohhira's. Some specialty health stores may carry it, and it can be bought online. I like it more than other similar products, as it has fermented cultures, and I've noticed these are helpful for my sleep.

I've also used one called Critical Care 350 billion. That is right, a whopping 350 billion beneficial bacteria per serving! I've had to buy it straight from my naturopath's office, so I cannot say you can find it online. Many naturopaths will most likely have a highly potent probiotic for clients with severe intestinal issues, or they will be able to order one for you. I began by taking an entire serving, and after a few months, I moved it down to one quarter of a dose. The best one I've found for dealing with zero beneficial gut bacteria or after taking antibiotics is something like Just Thrive, 100 percent spore-based probiotics.

I also like including some fermented foods and veggies in my diet. And while many have allergies or intolerance to soy products, when it is fermented, such as tempeh (fermented soy product high in protein and B vitamins), it often becomes much more tolerable. Tempeh also lowers cholesterol and increases bone density. In addition to tempeh, at times I also eat a nondairy yogurt, fermented vegetables like sauerkraut, fermented coconut water, or kombucha. Other fermented foods you may find helpful and delicious to include in your diet are miso, kefir, umeboshi plum paste, kimchi, buttermilk, and natto. Fermented foods improve digestion. They can help to raise your levels of B vitamins, digestive enzymes, and lactic acid, which helps to eliminate bad bacteria.

For anyone who has been tested and has zero good bacteria, or if you feel you may have very low beneficial intestinal flora, my advice is absolutely no fermented foods, simply because these foods can occasionally become contaminated with a bad bacteria that can easily overtake your system without any beneficial flora to fight it off. You should wait until you've rebuilt your gut flora at least three to six months before attempting fermented foods.

Helpful Supplements

Here is a list of some supplements I have found helpful. Do keep in mind we are all different, and your mileage may vary considerably, so please be careful and start by using your intuition and taking very small doses. Many of these are great antifungals as well as antibacterial and antiviral. A few may even be antiparasitic. Most have multiple beneficial properties.

ACZ Nano Zeolites: A volcanic mineral that is a heavy metal binder or chelator, immunomodulator, alkalizer, antioxidant, and antimicrobial and supports a healthy gut.

aloe vera juice: It helps to heal the intestinal wall, and in addition to being anti-inflammatory, it's an antimicrobial that has antifungal, antibacterial, antiparasitic, and antiviral properties.

ashwagandha: Reduces cortisol, reduces stress and anxiety, and helps with the adrenals.

astragalus: A great antiviral immune booster, and it contributes to telomere growth, which protect the chromosomes from aging and decline. It also helps detoxify the lymphatic system.

Berbercap by Thorne: Supports heart health, healthy cholesterol levels, immune function, healthy blood sugar metabolism and insulin sensitivity, and beneficial gut microbial balance.

Beta-TCP by Biotics Research: Gentle but potent. It has taurine (good for heart and nervous system), pancrelipase, beet concentrate (liver detox), superoxide dismutase (strong antioxidant), and catalase. It helps with bile flow and digestion. It's good overall and quite pure. I found it quite helpful for gall bladder issues.

black pu-erh tea: Helps prevent heart disease, reduces bad cholesterol, and is a detoxifier that helps remove toxic plastics from the body. It is a fermented tea and has lower tannin levels. It helps healthy digestion, metabolism, and body weight. Closest taste to coffee, especially chocolate pu-erh tea.

boswellia: Frankincense, which is also helpful for inflammation and pain. I know many prefer turmeric, but I seem to have the opposite effects from turmeric. It helps with protecting the liver, arthritis, and other inflammatory diseases.

Burbur by NutraMedix: It is similar to lymphomyosot but is an herb. I love this supplement for toning down a bad detox, especially one that keeps you wide awake. Burbur usually helps my sleep immensely. It is the same thing as Manayupa herb.

camu camu powder: Amazon rainforest fruit that contains higher levels of vitamin C than any other known botanical source.

cat's claw herb: Good for arthritis relief. Anti-inflammatory, anticancer, immune booster, and red blood cell benefits. It prevents oxidation of lipids and preserves integrity of red blood cell membranes. It helps with digestive disorders and is good for arthritis relief. Cat's claw has been particularly effective with persistent infections such as Lyme, candida, EBV, herpes, and numerous others.

chia seed: Lots of nutrients, fiber, protein, antioxidants, and omega-3 fatty acids.

Chloroxygen: Helps increase the oxygen-carrying capacity of your red blood cells and therefore your energy levels and brain function.

coleus forskohlii: Good for allergies and increasing energy.

collagen: Collagen protein powder is great for helping rebuild the mucosal lining of your GI tract, which means not only will you absorb nutrients better, but it seals and heals a leaky gut and gives better immunity and less problematic food allergies. Many consume bone broth for the collagen.

colostrum: Great for healing the intestinal lining and boosting your immunity and energy levels. Be careful, as there is a die-off with this (as with most supplements).

cranberry: Antifungal and antioxidant that also helps the kidneys and bladder. Some detoxification takes place through the renal system. A kidney herbal blend can also be beneficial if you feel you need help in this area.

dandelion root: Promotes a healthy liver, is antioxidant and anti-inflammatory, and soothes digestion.

Digest More with L-glutamine by Renew Life: This is a favorite of mine. You can take this to help with digestion and gas and bloating. It can also be taken between meals to act as a healing enzyme for your entire body. Glutamine also helps repair the intestinal lining.

I use a bitters herbal formula and anise, which both help with digestion. Being able to digest your food well enough is crucial for good health, absorbing nutrients, and preventing decomposing food being left in your intestines, which can provide food for yeast and bacteria.

Dysbiocide by Biotics Research: Supports healing of damaged intestinal walls and treats SIBO (small intestinal bacterial overgrowth). Good to use in tandem with FC Cidal.

FC Cidal by Biotics Research: Helps restore microbial balance and digestive health.

ginseng, schisandra: Consider taking at least one of these to help boost your adrenals while you detoxify. They can also help a lot with sleep and energy.

hemp seed: Lots of vitamins, minerals, fiber, protein, and omega-3 fatty acids.

Interfase by Klaire Labs: Enzyme supplement for biofilms that encourages healthy intestinal microbes. I found this one to be very potent, so start off slowly!

Lauricidin Monolaurin: A coconut-based antiviral supplement, very helpful for CFS.

liposomal vitamin C: More bioavailable vitamin C that provides good cardiovascular support, improved collagen production, and reduced oxidative stress.

Lymphomyosot: A homeopathic and gentle lymph detoxifier, one of my favorite products for supporting the immune system. Keeping the lymphatic system operating more effectively has a cleansing and detoxifying effect. Lymphomyosot reduces swelling, infection, pain, and inflammation. It is very effective for swollen glands and edema. Lymphomyosot is a synergistic blend and can be used for a variety of sluggish conditions and glandular dysfunction. Helpful for general malaise and fatigue.

lysine: It is antiviral, very good for Epstein-Barr and the herpes virus, and helps with calcium absorption. I find it good for sleep as well.

I will occasionally try a different antimicrobial from Nutramedix since I had undiagnosed Lyme disease for so long. There are usually coinfections to eliminate with Lyme. If I have a die-off or herxheimer, I know it's something I need. I always start with the smallest possible dose, then gradually increase, and how I feel will be my deciding factor as to whether I continue or not. If I have a die-off that slowly improves, I continue past the point at which I have no die-off for a short time, maybe a month or two.

maca root powder: Loaded with nutrients and high in iron and iodine, it boosts energy, vitality, and endurance, balances hormones, stimulates and balances the hypothalamus and pituitary glands (master glands of the body), improves mood, reduces and manages stress, improves quality of sleep, and increases libido.

magnascent iodine: Start with just a drop on your skin and work up slowly until you can tolerate four to eight drops topically. Only after you have no noticeable effects from this should you take it internally. It is very antifungal and will create a big die-off in most cases, as well as help your thyroid and endocrine system. Be very careful with this one, as some are allergic to iodine, and you can get your levels too high.

magnesium malate: It is also quite helpful for CFS. The malate is malic acid, which is a crucial component of the Krebs energy cycle. Magnesium glycinate is another one of my favorites. One can hardly get enough magnesium, especially in these highly energetic times we are living in. It is a crucial electrolyte for the nervous system and many bodily functions.

manganese: Needed for a healthy nervous system and brain function, necessary for healthy bone building, crucial in hormone production, including thyroxine, part of the antioxidant enzyme superoxide dismutase (SOD), and one of the most important antioxidants.

Manjistha: Another ayurvedic lymphatic and blood purifier or detoxifier. I began taking this because of spleen issues. The spleen gets overloaded when there has been an unresolved bacterial infection for a long period of time. It is known for helping reduce or eliminate herxheimer responses. It is also helpful in supporting the liver and kidneys. I have found it to be very gentle, as I usually d find most ayurvedic herbs.

methylcobalamin B$_{12}$: It is in the form of high-quality sublingual drops. You can get this from a compounding pharmacy for purity, or Pure Encapsulations makes a pretty good one. The one from the pharmacy will most likely be paid for by your insurance and can be highly concentrated. If you are sensitive to the methyl group of B vitamins, there are other forms of B_{12}. One is hydroxycobalamin, and another is adenosylcobalamin.

molybdenum: A mineral that helps to eliminate excess ammonia and formaldehyde from the system.

olive leaf extract: Antifungal and antiviral.

organic cold-pressed coconut or sesame oil: Used for oil pulling, which greatly reduces dental bacteria and caries. Supposed to be great for pulling toxins out through the mouth. It also whitens the teeth.

ornithine: This is an amino acid and has helped me sleep better many times after exposure to formaldehyde, mold, and other toxins. It has a very calming effect. It especially helps the body detoxify when there is ammonia buildup after a chemical exposure. It is so helpful to those with the mutation of the sulfur detox pathway and probably to anyone with sulfur allergies.

pau d'arco tea: Antifungal, antimicrobial, anticancer.

Pure Planet sports salts: Electrolyte supplement with pink Himalayan sea salt, potassium, and magnesium.

red clover: An anti-inflammatory, it treats skin disorders like eczema and respiratory issues. Most of the herbs I take have some detoxifying effects for the body, which I find really helpful in the process of creating a healthier body that is less prone to chemical overload and reactions. It also helps with a stronger immune system, and you are less likely to have other various health issues as you grow older.

red raspberry leaf: Loaded with vitamins and minerals, including B vitamins, vitamin C, potassium, magnesium, zinc, phosphorous, and iron. Anti-inflammatory, female hormone balancer, immune booster, good for skin and digestion.

ReMag: A liquid magnesium that is the most easily absorbed form of magnesium I know of. It claims to not ever cause diarrhea, as it never reaches the large intestine. Mix with juice, as the taste is not easy to tolerate.

rhodiola: Reduces stress, helps bolster the adrenals, increases mental and physical performance, and helps with the CNS, CFS, FM, and ADHD.

rooibos tea: Antifungal, antioxidant, and anti-inflammatory. It also contains quercetin.

serrapeptase: An enzyme from silkworms that I like a lot. It is helpful in breaking down nasty things that cause a lot of inflammation. So, it's good for pain, and when you detox, you can stir up a lot of inflammation and pain.

silica: Wonderful in many ways, it helps calcium get deposited in the bones and teeth, moves toxins out of the body, helps your skin, joints, ligaments, and connective tissue, and helps strengthen the connective tissue of your brain and nerve cells. Our bodies are operated by an electrical impulse system with the nervous system, and silica helps to maintain the health of the entire nervous system. I have felt this one is detoxifying, so go slowly.

spore-based probiotics: These have been the biggest help to me in recovering my intestinal flora, especially after a round of antibiotics.

theanine: It is a great neurotransmitter, helping you to be more alert and calm at the same time. It is good for sleep too. Anything you can do to calm your mind is helpful to your body. If you can find nothing that helps you to do this, ask again for your spirit guides and helpers to assist you. And always remember to thank them. Show your gratitude!

Trace Minerals Relax by NutraMedix: These have been the easiest for me to tolerate. I've always had trouble with synthetic supplements, so I finally learned to turn to food-sourced super herbs and foods that are packed with vitamins and minerals. There are plenty of those. Examples are maca powder, lucuma powder, baobab powder, acai, camu camu powder, and bee pollen. I've found them far easier than lab-formulated vitamins and minerals. There are also homeopathic enzymes, minerals, and vitamins if you have trouble tolerating a more dense form of these things.

Vitamin D Garden of Life Raw D3: I've had lots of trouble tolerating vitamin D. The best one I've found is this one, and I have to take it with K_2; otherwise my blood doesn't clot as well.

vitamin K_2: Promotes proper calcium metabolism, calcifying bones and preventing calcification of blood vessels and kidneys. Promotes blood clotting and heart health.

zinc: Boosts immune function, anti-inflammatory, antioxidant, blood sugar control, slows macular degeneration.

Laxatives and Bowel Cleansers

You may also require help in moving toxins through your digestive tract so they can be eliminated more quickly. We all know there are lots of laxatives and fiber supplements out there.

Some are good; others are not so good. I don't use senna, as I feel it's way too harsh. Psyllium can be too harsh for some; it can feel as if my gut is being shredded somewhat. I find flax seed to be fairly gentle. Put a quarter cup into a cup of hot water and let it sit for twenty minutes. Then eat/drink it.

cape aloe: Another gentle purgative that is bowel cleansing and used to help with IBS (irritable bowel syndrome). It is different from regular aloe and doesn't have nearly the propensity to cause stomach pain as typical aloe.

Essiac tea or tonic: A combination of four herbals, sheep sorrel, burdock root, slippery elm, and turkey rhubarb, which all help to detoxify the body. With any autoimmune illness or MCS, you need to be working on detoxing all the time in any way you can tolerate.

triphala: I like this, as it's a gentle three-herb ayurvedic laxative. It helps keep matter moving through the colon at an optimum pace, matter that is filled with toxins you do not want in your colon for very long. It is also known for removing parasites.

yellow dock: It is also a laxative, is anti-inflammatory, and treats bacterial and fungal infection and arthritis.

Homeopathy

Homeopathy is energetic or vibrational medicine. In many homeopathics, there is none of the original substance in the pellets or tinctures. The potency of these would be 30C or higher. You may be more susceptible to reacting to the lower potencies, such as 3X, 6X, 3C, or 6C, as they do contain some of the original substance. I found homeopathy was easier to tolerate when I was very sick. Some can't deal with the alcohol or lactose in homeopathic remedies. I would put the lactose pellets in about a quarter or half cup of water and let them dissolve and then take a *sip* of the water. This was enough to create the desired changes in my physiology.

It can work with such a small amount as it is actually more potent than denser supplements because it is energetic in nature. Just as spirit trumps matter, this form of healing is stronger, works on the higher levels, and is easier for some to tolerate. When I have a remedy that is preserved with alcohol, I might put the tincture into steaming hot water and let the alcohol steam off. Some have said that holding the tube of pellets was enough to create the desired effect. It's very subtle, and you may have to wait several hours to notice anything. You can also learn how to make your own remedies without either of these possibly offending substances. There are sites online that can help you. It really is quite simple.

Try to stay out of the mindset of "I can't tolerate any of these supplements, so how can any of this help me?" A huge reason for intolerance is that in addition to a toxic, overloaded liver, one has too many untreated infections—bacterial, fungal, parasitic, and viral. Once you get this load down, you will find your level of tolerance for most things vastly improved. I can count on one hand the amount of supplements I could tolerate in the beginning. It felt like I was never going to get anywhere. I now know that much of the time I couldn't tolerate even the purest of supplements because they were causing a detox response, which many alternative health care professionals didn't recognize.

Also, keep in mind that so much of the early healing can be done without taking a single supplement. So much can be done on the spiritual, emotional, and mental levels, as well as being careful to consume the highest-quality organic whole foods, packed with nutrients. And, of course, make sure your home environment is the safest it can be for you, not only on the physical level, concerning chemicals, mold, pollen, dust, and animal dander, but on the emotional and spiritual levels, as these are very conducive to overall good health.

Safe Ways to Clean Chemicals from Belongings

EM1, or Effective Microorganisms 1, is very effective at removing scents and pesticides from fabrics and walls. It is a beneficial sort of liquid probiotic farmers use to enhance soil. It also eats up pesticides, converting them into nonharmful matter. I put some into a spray bottle and use it that way. It basically eats up any organic matter. I've had great luck using it to eliminate the odor left from skunk spraying. The only downside is that it is made using molasses and leaves the odor of molasses behind, unless you can wash it off with soap and water. But it is powerful enough to get rid of even skunk odors very easily.

Vodka was a great help to me in removing petrochemical machine oils, such as from an organic cotton futon mattress I couldn't tolerate because of the petrochemical machine oils left on it. One light spraying with vodka removed the entire issue for me. I've also used it successfully on new wall unit air-conditioners to remove residue from machine oils.

One cup of vinegar in a wash load greatly helps to remove formaldehyde from new clothes and fabrics. It's great for cleaning glass and other surfaces too.

The Importance of Energetic Hygiene

Soon after my awakening, I became a master of an Atlantean Reiki called Arolo Tifar. This Reiki came from the ancient

Atlantean masters and was channeled by Eckard Strohm from Germany. I received these attunements from two different teachers who had learned and been attuned directly from him. I finally attained my Usui Reiki master level attunement from another local Usui Reiki master. I also received attunements to be a kundalini Reiki master. I've since become an ENLP (energetic neuro linguistic programmer), a Psych-K practitioner, a colon hydrotherapist, and Marconic Recalibration practitioner. Each attunement I have received as an energy healer has opened me up more to becoming a better channel or clear vessel for the energy to come through, as well as learning how and why to protect myself psychically.

One of the best ways I've found to protect myself is visualizing myself surrounded by a pyramid shape. For me, that works far better than an egg of light around me or a metal shield with outward facing mirrors, which so many others find beneficial, or asking for the help of Archangel Michael. He is an archangel known specifically for energetically protecting those who ask for his help. I was terribly frustrated by this for many years until I discovered what worked for me. This may seem like a far-out thing to do unless you are aware you are affected by negative energies. Put it into action and see the positive benefits.

Apparently this is an area many empaths and those who are very sensitive (including chemically sensitive people) need to take seriously. They need to learn to energetically protect and ground themselves. This is what energetic hygiene is. It is a practice of regularly clearing or cleansing your energy bodies. Although unseen, everyone definitely has them. It can make an amazing difference in how well you feel. It also keeps your auric field more intact, with fewer holes so that you become less reactive to chemicals and other toxins, such as radiation and toxic emotions. I finally learned that I receive the most help by calling on some of the extraterrestrial star beings, more so than the angels or archangels. And yes, apparently these do exist. As they say, we are not alone in this big universe. There are many far more advanced beings than earth humans.

The Arcturian extraterrestrials have provided me excellent protective benefits. I know that may sound far out, but being exceedingly energetically sensitive, since calling on Jesus, angels, and even archangels was not giving me full protection, I began to experiment to see what did help or who would step up to the plate to help me in the way I needed it. The Arcturian race are known as Christed Beings of Love, working with humanity and the earth in these current times. They are a fifth-dimensional civilization, and their energy works with humanity as emotional, mental, and spiritual healers. They originate from the giant star known as Arcturus (Arcturianlight.com.au).

I have also received vast amounts of help from what is known as the Galactic Federation of Light or the Great White Brotherhood. The Galactic Federation of Light was founded over four and a half million years ago. It was created to stop interdimensional dark forces from taking over the galaxy. They are made up of thousands of civilizations or Star Nations and are a vast galactic network of love and light beings (Intothelight.news). Earth is on an ascension pathway to one day join this galactic federation. There are many intuitives who channel quite helpful information from sources such as these. Recently, the Israeli official Haim Eshed, the former head of Israel's space security program, spoke of a galactic federation that has a secret pact with Washington, DC, which may not be so secret in the near future (Dailymail.co.uk).

As I became more attuned to the world of energy, I began to have a deep knowing that everything is energy. Before I was aware of this, I perceived these energies as solid events or masses of matter that could harm me, and therefore my flow was more blocked by fear. When this awareness developed, I began living in much less fear and became more open to the flow of life. I had received the first two levels of attunement to do Usui Reiki many years before but had only used it to help myself through difficult, unresolvable symptoms or for my children when they weren't feeling well.

As I learned more and began to understand energy on a deeper level, I was able to understand how I needed to shield myself from all sorts of unwelcome energies. One of the best things I've learned is the importance of grounding oneself, especially if you are very sensitive on many levels. Favorite ways for me have been earthing or grounding shoes without rubber soles, soaking in a sea salt / baking soda bath, spending time outdoors in direct contact with the earth or trees, and meditating. Also, eating grounding, heavier foods can be helpful, I prefer root vegetables, winter squash, sweet potatoes, and thick, hearty, wintery type stews.

It is crucial to add some of these practices to your daily life, as it helps keep your energy field cleared, and energy is able to flow optimally. Our society does not teach these things because we've been a very three-dimensional world focused on what is able to be seen right in front of us. To progress and ease into a more 5-D world, we need to begin to understand there is so much that is unseen and open our minds to the fact that there is truly so much more. Operating as if the only things that are real are what you can touch and see physically is akin to a toddler feeling his parent is no longer in existence because they've left the room.

We haven't been able to see these things, as our systems have not been wired or programmed to do so. However, there are now amplified photon light energies flooding the planet that are designed to help rewire or reprogram us on the cellular and DNA level. This has a dramatic effect on your spiritual evolution, so the time to make use of higher-level energies is upon us. More and more people are going to find that, little by little, abilities come to them that previously seemed foreign. To remain closed to unknown possibilities will shut down your energy flow and restrict your ability to heal and transcend 3-D level issues. It is in our best interest to learn how to heal and transcend, as it's either that or lose your marbles and be stressed out constantly.

Internal Energy Cleansing

Here's something I like to do to remove negative energy from my being, daily or as often as needed. Imagine that intense golden light from the heavens is infiltrating the crown of your head, as if you were wearing a crown of golden light that then showers down into the rest of your body. This is not only very cleansing; it lifts your vibration and activates your connection to Source and all that is, helping to plug you into universal life force energy. Your personal supply can become limitless, there for the asking and taking. Intention and a bit of imagination are key in creation on the spiritual level.

Another easy exercise to activate your life force energy is to lie on your back with your knees bent and feet on the floor, or it can be done even while lying in bed. Next, pump your hips just slightly up and down, an inch at most, as much as you can easily do, maybe twenty to a hundred repetitions. This stimulates the energy at the base of your spine, which is where the kundalini serpent lies coiled and sleeping, waiting to be activated. When awoken, it will rise up the spine to the crown of the head, supplying us with our full connection to our birthright of universal life force. This exercise by itself will not cause your kundalini to awaken; it will simply increase your energy level. This is also a very good exercise to build bone and keep osteoporosis of the spine at bay.

Also, while lying on your back, you can lift each leg alternately, breathing in deeply with each lift and exhaling on the decline. You can do the breath of fire, a rapid panting breath with the mouth wide open and tongue hanging out, or mouth closed and through the nostrils, for ten to fifteen seconds with each leg lift. You don't even have to be sitting up, let alone standing, to do these exercises. This also activates your life force energy and is highly energizing. It may be hard to believe, but try doing this upon awakening each day in addition to the one above. The more you can do, the better, within reason of course, and never going beyond what feels good to you. If something doesn't feel right or good, by all means avoid it completely. There are many other things you can do instead.

There are many ways to create, increase, and facilitate a fairly consistent flow of life force energy. However, anytime you are working on detoxifying your body, emotions, and spirit, you will have less energy than when you are not. Knowing this, it is even more important to do at least a few of these exercises on a daily basis, if not several times a day.

The process of healing and integrating the shadow side is almost inevitable with such an awakening. It was not the fearsome thing that many find it, although it can be very unpleasant and even difficult at times. I say it's difficult because a lot comes up for healing, most of which has been repressed in our subconscious during painful childhood events—or simply suppressed due to not feeling OK with certain aspects of our personality. It's never fun to suddenly realize you may be self-centered, controlling of others, arrogant, or feeling a lot of fear or shame. The truth is we all carry some amount of these aspects and feelings within ourselves. It is also true that we have to become aware of the shadow parts of ourselves and feel the pain of those parts and their origins to begin to integrate and heal.

Feeling emotions is not a foreign concept for me, and I discovered in my twenties that I was far better off letting these emotions pass through me without resistance. I began this process when I left home and realized I'd grown up with an alcoholic father. I really wanted to heal the damage that resulted from living in that situation. It is so much easier to do this work when you let go of the judgment you may hold for yourself and treat yourself kindly and with compassion, realizing that you are human like everyone else. It can be very difficult once you've done this kind of work on yourself to be around others who have not, as they often still want to project onto others what they do not wish to look at within themselves. Their lives are often filled with more drama, each drama an opportunity for them to look within and discover why they feel so triggered and finally heal their wounds or shadow side.

This is another reason energetic hygiene is so helpful. It clears others negative emotional energies from your being. As an empath, I feel them all, and they can wreak havoc on my body, mind, and spirit. This is part of how I became as ill as I did. I had to learn to recognize what was mine and what was not, and the only way to do that was to sit in silence and meditate. When I access my inner being, my truth, I always know, if it is mine, whatever it is will still be there. If it is not, it simply falls away, back to its rightful owner. Meditation and lots of alone time is crucial for people who are this exquisitely sensitive to all kinds of energies. After being in stillness, when you've determined if you are holding others' lower-vibratory energy, you can perform the energy hygiene methods that work best for you.

Another thing you can do is chant a mantra daily, especially whenever you are upset or disturbed in any way by anything at all. It can be so simple. You can say out loud or silently, "I love you. I love you. I love you," proclaiming to your conscious and subconscious mind that you love yourself. Watch and see what happens in your life. It can be miraculous how much this can change for you. Or it can just be the word *om*, which I've done many times, especially when I'm stressed. It is a calming yet simple thing to do. Om is the most sacred mantra in Hinduism and Tibetan Buddhism, signifying the essence of the ultimate reality or consciousness. It's centering and brings you back into yourself, which is why it has such power to calm you.

Being in alignment with Source, or who you are and who you came here to be, alleviates all fear and puts one into a state of *love*, which is the healing and activating force of the universe. Fear is destructive and negative. Love is the building force of creation. It is truly love from which all flows. Once you begin to realize and put this concept into action, the positive power of it is life changing.

Fueling Your Body for the Ascent

In considering how to consume the highest-quality nutrients for your ascent back into a healthful, vital state, I cannot stress enough how important live enzymes are for your entire system. They are the foundation on which everything functions. Hence, a raw food diet becomes crucial for someone trying to regain their health. Many who are ill, however, and some with GI diseases have trouble digesting raw foods. If you absolutely cannot digest raw foods, I would begin taking digestive enzymes before every meal and proteolytic enzymes in between meals. These are known for decreasing inflammation, easing pain, and possibly reducing symptoms of IBS (irritable bowel syndrome).

However, if you feel intuitively that eating raw foods could help you, you can start very slowly, with one raw meal per day for several months. You can also put your whole meal into a Vitamix blender and make vegetable drinks this way, adding a variety of nutrients, superfoods, and herbs if you choose. Sometimes raw foods seemed easier for me to digest when they were broken down in this way first. My Vitamix blender gave my body less work to do. This way of consuming food when you are very ill can give your body a tremendous amount of vitamins, minerals, and enzymes, supplying you with a vast amount of nutrients for healing in a way that takes an incredible amount of stress off your body in needing to work as hard to digest the food.

I put everything in my vegetable smoothie that I would put in a salad, plus lemon juice, olive or coconut oil, and sea salt. For fruit or veggie smoothies, I also add aloe vera juice, raw ginger, camu powder (for the vitamin C), hemp seeds, pumpkin seeds, flax seed, chia seed, and/or pea protein powder for vegan protein. Sometimes I will add barley grass powder or a greens supplement. Chloroxygen and cilantro are nice additions. I will often add royal bee jelly or pollen for the B vitamins. Sometimes I add sunflower lecithin powder or some of my herbal tinctures, provided they don't mess with the taste too much.

I use maca root powder, which is high in calcium, amino acids, and many vitamins and minerals. I include oil and sometimes a quarter of an avocado. Oils are essential for your nervous system, but it's important to use the right kind, such as from seeds, nuts, olives, avocados, sesame, coconut, or olives. Those are the only kinds I use. I do try to limit my fat consumption so as not to overwhelm my liver and its ability to produce enough bile. If you're having trouble with your liver, digesting food, or losing weight, I would try to limit fats as much as possible. Stay away from canola oil; it has some negative cardiac effects as far as I can tell, and the research does confirm this. I had heart palpitations whenever I consumed any. See "9 Reasons to Throw Out Your Canola Oil and What to Use Instead" (www.bulletproof.com).

Other than this, I try to eat as many fruits and vegetables as possible. My cabinets are sparse, and my refrigerator is mostly always full. The dividends and bonuses are so high for me that I just can't ignore it. There are so many good recipe books to enjoy from any health food store or online. Food, nature, and being in alignment with the natural order of life are my primary medicines.

Sometimes even when you start with a very small amount of something, you'll need to wait two to five days before trying again, as the die-off for some will be so strong (even from a very tiny amount) that you need this time to let your body process and eliminate the infectious matter that has been killed, otherwise known as the herxheimer response. Most practitioners know you want to get well fast and so ask you to go at a much faster rate than your body is capable of. It behooves you to push yourself (to a degree) to do some things you may have been fearful about doing in the past, but you also need to take your time and be gentle with yourself. It took a long time to become as sick as you are, and there is no magic pill. It will take some time and effort.

Many of the supplements I've mentioned can be found in forms that are quite pristine and free of all allergens and contamination. Thinking of everything as a reaction can cause fear and then a never-ending, energy-consuming cycle of looking for things to which you may react in the future. It can become an endless negative cycle and affects the amygdala in your brain, setting it into a fight-or-flight mode at all times. No wonder I used to wish futilely for a day when I didn't have to think about all the horrors I had to deal with all the time. I had gotten myself to that state. No one else did it to me or for me. I did it by myself.

At the time, it seemed it wasn't a choice, but once your perception shifts, you begin to see how much power you have, and you take your life back. I will not lie; it is a deep, dark hole you must crawl out of—and pretty much by yourself. No one can do it for you. It is not a cakewalk to get out of a hole this deep. You must be willing to put the effort in, be willing to be open up, and decide to have a life based on positivity and love and spirit instead of negativity and fear. You get to choose what comes through your being. When you do this, you will know you're in alignment with the divine. You will know because you will feel a surge of super powerful energy moving through you and your life, and you will sense that there is so much more to life than what you've been led to believe.

When you've taken a supplement that helps to eliminate candida or any other coinfections (the other bacterial, viral, and parasitic infections that occur when one's immune system has been overburdened with toxins), you are going to experience a herxheimer, or die- off. This is good evidence that you have work to do with eliminating toxins. Typical die-off symptoms follow:

- increased inflammation
- more fatigue
- memory impairment or brain fog
- nerve and muscle pain
- headaches
- nausea or queasiness
- chills/sweats
- fever
- weakness
- rapid heart rate
- rashes
- lowered blood pressure

I probably spent a good three to four years in a fairly constant state of die-off. I found ways of dealing with it that made life doable, some of which were the binders previously mentioned. You simply have to find a binder you can tolerate and take it consistently when you start to feel the ill effects of die-off. If at all possible, get past any squeamishness or fear over doing enemas and colonics. You simply must support the movement of these toxins out of your intestines as rapidly as possible; this is where they are being dumped after being processed by your liver.

To leave them sitting there for any length of time is a mistake. Your body will thank you for helping to move them out as quickly as possible. Even in a sauna, the toxins are released from the cells into your bloodstream and hopefully out through your sweat; however, some will go through the liver into your intestines, and it is still wise to employ a method of removing them from there. Having a bowel movement, even regularly, is not nearly as beneficial as deep cleaning your intestinal tract with enemas or colonics.

Your adrenals will need a lot of support during this whole effort and beyond. First, there are the B vitamins, which I mentioned. I get my B vitamins from bee pollen, nutritional yeast, legumes, peas, nuts, seeds (hempseed, chia seed, flaxseed), sea vegetables, avocado, leafy greens, tempeh, turkey, salmon, and grass-fed meats. Vitamin C is crucial for the adrenals. I addition to rhodiola, herbs such as ginseng or eleuthero and schisandra or ashwagandha are helpful. I like these, as they are solo gentle herbals. I have found most of the adrenal support herbs to be very tolerable, gentle, and helpful. Putting a pinch of sea salt in your lemon water is helpful for exhausted adrenals. Also never forget your electrolytes.

If you need help with your neurotransmitters or are having issues with your nervous system (fatigue, insomnia, anxiety, depression, addictions, brain fog, loss of appetite control, or hormone imbalances), I suggest you find a naturopathic physician or ND in your area to find out which ones you need. Or you can ask for recommendations at your local health food store, in the supplement department. If you have a chiropractor or acupuncturist, you may ask them, as these are all alternative health professionals. Neurotransmitters an become exceedingly out of whack as a result of all the stress your body has been under.

Once I started eating only whole, organic raw foods, with their unaltered live enzymes, my body seemed to not need help with neurotransmitters anymore. The terrible anxiety I'd had for years dissipated within a few days of beginning to nourish my body this way. It was amazing validation for what many alternative health food advocates had been saying for a long time. If you find it too detoxifying, that's because it may be for you, and you may need to start off with one raw meal a day for up to several months. Then increase to two for a few more months, and then you can become a total raw foodist if that is your choice.

However, each person has varying needs, and I will not say it will work this way for everyone. I am not a die-hard anything. I am a supporter of what is the best foundation for health and well-being for each person, and this is something that only you can decipher and know within yourself. Learn to go within and ask often, as needs change over time. Also, it is important to have faith that you can do this. You certainly will not start off doing it all at once. But little by little, adding what you are comfortable with and getting used to that, you will succeed. You will most likely amaze yourself after just a few months.

I have had problems with my spleen, as it was affected by the Lyme, and I cannot consume super cold foods much. During these times, I need to go more into a TCM (Traditional Chinese Medicine) style of eating for my spleen. I simply include more soups, stews, cooked root vegetables, and lightly steamed vegetables. And again, no processed foods, sugar, or high fat. It is one of the best practices to assess where you are, and then adjust your diet, protocol, or health care regimen to what your body wants or needs. This is a major component to living in alignment with your spirit, as your body will always tell you what it needs when you listen to it.

Living in Alignment

True freedom is living as if you had completely chosen
whatever you feel or experience in this moment. This
inner alignment with the Now is the end of suffering.
—Eckhart Tolle

Living life as a well person has been almost nothing like I
imagined and so much more than I ever could have imagined.
I am so full of appreciation, gratitude, joy, and bliss. These are
the key ingredients to having everything I desire and need, and it
helps me remain in that state of being. Gratitude opens me fully to
the infinite waves of abundance and good that flow magnetically
toward me from every infinite source in the universe, from all
that is. I now have a true understanding of how that works, and I
make it my business to access a state of gratitude daily.

I did end up leaving my marriage of almost twenty-six years, the
spiritual reason being that since I became reconnected with my spirit,
it was like being reborn and becoming whole, and it made me a new
person. The person I am now is very different from the repressed,
disconnected, automated shell of a person I was previously when
disconnected from Spirit. When I say spirit, I mean my higher self,
which I see as directly connected to God, Source, the divine or prime
Creator. I could finally admit to myself that I had been living a truth
that was not my own. It was painful for all involved, but sometimes
when there is a need for change, it is not always comfortable or easy,
even though ultimately it leads to living more authentically.

In truth, you will always have a guiding light shining where there was none before. The first year of being on my own was a huge learning curve for me. I was playing catch-up, not only because I hadn't been single or had to take care of all of life's responsibilities and issues on my own but because I was catching up on the ways of a world I hadn't been part of in twenty years. I didn't even know how to operate a computer, as I had been so electromagnetically sensitive for all those years, so I had given up trying. Whew! I can't begin to tell you how much there was for me to learn and take in.

I remember going to the Apple store to learn the basics of operating a Mac computer, and there were mostly people who were decades older than me in the class who'd just bought their latest, most expensive Macs, and they already knew a lot more than I did. So, the beginner class seemed to start above my level! I had to ask for the teacher to go back to the starting level for every single thing he tried to explain. He had a bit of trouble understanding my lack of knowledge in this area, I am sure. It was as if I had just arrived from a previous century or from a different planet! In any case, about a year later, one of my daughters was quite impressed with my computer knowledge and progress. I can't say those months were without a fair amount of frustration and at times a lot of tears. It was like rehabilitation and physical therapy; when you aren't able to do something at first, practice and repetition makes perfect.

Meanwhile, it was also somewhat overwhelming to take care of an entire house and eight-acre property by myself, plus reacclimate myself to the world and learn so many new things. I was also learning how to be in business for myself, doing energy healing work and spiritual guidance for others. On top of all that, I was dealing with my newly awoken kundalini. That gave me unlimited supplies of energy and new insights into all of life. At times, this blew my mind enough that I had to stop in my tracks to ponder my new awareness and integrate it more fully into my being. This was my hero's journey, a new, exhilarating level of freedom that came with a phenomenal amount of responsibility.

I had been told this by Aragon, who had many gems of wisdom to share with me, but it took a while for me to fully understand it. You cannot be in this state of being awakened and healed without the knowledge that with it comes a level of power and therefore the responsibility to remain in truth and authenticity for and with yourself at all times. This can make it look like you are not living in accordance with the social mores of your time, place, or era. However, as long as you know you are remaining in authenticity with your inner wisdom and being, to the best of your ability at any given time, you are in alignment with Spirit, and all of life becomes miraculously synchronistic and supportive of your existence.

I began renting out rooms in my chemically safe home at this time not only to help me with expenses but to help others who were still sick with MCS or Lyme disease. I got to experience firsthand, repeatedly, each of my renters manifest the issues they were most focused on and frightened about. It was an incredible experience that I will never forget. It seemed the universe wanted to cement in my being the truth of this law of attraction by showing it to me in a negative way over and over. It was most assuredly easier to watch it this way, instead of in my personal life. It made me more determined than ever to focus only on what I *did* want to manifest in my life. And not only that, but to focus on feeling as though I already *had* it, to bring up the feelings one feels when they *know* they already have exactly what they want. At the same time, you let go of the *need* to have it, because you know that God has heard you and is backing you up, in every way possible and more than you can know. You simply trust this.

The more you can allow yourself to trust, the more incredible the peace is you will experience. It was a concept I learned after many years of pain and suffering and coming to a dead end from running away from all the negative things I had come to fear and see as harmful to me.

When you've been sick for a while, sometimes sickness itself becomes comfortable, or at least easier than breaking out of that comfort zone and pushing through your limitations to make real progress, shake it up, and change things thoroughly. This is what you're going to need to do if you want to heal. Many things will change, and though it is not always comfortable or secure, this is not a bad thing. It can be a very a good thing and most often is. My life after my awakening and subsequent divorce is a prime example. Not much about the year after all of this was easy or comfortable, and at the same time, I felt happier and more free than I had imagined possible.

If nothing else, change creates transformation and growth, and to me, this is always good, as humans need growth to evolve and become more of who they are. This is where that trust in a higher power really can come in handy. This is one of the first premises anyone who becomes involved in any twelve-step program for healing from addiction or codependency is taught— how to have faith in and trust a higher power, whether to you it is God, your higher self, angels, ascended masters, or your spirit guides. There is a force greater than ourselves at work, and coming to an acceptance and understanding of this produces profound results in your path and on your journey to wholeness and health.

Wolf Encounter in France

To heal is to touch with love that which
we previously touched with fear.
—Stephen Levine

I wanted very badly to have as many experiences as possible for
the first few years I was well, so I began planning a trip all over
Europe for an undetermined amount of time. People thought I
was a bit over the top, but I had an abundant amount of energy
and hadn't really participated in life for two decades. Of course I
was going all out! Others had no idea how it felt to be granted a
reprieve after two decades of imprisonment. At times, when I was
confined, I would listen to someone complain about having cabin
fever after being stuck at home because of a few days of snow and
icy roads. I would think, *Oh, you're unequivocally complaining to
the wrong person about that one.* But they had no idea. Most are not
capable of fully putting themselves into another's shoes, especially
when that other's shoes have walked a very different path.

In my decision to travel to Europe, I think I chose to go out of
the country in part just to prove I could do it. I was a bit nervous
to go by myself, so I asked some friends if any of them wanted to
go. Most everyone wanted to, but only one, my girlfriend Chloe,
was able to come meet me in Italy for a couple of weeks. I knew
at this point it was truly to be a spiritual odyssey I needed to do
alone. So, I committed to going to Europe alone in August 2012.
I bought a one-way ticket. I had no idea at the start how long I'd

be gone. I rented out my house to two people with MCS who had met and lived successfully in my house with me for a month before I left. This was in order to help me fund my trip.

I visited with my mom and stepfather for a few days on the East Coast before leaving for England. I was just two days away from my flight when I got a call from my renter Elyse, telling me that the other renter, Margot, had been on antipsychotic medication (unbeknownst to either of us) to help her with her reactions, and she had stopped taking it. She said the other renter was going crazy, putting some of my valuables in the trunk of her car and the garbage can outside, breaking things, and being threatening to her. My mom and her husband wanted to tell me what to do, based on their fear and logic. My mom frantically said, "I really think you should cancel your trip and go home to deal with this situation so that all of your things aren't destroyed and the other renter isn't hurt."

I did consult several lawyers and a paralegal to ask what could be done. The answer from all was that the best I could do was give the unstable renter a thirty-day notice. If I went back, I'd have to live there with her for those thirty days or find someplace else and pay rent there, still unable to do anything other than wait out the situation. It was not an ideal thing to happen by any standards. I did not relish the idea of giving up my plans to travel and all the money I'd sunk into the trip already to go back and live with a psychotic person in my home for a month.

I told my mom and stepfather that I needed quiet time and to go within to determine my own answer. So, I centered into quietness and the knowingness of my spirit and almost immediately received my answer. I was to go ahead with my plans and let Elyse know there was nothing more I could do there than I could do from afar. I told her to find another place to live, to take care of herself the best she could. She needed to be responsible for her own well-being and safety. There was nothing I could've done legally to change what was going on. My hands were tied. I saw then that this was a life lesson for her as well. I was in my own process of letting go of the importance of all my material and worldly possessions and leaving matters in the hands of God. I saw that it would accomplish nothing by putting myself in danger and living with an unstable person.

I had gotten a book, *The Power of Shakti* by Padma Aon, just before I left and was reading it in the airport while I waited for my flight. I opened it to a page, and my eyes fell on one sentence: "At times in life, one must practice ruthless compassion." This spoke to me more loudly than anything else could have in that moment. I knew when I opened the book to that page, seemingly by coincidence, and read that very sentence, it was Spirit's way of letting me know that what I was doing seemed ruthless, even to myself, but that it was also coming from a spiritual level of compassion for the entire situation. I had offered up my home to two people to work out, albeit in a very dramatic way, some issues that they both had chosen, on the spiritual level, to work out together.

I knew from living with Elyse, the one who had informed me of the situation, that she needed to become more fully aware of her own power in her life and use it. She was still firmly entrenched in that role of victim to all of life and so was playing her part perfectly with the mama bear (me) gone. I could see the whole situation was there to call her to stand in her power and use it. She did this to some degree by having the other woman committed to the psych ward of a hospital. This only lasted a few days, and she still had the issue to deal with when the woman returned.

I repeatedly stressed to her that if she was concerned for her safety, she absolutely must go, and I would not hold her responsible for the rent. It was amazing how much of this I could view from a higher perspective, as if I could see spiritually what was at play and how it was ultimately for everyone's benefit and good, although it looked like a calamitous mess. This situation also triggered my own healing around taking too much responsibility for all the others around me. It was something I'd done almost since birth. I kept reminding myself that it was indeed compassion on the highest level, albeit a ruthless sort of compassion.

For the first few weeks of my trip in England, Scotland, and Ireland, I was tied up in knots from the constant worry about what was happening in my home to both of the renters and my belongings. This made it harder to enjoy my time there. One day I was walking down the street in Galway, on my way to the bus station. It was raining, and I had just received another email from Elyse. It made my heart jump into my throat and brought up all my fear. I felt truly tormented, and I prayed to God to help me, telling him I just didn't know what to do. I decided to stop in a cafe to get out of the rain, as I had plenty of time to catch my bus. I sat down on a cushy love seat next to a lovely Irish woman to have tea and crumpets.

After a couple minutes of sitting in silence, she began talking to me in the friendly, open, and loving way the Irish seem to have, and it wasn't long before she had me telling her what was uppermost on my mind. She simply said, "So, you're traveling. Where are you from, and how is it going so far?" I immediately felt so comforted by her presence and knew she was sincere in wanting to know about me on more than a superficial level. I responded, "I'm from the Southwest of the US, and I'm very stressed at the moment, due to some issues happening back home with renters I left in my home with my cat." She asked me what was happening, and I told her all of it. She must've been an angel God sent, as she instructed me to not open another email from the renters while I was in Europe. She said it would all work out in the end and there was nothing I could do about any of it anyway.

We talked a while longer, and she was so warm and loving to me, an angel and mother at once. I wanted to nestle my head in her bosom when we hugged goodbye. Off I trotted to the train station, vastly relieved to have met such a wise and caring soul on my solo journey. However, from the weeks of pent-up tension, I truly needed to let it rip. In other words, I needed a good cry. I got to the train station, where I locked myself in a bathroom stall, waiting for the bathroom to empty out so I could let the beginnings of my weeks of torment start to flood out. There was a woman at the sink, and I waited for her to make her exit, only she didn't. I did cry a little, not nearly enough, and it finally dawned on me: she was waiting for me to come out.

When I did, she looked at me and said, "So, travel's been rough for you, huh?"

I said, "Yes, but not how you think. It's about stuff going on back home I have no control over."

She said simply, "Well, you can never pray enough." She then walked with me to my bus, waited for me to get on, and waved goodbye. I was incredulous at the loving ways of these Irish women who had just appeared out of nowhere when I needed support the most. I knew then that God had heard me and had sent them as his angel messengers. I will never forget them as long as I live.

Before I departed, I must've had some slight intuition about my belongings not being OK because I took pictures of everything, letting my renters know I wanted things to be the same way upon my return. I took a picture of my grandmother's beautiful antique chest and recalled thinking I wanted that to be safe. When I returned four months later, I looked at the photos I'd taken before leaving, and I saw that there were orbs of light in the picture, directly on top of the chest. Orbs of light are considered to be spirit beings there for our help and protection. I had also taken photos of myself in some of the clothes I had bought for my trip to show my best friend who lived at a distance. I now noticed that in most of these photos, I had orbs covering my legs. This spoke loudly to me that I had protection around me for my travels, my movement forward out into the world.

Ultimately, everything did turn out for the best. When I arrived home, both women had moved on, and my house was fine, minus a few pieces of pottery or glassware, which I never missed. I knew that in the overall scheme of things, possessions meant very little, and letting go of them was more freeing than holding on and having that disturb my internal peace. But what a wild ride my life had become since my healing. I wouldn't trade it for being sick or anything else. I now realize that everything that happens in life is to lead us to our own awakening, and if you already consider yourself awake, then to a deeper awakening.

Everything happens for our learning, awareness, spiritual progression, and enlightenment. It does seem intense at times, but the more awake and aware you become, the more the universe seems to accelerate your path, testing you all along the way about whether you will choose to remain centered in the light regardless of any chaos taking place around you. The universe is aware that you are more in your power, and therefore it gives you more to practice with, learn, and grow from. So, if you don't feel ready for that, certainly don't try to awaken your kundalini.

If you choose to be complacent and remain in whatever situation you're in, your growth and any change in your life will slow down exponentially. I choose to live a life in which I feel alive, constantly transforming, changing, and growing. To me, that *is* life. That is letting the life force energy flow through you unimpeded. It takes a vast amount of trust and letting go at times. Many choose to remain as still as possible, with nothing changing. In this way, they stop the flow of universal or life force energy moving through them and their lives. It seems safe, and it seems it will be comfortable, but to me, it is not truly living.

Trying to control the flow of life effectively shuts it off. It creates illness and blockages, like an overflowing, backed-up toilet you are afraid to flush, because you are so fearful of nasty stuff that may pour out of that toilet. Of course, it's best to figure out where the blockage is and eliminate that first. This is essentially what healing is about. This is what will open you up to healing and the light. Have you heard the saying, the cracks are where the light gets in? Life is change. Be open to it. There will be good, and there will be what appears to be bad, but if you can change your perspective and see bad as the ruthless compassion of something being put in your path for your benefit, you will be able to allow it with greater ease and learn from it.

Of course, I wouldn't view all the years of suffering with MCS as necessarily *good* from a logical standpoint, but it was all for good in the end, because it taught me so much, as I am sure having any prolonged chronic illness has taught you on your path. There is always a reason we have the hard stuff to deal with. A wonderful place to come to in your process is one in which you no longer judge anything as good or bad and have no written-in-stone opinions on anything. This is a place of openness and allowing all things to be in their natural state. I heard in one of my meditations after my healing that I was never actually sick; I was just living that illusion very fully and completely.

I know I chose that illusion in order to learn what going into the darkness of the abyss of hell was truly like, and to fully experience the state of fear that led to. Once I did, I could experience fully what love and light are. It was only then that I seemed able to help lead others out of that hellish pit of illness and lack. On a spiritual level, you have also chosen it for one reason or another. Once you accept this, you can no longer be a victim to it. You begin to take full responsibility for your life. We are all here, having our own individual experiences, to eventually come back into a greater understanding of oneness with one another and the light and to remember how not to fall into the dark abyss again.

I do realize there is much in the world that is still not of the light. I am not in denial of this, yet I am fully aware that the darkness only persists because not all have chosen to come into the light yet. None of it is right or wrong. People simply are where they are on their journey, and the more of us that wake up to the truth, the more light we can and will bring to the planet. This will be what creates change at the most profound level and the place from which we can create a new Earth.

The first place I stayed was the most unique Moroccan-style flat in London, near Camden Town, owned by a man who was a rebirther using breath work. He had had an illness that he'd recovered from as well. We instantaneously clicked. In his quest for health, he had instinctively veered away from using chemical products. He was a wonderfully entertaining man, full of love and joy. When I first arrived, I was quite upset about the renter situation back home, and he sat me down and said, "Let's talk." I spilled it all to him.

I noticed that I kept blowing light bulbs all over his flat, almost every time I'd walk into a room. He couldn't help but notice. This is an indicator of how we carry a lot of electrical energy, and even more when we are emotionally stressed, especially when we are well and running a lot of life force energy through our bodies. This phenomenon stopped once I calmed down and got more grounded and centered, which I think he was happy about.

I had no fear of exposure to harmful chemicals, to the point I never even bothered to ask anyone about any of it, which I found amazing, and there were none in his flat. I was discovering that when you are focused on everything being safe and free of toxins, that is primarily the way things are for you.

Yes, it seems very odd, but I have continued to find much truth in this. The less I have been focused on fear of chemical exposures and just happen to mention my severe sensitivity in the past, the more people have been willing to bend over backward to accommodate me. They seem far more concerned that I'm exposed than anyone ever was when I was truly ill. That has definitely been one of the oddest things, and although I am grateful, it has also felt slightly annoying at times. Here I am, healed and not wishing to be fussed over in the same way that would've been not only nice but so desperately necessary when I truly needed it. Life is good, although strangely paradoxical at times.

All I can surmise is that somehow the fear and desperation pulls in energetically from the universe a certain likewise negative energy that really turns people off, to the point they can't even hear you. This is unfortunate, and I won't even say it is how people are, as much as I know it is how the entire universe operates on the metaphysical level. The more you understand this, the more you can begin to correct it for yourself. When you are at your sickest, it can tend to create feelings of desperation and fear that the next exposure will be the one that is the end of you. This is where you most need to watch your thinking and correct it, since whatever you are focused on will be brought to you promptly, courtesy of universal energies. Some of us may be better at manifesting this more rapidly than others, as it has also to do with a certain level of profoundly felt emotion combined with the focus.

I stayed primarily in people's homes or apartments rented through a popular bed-and-breakfast site. Europe does have a fairly widespread chain of affordable green hotels, which were also very good—no chemicals and no smells, comparatively speaking. I used those too. I know I have said that I forgot to ask about chemical usage in places, but I certainly attempted to live as cleanly as possible, so the green hotels were a nice find. The hardest thing was breathing in lots of cigarette smoke, as people there smoke incessantly out in public. That does get old, even for a well person who hasn't smelled that odor in many years. I had no reaction, but the smell is incredibly heavy and disgusting. In some cities, I would walk between eight and twelve miles a day. I think people are in better physical shape there, despite all the smoking, because they walk so much.

I did try to stick to my raw diet where possible. It was easy in the English-speaking countries but not so much in France and Italy. However, the food is not genetically modified over there, so the effect of eating wheat and dairy from restaurants was not as problematic as it is in the US.

After I'd spent about a month in England, Scotland, and Ireland, it was time for me to take the Eurorail to Paris and more adventures in France. It is quite a wild ride going to Europe by yourself when you've been sick for two decades and sequestered in a rural location for ten years. Fun, exciting, new, empowering, educational, and enriching are just a few words that describe it. I loved England, Scotland, and Ireland. The people there were fabulous. I fell in love with everyone I met. I did all this without a thought about what I may or may not be able to tolerate or what might make me sick.

It was so incredibly freeing. "Free yourself" is what Aragon had said to me several times. Here I was doing just that in one of the biggest ways I could imagine, after all I'd been through. I believe what he meant was to free myself from my mind and its illusions. The mind will have you thinking everything in your life is reality, but it can all change in an instant with a change in your perception.

The day I traveled from London to Paris in early September 2012, I went on the Eurostar, the part of the Eurorail that goes under the English Channel. It was exciting! As soon as I got to

France, the whole system seemed to change. The voices on the intercom became much softer and more genteel than they had been in England, lulling me. Unfortunately, it was so soft, and I wasn't accustomed to the French language, that I missed my stop. I had to get off and catch a new train for which I had no ticket. This was a bit stressful. At the station I got off at, there was a German woman looking to put her two young boys, about eight and ten, on by themselves. They told her the boys needed an escort, so she asked if I'd be willing. We were just about the only people in the station. Without understanding the system fully, I said yes, somewhat to my detriment.

Little did I realize what would ensue on the train ride. The boys had no assigned seats, and the train was mostly full, so the conductor led them to a first-class car. I wish the mother had been able to communicate beforehand to the conductor what was happening. But that was not the way things were done there. Those trains pull in, and it's all a big, mad rush, and then they pull out as rapidly as possible. I went up to first class with them, having agreed to supervise them and look out for them. I sat down in an empty seat. After about ten minutes, the conductor approached me, barking at me in French. I tried my best, through gestures mostly, to explain to him what I was doing there, pointing to the boys.

He was not having any of it. The barking turned into threatening yelling in French. I tried again to let him know the situation to the best of my ability. It was clearly not going to work. I started to have visions of being hauled off the train at the next stop and being taken to a French jail. It freaked me out. It's scary when someone is screaming at you with an angry face in a language you can't understand. So, knowing I was breaking the rules and unable to make him understand why, I got up and moved to the next car, where I stood for the rest of the trip. At least I could still somewhat keep an eye on those boys.

Because of missing my stop, I was late getting to my flat in Paris. The owner told me she'd leave the key with a shop owner around the corner. Again, the shop owner spoke no English. I speak very little French. She did finally give me the key, however. I went back and tried to open the door, to no avail. So I went back to the shop, and finally a customer came in who could understand the issue and very sweetly walked back with me and got the door open. I went upstairs and after a bit realized I needed to go out and buy spring water, as I had no drinking water there. When I tried to get out of the building, I had the same issue; I could not get out. I started to feel a bit frantic, needing water and knowing full well not to drink water out of the taps there due to the possible parasite contamination. I simply could not figure it out, and the owner was at work, so I couldn't get her over there to help.

I finally realized there was a mail slot in the door, so I opened it and could see people walking by on the street. I called out for help, and a sweet couple strolling by with their baby stopped. The father reached his hand in through the slot and opened the door for me. It was simple but extremely different from any door I'd ever seen before. The building was ancient. Even though it was so old, there was no issue with mold. Those buildings are so well built. They laughed, and I was just grateful the problem was so easily solved. That was easily one of my more trying and exhausting days on my trip. Although I never understood the doors well enough to describe what exactly happened with my door situation there in Paris, I found plenty of other evidence online that many tourists have the same issue. In fact, there is an amusing article, "How I Came to Fear French Doors," on bonjourparis.com.

While I had been in London, I made a point to locate a colon hydrotherapist so that I could continue keeping my body as detoxed and clear as possible. The therapist I found said she was facilitating a detox retreat about two weeks after I'd be leaving London, in the South of France. When I calculated the cost of the detox retreat, it wasn't significantly more than what I was spending on room and board already. So, I decided it would be a haven for me and possibly enable me to be on my journey for a while longer if I paid strict attention to my health. After Paris, I headed by train to Carcassonne, a small town in the South of France, near the Pyrenees Mountains, where the retreat was held.

I got off the train, starving, in a small town, to discover that Sunday was the town's day of rest, so no restaurants were open, at least not to serve food. There were one or two open to serve alcohol, and that's what the locals were doing on their day of rest, drinking and smoking. I found a grocery and went in and bought some apples, kiwis, avocado, cheese, and lettuce and made a nice salad with these. The next day, all of the retreat participants met in this town to ride up to the detox retreat located in a beautiful, huge, old home up the mountain. The home was built right on top of a sulfur spring. My room was luckily on the third floor of the building, because the bottom floor was moldy due to the house having been directly over a water source for hundreds of years.

I noticed my mood suffering somewhat while I was there, but I didn't know if it was due to not eating all week and intense detox or the moldiness. I learned that my body doesn't like going without food for longer than about two meals. To be honest, we did have a glass of vegetable juice with lemon juice twice a day. We also had warm vegetable broth nightly and herbal teas. Toward the end of the week, we were allowed protein powders if we were not able to shake the constant hunger, which I gladly added to everything. There were also several colonics, yoga, hot sulfur tub soaks, sauna, steam room, ear candling, and energy work offered.

Everyone said the weakness and incessant hunger would vanish after a few days. That didn't happen for me, although the others did lose their hunger in a few days. Neither got worse, but both were a constant the entire week. By the time food was offered again, at the end of seven days, I was the first one at the table, waiting in a bit of torment for the others to arrive, lest I devour everything on the table before they had their chance at it. Even after leaving, I ate everything in sight for the next several days, gaining back any weight I had lost and then some. I just could not seem to stop eating. They warned against this, saying our bodies would not be able to handle it, but mine seemed to need it, and I handled all this eating far better than I had handled the period of deprivation.

I cannot honestly say I feel this method of detox worked well for me. It was too severe to go without food for that long. Not everyone finds fasting for prolonged periods especially beneficial. My body seems to prefer a more gentle form of detox and is truly happier having whole food, especially if it is only fruits, salads, avocados, olives, seeds, and nuts—and not a lot of these either. I just need something! I think the juices actually made me hungrier than eating very lightly would have. I think many of us who have had MCS and had our nervous system affected need oils and fats in our diets. It's very calming to the nervous system and helps coat the myelin nerve sheath, enabling one to deal more easily with stressors.

In fact, when I had been sick, I noticed that eating especially dairy fats, I could endure more exposures. The fattier, the better. Whole cream and milk or yogurt were the best. I found later it had something to do with the butyric acid in the fat. Apparently, it keeps toxins from being released as rapidly in the bloodstream. Butyric acid can also help maintain a healthy intestinal lining and has relieved symptoms in people with inflammatory bowel disease. As I stated, I found it helpful in reducing symptoms when there would be a known exposure, making my life a bit easier.

Not that I am a proponent of keeping dairy in the diet, as I feel there are negatives here, and I do notice an increase in liver and gallbladder issues if I consume it regularly. Sometimes, almost anything can be used as medicine.

While I was at the retreat in the Pyrenees, I got in touch with a Mary Magdalene center, as I wanted to visit it while there. I was told they were not open at the time but that there was someone there who would do distance energy healing for me. It was not exactly what I had been seeking, but I agreed to it. The woman who did this for me called me after she finished and told me she had found a karmic knot in my heart having to do with a failed love relationship. She asked if I knew what she was referring to. Oh boy, did I ever know what and who she was talking about. I felt nothing for a couple days after the treatment, and then suddenly, it hit me really hard.

I had moved on to the town of Arles, Vincent Van Gogh's favorite spot, when the grief that I'd previously been unable to access, began pouring out. It was uncontainable, as if several lifetimes of grief had worked their way up to a level that could finally be felt and released. This was not fun, for sure, but very needed. I spent at least one afternoon sobbing in my flat, as if my heart would physically break. I walked around the town of Arles endlessly for several days, just feeling this incredible amount of sadness coming up and out of me.

Miraculously, beautiful, angelic little children kept approaching me and engaging me in their antics, in their sweetness and innocence, as if they could feel my pain and wanted to lighten it intuitively. There was one in particular who was outside on the sidewalk while I was indoors on the other side of the window, sitting in a cafe. There was a painted area from the floor that extended up a couple of feet. This child, probably about four years old, kept crouching down and then popping up repeatedly, playing a game of peekaboo with me. Of course I couldn't help but smile. It was a beautiful reminder that we always have everything we need, even if it doesn't come in the form we thought it should or wanted it to.

One day while in Arles, my host mentioned I should visit the Cryptoportiques of Arles. There wasn't a lot to do in this town except be, which was kind of perfect for the grieving state I was in and wandering aimlessly, so I decided I would go. I got there one day kind of late, and it was about fifteen minutes before closing time. I went down and was completely alone. There wasn't a lot in the crypt, just a long hallway that I walked down, maybe close to a mile. I was fine being down there alone. I approached the end of the hall, and there was an archway opening out onto the street, with the daylight shining in.

Suddenly I noticed in the archway an animal I hoped was a dog, but it looked for all the world exactly like a wolf. It paced back and forth in the arched opening, each time turning its head in my direction. I froze. I quickly thought over my options, which weren't many, and quickly decided to turn and walk as rapidly and calmly as I could back in the direction I'd come from, making every possible effort to contain my rising terror. I got back to the steps that led up to the office and flew up them. Panting when I arrived back to a safe place with a door to close behind me, I tried to convey to the office woman why I was breathing so heavily in a terrorized state. She laughed, not understanding a word of my English. I'm sure she simply assumed I had been fearful of being alone down there. Not exactly alone, and she had not a clue as to the real reason for my frightened agitation.

That evening, I went out to a cafe and tried to order a single glass of wine. Perhaps this is not the custom in France? The waiter obviously had other ideas. He was convinced I'd be better off with a half carafe, as it was more for your money. That is a problem at times in a foreign country. You cannot make them understand you may want something different from what is customary there. So, a half carafe came, against my wishes. You learn it is just better to go with the flow in some circumstances. In my state of grieving and trying not to waste money, I ended up drinking far more wine than I would have normally. It was really hard, to say the least, walking back to my flat in complete darkness, in heels, on cobblestone streets, and not really knowing my way in this more than tipsy condition.

When I got back, my flat owner was having a very small intimate gathering of local artists and photographers in which wine, of course, was being consumed. She offered me a glass. Knowing full well I'd already had too much, and also knowing full well I'd already made some faux pas along the way from not understanding what people in other cultures may find offensive, I tried in my more than slightly inebriated state to make a decision on how best to handle the situation. Not being as firmly grounded in what was right for me as usual and also wanting very strongly not to offend, I took her up on her offer. It was a nice party and a very chic and artsy group of young people. I was amazingly well the next day. French wine doesn't seem to have the same detrimental hangover effect as many in the US do.

A week or so later, my girlfriend Chloe met up with me in Italy, where we went to Lake Como, Bellagio, Cinque Terre, Florence, Venice, Milan, and Rome together. Soon after her arrival, I told her about my terrifying ordeal in the crypt of Arles. She suggested we look up the meaning of the wolf as a spirit animal totem. We did, and the key word that jumped out at me was *strength*. The wolf totem is known not only for being a teacher but also for strength. I recalled how I had drawn the strength tarot card repeatedly before my trip to Europe when asking the tarot what the trip was about for me.

The next day, we were strolling through the gardens in Bellagio, and we sat down to pause on a bench. That was when she asked me, "Talcyona, why did coming face-to-face with this wolf frighten you so much?" As soon as the words left her mouth, I burst into tears. I knew why instantly. I said to her, "Because I am afraid of my own strength." We both just sat silently for a few moments, and I knew had to look at why I was afraid of my own power, my own strength. The wolf appeared to wake me up to that fact. I had known since I was young that I possessed an incredible strength and power that I thought everyone had, and I still think they do, but that any display of it always resulted in making others uncomfortable or even fearful. I learned early on to pull it into myself and sit on it, repress it. It still served me well on some levels, such as having an incredible amount of staying power and fortitude for whatever I felt most passionately about. I have an inner knowingness that I can and will achieve whatever I decide.

Of course, along the way, I have learned it works best for me to never neglect the spiritual component of asking for help and doing whatever I do from the highest vibrational level I can. It is a firm resoluteness, which I wouldn't call stubbornness, that is fairly unshakable. It is a quiet internal strength that is not always visible to others. It's not always gentle and can come forth quite suddenly. This is when people become uncomfortable, as it probably feels as if they're being steamrolled by some unexpected force. It's taken me this far in life to know exactly how to use this strength, and I've been afraid at times of unleashing the power of it, since I've seen the results—people gasping and looking shocked, saying, "Couldn't you have been gentler or less forceful in getting your message across?"

Being the empath I am, I have a very high level of sensitivity to others, wishing not to harm them or bring them discomfort in any way. But Mars in my natal chart is in Sagittarius conjunct the Galactic Center. Oh dear, this gives Mars extra force and strength, and Mars is already the planet of male energy, aggression, and ambition. So, at moments, I probably have greater trouble containing that energy. However, I now know this is part of my gift. I am meant to use this power in connection with my expression and always trust in my inner knowing about when and how to use it. For those who know human design astrology, for my design, it is a sacral response or intuitively felt and connected directly to my throat chakra (speaking and expression) and will at times help me to verbalize exactly what comes up without any thought, which became more pronounced with my awakening.

This can verge on being shocking not only to me but others. With age and wisdom, I've learned that whenever this urge hits me, it is something that needs to be said, and the person I'm saying it to needs to or is ready to hear it. I've learned I've been blessed in my astrology with the wounded healer planet, Chiron, being conjunct Mercury, the planet of expression and communication, or the messenger of the gods, in my ninth house of spirituality, religion, and travel. That means I have an ability to heal through my words, if used with wisdom, strength, and compassion. It took me until I was fifty-nine years old to integrate all of that successfully and not be afraid of using it. I am so gratified for having learned astrology, as I can see now how it lays out the framework for each person's purpose and life path, their growth opportunities and evolution in this lifetime.

This revelation concerning the wolf encounter in the crypt in southern France was a grand spiritual culmination of my entire trip. What a huge revelation for me and, finally, a huge acknowledgment of my power. I am in love with the synchronicity of life. I feel if you really pay attention, it is all there, always— life speaking to you in the ways you most need to hear. It was interesting that the beginnings of this awareness, this both horrifying and miraculous event, should occur in the South of France. This was precisely where Aragon had asked me to collaborate with him, doing a shamanic healing journey with a group of people at the very time this event happened.

That did not happen, however, as I had ended my relationship with him prior to my trip. He had told me at one point in our relationship that I had everything he had; I just needed to discover it for myself. What was most amazing to me was that I had seen him as having this incredible power that I did not think I had, and partly, I was attempting to obtain it through my association with him. Also amazing was the fact that I hadn't even planned to go to France at all, yet I went because of the healing retreat in the Pyrenees, which I'd found out about in London. And then I ended up doing the intense grieving in the South of France. It really drove the point home that the universe has a greater plan and order than we can begin to imagine.

The next part of my trip was quite memorable and not only because it was in the beautiful country of Switzerland. Idyllic countryside viewed while traveling by the Eurorail makes one understand more completely the romance of trains. I've been in love with travel by train since. I stayed in Lucerne in a beautiful home overlooking Lake Lucerne. I decided I would make the trip up Mount Pilatus for the breathtaking views it offers and ride the cogwheel railway to the top. First I needed to board a steamboat to cross Lake Lucerne, and once I boarded, I had difficulty figuring out where to pay for my ticket across the lake.

So, I sat down at a table and decided to wait and watch others to see what they were doing or where they were going. I found observation to be very helpful at times when I didn't speak the language. Suddenly a uniformed man appeared and said to me, "You didn't pay for your ticket." I said, "Yes, I know. I didn't know where to do that." Then he flirted with me a little and engaged me in some light conversation. He finally told me where to pay for my ticket and started to walk away. As he got a few steps away from my table, he turned abruptly and said seriously and firmly, "No, I'll come back for you." The second he said this, I felt, for lack of a better word, slimed. Energetically very slimed. So very bizarre. It felt like I had a heavy, thick, sticky, slippery substance thrown over my head that encapsulated my entire being.

Not only was there this physical feeling; there was a horrifyingly immense depression that settled over me that I could not shake. I could not figure out for the life of me what had just happened. I went out to the front of the boat, hoping the breeze would blow off whatever had just settled on me. It did no good whatsoever, although I stayed out there for the rest of the trip, hoping like crazy no one would try to talk to me, as I felt more off than I've ever felt in my entire life. When we arrived near the base of Mount Pilatus, I disembarked from the steamboat, and the second my first foot hit the ground, the feeling vanished as suddenly as it had come in.

I'll admit there was a lot of stimulation with traveling constantly that I wasn't used to, and my nerves were on edge often because of all of that extra stimulation and the need to figure out where I was going, the public transportation systems, and the money in each country. Traveling out of the country for the first time can be a bit mind-boggling. As I said, in each country, everything is somewhat different, and I was also trying to communicate with people who didn't speak my language, nor I theirs. Doing it alone added another layer to this dynamic, but what a boost, knowing I could manage in the world at large on so many levels at once.

Many times, walking through a noisy, crowded train station, I would find myself repeating *om* out loud, to myself. The noise made it impossible for anyone to hear me. It was very grounding and centering and basically eliminated any fear or anxiety I might have had. It kept me on track and able to figure out what I needed to do and where I needed to go. In fact, I started to notice that near the end of my four months in Europe, other English-speaking travelers would approach me in train stations, fairly frantic, looking to me to help them figure out what to do and where to go. I guess they sensed the calm coming off me, as if I knew what I was doing. It was fabulous confirmation that I was doing very well. I also knew I was doing exactly what I needed to be doing to gain a renewed sense of confidence in myself after so many years of being sequestered and isolated. I pushed past my former boundaries and what I had been comfortable with. There isn't anything quite as exhilarating and conducive to one's personal growth.

My Ascension Path and Spiritual Revelations

Live your life from your heart. Share from your heart.
And your story will touch and heal people's souls.
—Melody Beattie

Not long after my return from Europe, I heard, clairaudiently, that I was to go live in northern Arizona—not once but three times. It took that many times before I listened. My mind wanted to tell me that I could not go live somewhere else for logical reasons, such as living in and owning a house I needed to make mortgage payments on. The first time I heard this message, I simply paid no attention. The second time was almost eerie. I had gone to a movie with a friend, and at the end of the movie, before the lights came back on, I clearly heard a voice say, "You need to go live in northern Arizona." It shocked me, and at that point, I paid enough attention to put my house up for rent so that I would have enough income to realistically do what I was being told I needed to.

It wasn't long before I had a couple who was interested, but the situation wasn't right, and it quickly fell through. I had a conversation out loud with Spirit and said, "I guess I'm not going there since I have no renters yet." And, lo and behold, I literally "heard" a voice *scream* back at me, *"You will go!"* This unnerved me to the point that I looked at rentals that allowed a monthly lease and signed up for one that day. Within a couple more days, I had a renter show up who allowed me the means to go in the direction that Spirit had given me for the next nine months. My awakening and reconnection to Spirit enabled me to perceive things on many different levels that I previously would not have been able to do.

I don't always hear voices, but when my higher self is trying to guide me and feels passionately that I must do something, I will hear it. I also hear it during energy-healing sessions with clients at times. I hope in reading this, you are able to understand that your own inner knowing and connection to your higher self and God is a very valuable gift that can help you far more in life than any amount of logic or good strategic planning is actually able to. Focus your intention on making this connection be a real and strong one.

When you are open to it and pay attention to the signs, you will see how real and valuable it is. There are signs all over. Some of my favorites have to do with nature. You may find a bird's feather in your path, or a certain animal shows up for you, even a scorpion or ants. I always look up the spiritual meaning of such things, and it's usually right on target for where I'm at in my life. Sometimes it gives me validation that I'm on the right track. Also, numbers showing up in sequence, such as 1111 or 555, have significant spiritual meanings.

Sedona is a magical and magnetic red rock vortex location that draws psychics, healers, and spiritually minded people as well as the avid outdoor hikers from all over. It is largely a transient place, and I believe it is because the energy is so intense there that if you have too many issues you have not dealt with, it is exhausting very quickly. The energy of the vortexes magnetically pulls these issues up and out of you if you are open psychically to that sort of thing. If you are energetically sensitive or an empath, being there for too long can be exhausting.

Native Americans have been known to say it is a place for ceremonial purposes only and that one should never live here. I felt the strength of the energy immediately after arriving and learned that to be there for any length of time, I needed to keep my crown chakra open and stay very grounded. I learned this due to the fact that I felt pressure building in my head that nothing relieved until I visualized my crown chakra opening like a lotus flower. Because of my heightened energy sensitivity, as soon as I arrived in this high-energy vortex location, I could feel a very low-level vibrating feeling moving along my inner core.

It was constant and at times felt almost like it was a fire inside, simmering. It could also instigate a feeling of low-level anxiety, which I found unpleasant. I learned from a psychic there that I was running a huge amount of electrical energy (this was later corroborated by an astrologer, based on what he could see in my chart). The psychic taught me how to ground this electrical energy so that it was not accumulating inside of me and could be used to help heal the earth. I ground it into the earth by visualizing that I had chains grounding me from my root chakra down to the earth's center and bolts of lightning coming out of each foot into the ground with each step I took. This helped quite a bit, but I also found it an absolute necessity to spend as much time as possible outside, sitting, lying, or walking barefoot.

Doing this greatly relieved the buildup of energy in my body. This doesn't seem to have a lot to do with chemical sensitivities, although it may have more to do with it than I fully understand. I truly feel that when you have healing and energy-sensitive abilities and you have repressed or ignored that part of yourself for a long time, you can end up being quite sick from that repression, and it ends up being quite a different thing. I feel now that a lot of my illness was from taking on far too much energy from others' maladies that weren't my own and not knowing how to discharge it or let it flow through me. I felt that if I continued to do these practices the psychic taught me, I might be able to handle staying in this intense location even though she told me I was far too sensitive to stay and that I should move to a neighboring town.

I did stay, and what a trip it was. The healing and the ways in which it happens there are nothing short of phenomenal, not to mention magical. If people are not psychically in tune before they move to this area, they will very likely become so after being there a while. Life is lived in a sort of bubble. Everyone is attuned to one another, very empathic and compassionate souls primarily. It seemed that all I had to do was think of something I wanted, and it appeared. Not everything but many things, and probably the ones I most needed. I recall one evening just feeling the desire to watch a movie, and within five minutes, a friend called and said, "Hey, want to come over and watch a movie?" This was not a normal occurrence for me, as I hadn't watched much TV or many movies since my awakening. In short, the powers of manifestation are amplified there. I received a vast amount of healing. The most major was around the trauma I had felt over meeting my twin flame and the profound grief I felt over our separation.

I mistakenly thought at the time that a twin flame relationship would be everything a conventional relationship "should" be. How funny this is to me now. Although I will always feel the profundity of having loved someone more deeply than any love I ever knew I was capable of, and with the entirety of my being, I now know that encountering him was much more about learning to love *myself* on that level than I had ever been able to fathom doing beforehand. And for this I am eternally grateful. This is why I feel as I do about the false twin flame and their gift to empaths who are struggling in this world. Having been through this, I don't consider myself a victim any longer. I did at first. I cannot say how glad I am that I invested so much time and energy in my own healing and self-esteem rebuilding. I have finally transmuted the pain and the whole experience to something I consider very meaningful, my own healing at some of the deepest core levels. It has resulted in profound transformation.

Here is one example of the kind of synchronicities that happened regularly for me while living in this highly magnetic vortex town. I happened to attend a seminar about how the words we use affect and manifest things for us. I noticed a tall man sitting directly across from me who was gregarious and spoke a lot, and loudly, during the seminar. It was *almost* annoying. A few days later, I overheard from my open kitchen window my apartment neighbor standing outside talking to someone, and they mentioned this very seminar. My curiosity was piqued, so I went downstairs to meet these people, who were obviously interested in some of the same things I was. Well, with my neighbor was that very same man who'd been sitting right across from me in the seminar. His name was Sam. We talked for a few minutes, and then I went back home.

The seminar instructor had given us an exercise to do at home, which was to say to ourselves nightly before falling asleep, "I am my beloved, my beloved is in me." This was supposed to help manifest our twin flame, soul mate, or sacred partner. I did it, because I wanted quite intensely to find a partner I felt as deeply about as I had about Aragon. I was still very sad about the loss of this relationship and feeling a huge void, two years after I had ended our contact. I began making this statement out loud and did this for three nights. On the third morning, I awoke and realized I was overcome with sadness. I cried and cried and cried and couldn't stop crying the entire day. Later that day, I was still crying, eyes very swollen, when someone suddenly knocked on my door.

I didn't really want to see anyone, but I cracked the door, and there stood the tall man, Sam, from the seminar, and all he said was, "I have something that could help you." He told me that my apartment neighbor (who was very psychic) had felt that something was really off with me that day. I told him to come back the next day, which he did. He knew a technique called Hawaiian Huna Higher self-therapy. He got me into a trance and took me back to the earliest time I could remember in which I felt the same pain I was feeling the day before. I saw myself as a baby, knowing even then that I was a healer and wanting to help my parents to heal, as I felt the energy of their woundedness. I could not heal them, however, and my soul was absolutely crushed and felt the incredible weight of this pain all of my life.

I realized that this was completely connected to my perceived inability to help my twin flame to heal as he had done for me. The moment this session was over, I knew I was altered. I no longer had this pain or weight with me or in me. It was as if a giant malignant tumor had been excised. And thus, my journey into myself, loving myself ever more fully and completely, continued. It started with the simple phrase, "I am my beloved, my beloved is in me." Now I comprehend this on a level that is so very deep and sacred. I know I am never alone because I am there for me. And I love my self. And so it is with meeting a person who is meant to be your transformer.

There is no process I can give you that would be better than this mantra, "I am my beloved, my beloved is in me," to ready yourself for meeting your own beloved and bringing up and healing any core wounds preventing this. You may be able to recognize when you have met this person by how connected you feel not only to them but to yourself and how it leads you back to yourself time and time again. It is as if they are the exact mirror you need to do the most profound healing work possible. If you allow it, it can and will heal you. I did not say there would be no pain involved in this process, and the pain can feel as though it will take you out. But even though it feels that way, it will not, and if you are willing to allow this, the rewards are like nothing you could ever have imagined.

After about a year and a half of living in northern Arizona, I started to take the supplements ALA (alpha lipoic acid) and MSM. Both of these are sulfur-based supplements designed to help detoxify the body. ALA is widely used as a mercury or heavy metal chelator. I think my system was finally low enough in mercury, as I hadn't eaten fish heavy in mercury in many years, had all my amalgam fillings removed many years prior, and ate small amounts of cilantro regularly. I took the ALA and MSM for a few months but noticed no big benefit, so I stopped. Soon after stopping, I noticed that I was developing small patches of red rashes on both forearms. They didn't itch, which I found strange. I wondered if it was perhaps hormone related. I didn't know but also thought it possible it was smart meter related.

While I was living in northern Arizona, a few smart meters were installed on the end of my apartment complex of six units. I began feeling much more tired than usual within a week and not able to think as clearly. Soon after, a rash started appearing on my forearms. No symptom I had was made worse from the typical previous chemical exposures, however. After several months of these symptoms not improving, I decided my time living there needed to come to a close. I was not realizing yet what was to come.

I moved and began a short stint of housesitting in Tucson, Phoenix, and Colorado. I was asked by friends to housesit a few times in the area of northern Arizona where I had lived, and each time I did, the rash would grow exponentially worse, with no improvement after leaving. It was so odd. I found myself wondering if the vortex energy there combined with and amplified the smart meters and was something my body simply cannot tolerate. The last time there, my intuition definitely let me know it was time to try a different location, a more grounding one than this area offered. My intuition was pulling me to go to a location in Northern California. By this time, I was covered from my neck to my ankles with an angry, red, burning rash. It was very uncomfortable.

Then it started to become excruciatingly unbearable—a terrible burning and stinging with some itching. Getting it wet with water caused the burning to become more intense for up to an hour after. This was the most bizarre thing, and I could not get a handle on the cause. As astrology would have it, I was in my second Saturn return with my natal Saturn in the sixth house (the house of work and health) with hard squares to both my sun and Pluto. This all started a few months into my Saturn return, and at this time, I was well into it, almost a year. The rash issue had become nightmarish, and by now it was beginning to feel like I had radiation burns all over.

There was so much redness and swelling in my skin. The heat was all in the surface of my skin, to the point that I was shivering internally and had trouble staying warm. I went to several skin doctors who were of no help whatsoever. They all said psoriasis and gave me steroids. The only thing I could think to do was to cover the rash in a product called Un-petroleum Jelly, as this seemed to keep my skin from drying out too much. I became suddenly sensitive to almost all fabrics, except for a few articles of clothing that were extremely soft, thin, well-worn 100 percent cotton. I couldn't handle any metal jewelry. I felt I was being radiated by electromagnetic fields, and this increased dramatically with anything metal touching me. So, I seemed stuck in a living hell covered in grease, which quickly saturated the few articles of clothing I could wear. They darkened in color and hung like oilcloth on me. I was really a sight for sore eyes.

With my spirit urging me to go to a sacred place in California, I got in my car and made that drive and magically ended up in a house that used to be a healing center in a small Northern California town. Two young men were living there, one of whom was a licensed peyote shamanic medicine man. He told me he had healed himself from a similar rash with the help of peyote. I was so desperate I would have done anything for some relief. He gave me the peyote in small amounts at first and then left it up to me how much to take. I took it pretty much daily all day long, in teas and sucking the buttons until they disintegrated in my mouth, for the next two months. I never took enough at a time to hallucinate, and it didn't cure the rash, but it did help me to stay calm and meditative much of the time. At times, however, it did seem to make me feel extremely agitated. Such a challenging and interesting time in my life, without a doubt.

I realized that when I was meditating, or at least very calm and still, I couldn't feel the stinging and burning sensation that was now constantly present otherwise. I ended up spending most of my time during January and February lying barely clothed on a bed, in a sometimes meditative and sometimes severely distressed and agitated state. It was a cold, wet winter, and I had two space heaters running constantly in my room. I was shivering and shaking internally because so much of the blood in my body was on the surface of my skin instead of in my organs.

For much of this time, I listened to the Lakota Indian healing song repeatedly. The lyrics are "Father, help me, I want to live." Amazingly, I never knew this until much later. I just knew it brought me peace in my miserable state. One of the major things I learned from this experience was that the more I accepted what was and actually gave it love, the easier it became to deal with it. I finally did reach a place of pure acceptance, that if this was what the rest of my life was to be, then I would be the person I came here to be regardless of the suffering my mind wanted to believe my skin was causing me.

I started to go out in the spring with short sleeves on, making the intensely hideous redness of my arms visible to all. I finally found a naturopathic doctor who thought I had symptoms of the CBS (Cystathionine Beta-Synthase) sulfur detox gene mutation. I had the genetic testing done, and sure enough, she was right on target with her diagnosis from looking at me and hearing my history. She told me to stop eating *all* foods containing any sulfur and to stop taking any sulfur supplements. I did as she said, and within two months, the rash began to drastically improve. During the time I had this rash, I ended up spending almost seven months mostly in isolation. The rash cleared, and the isolation ended just as my Saturn return was ending. I am sure now this was part of the divine plan for my life path.

If you are concerned about ethical issues of genetic testing, you could try eliminating high-sulfur supplements, medications, and products to see if your symptoms improve. And if your symptoms are severe enough, you could try eliminating as many sulfur-containing foods for a couple of months to see if you can get the symptoms under control. Some of those products with sulfates are shampoos, dishwashing liquid, toothpastes, and laundry detergents. The highest foods are eggs, onion, garlic, and cruciferous vegetables. There are many supplements and medications to be avoided.

Some of the supplements include alpha lipoic acid, milk thistle, N-acetyl cysteine, and MSM. Some of the medications are Bactrim and sulfa drugs. You can do a Google search on supplements and medications to avoid with the CBS gene mutation.

The inability to properly metabolize sulfur and sulfates in foods, supplements, and cleaning products causes too much ammonia to build up in your body. Indeed, a young acupuncturist fresh out of school was determined to diagnose me properly so he could help, and after hours of poring through his medical books, he told me the best he could come up with was a chemical poisoning of sorts that could possibly end up being fatal. I would say that was fairly accurate even without being specific. With my body's inability to detoxify through the sulfur pathway, large amounts of ammonia were building up, poisoning my brain and organs. My body was valiantly attempting to remove these toxins through my skin, resulting in virtually the same thing as the worst baby diaper rash ever, all over.

I did meet a man named Donovan from an online dating site, since I wasn't getting out at all, who I know now was an angel sent to me. We became pen pal friends at first. After we met, at one point he told me to think of the seemingly incurable, appearance-destroying, and extremely uncomfortable rash as "my beautiful expression." At first, rolling my eyes, I thought, *How bizarre and unfathomable.* Even the way he said it was totally filled with light and loving energy, and because of this, it was so encouraging to me at a time when everything seemed to have been stripped from my life. I remember the first nice day, in a long string of overcast and wet days, I got myself together and went for a long walk around the lake. I talked to my body and my skin, telling it how beautiful it was and really feeling it. It became my mantra, to call it my "beautiful expression" instead of my rash.

It actually gave me the energy and space to receive a different perspective on my situation in many ways. I cannot minimize how difficult it was to get to this place. I fought it with everything in my being, despite all I had learned previously. My mind, or ego, wanted to make me think it had to run the show, or my life was in jeopardy. But there is something far greater than us or our ego/mind that is actually in control and maneuvers things to our benefit, if only we can surrender to it and receive all that it has to offer us. I cannot stress this enough, especially when you have what seem to be incorrigible health issues.

This is the epitome of a lack of resistance or nonresistance to what is. The second you stop fighting and resisting something, the less of an issue it becomes, and the less importance or influence it has over you. About a month after putting as much awareness into this nonresistance, I began to go out again, to dance and do yoga with others. I was still covered in this rash, and not knowing if it was ever going to be gone, I think I had gained courage from this simple exercise of self-talk, and that made me feel I had some power over my body. I could not go on letting my body have the upper hand, as I knew from past experience this was not even remotely helpful. It's a huge untruth we've been taught since birth. I felt like a warrior when I chose to show up at yoga classes and dance events even in this state. This is how I came to discard the idea I'd previously held tightly, that something seemingly negative in your world or body must be resisted and fought against. It actually makes whatever you are resisting persist and stronger.

Ignoring a tripped genetic mutation such as this can take you to a point where you can no longer detoxify much at all, as you are on overload to the maximum. Some people suggested I detox by fasting on water and refused to listen when I told them I felt any detox made the rash unbearably worse, not to mention it made me feel extremely weird. I had done a lot of detox before, so I knew something was terribly off kilter. You should always pay the utmost attention to your own body. This was a perfect example of being really sick and not able to do any intense sort of detoxifying, such as a water fast, without becoming even worse.

I am so glad I paid attention to my body and intuition. I still don't think there are a huge number of naturopaths, let alone allopathic physicians, who know much about genetic mutations in the detox pathways. My intuition was screaming at me to go to a place where the energy would be gentle and soothing, and I would find the right help! So I went. I have learned it's best to be in touch with this part of myself and to let it guide me, not to do just what my mind tells me or thinks intellectually would be right. It took a long time to right what had happened in my body from the overload of ammonia, which causes all sorts of things to go wrong. But I knew I had healed myself before, and I knew I could do it again. I have again done so successfully.

I can also see now in the overall scheme of things that this was predestined to happen for my highest good. It's very hard to understand at the time when things are at their very worst that they are actually happening *for* you and that it's all happening for a reason. "What reason?" you might ask repeatedly, and get no answer until much later. At the very least, I now finally had the biological reason for having been so chemically sensitive, as I am pretty sure this pathway as well as a few others were totally overloaded when I was sick with MCS.

I do feel this gene got seriously tripped not only by taking the MSM but also from living in the town in northern Arizona that I lived in when it happened, a place with high amounts of vortex energy, which was then amplified after the introduction of smart meters on the majority of homes and businesses in the town. This made the electromagnetic energy off the charts for me. That kind of energy in an overabundance can make anyone become incredibly toxic pretty rapidly. I feel we have been seeing some of this in the case of the coronavirus pandemic, as it seems to have been far worse in areas with a lot of air pollution and 5G cell towers already in place.

I can see and feel the energies here on the planet now increasing to a point where I am sure had I not had this experience and discovered the gene mutation, I'd be right back in that boat of being super sensitive to everything again. Having this happen helped wake me up to the fact that I am just going to have to really focus on the health of my mind, body, and spirit in this life or nothing will work for me. I came here as a super sensitive being, and I will more than likely leave that way. There is simply no getting around that.

After this episode, I did again employ some brain retraining, this time EMDR (eye movement desensitization and reprocessing) to recover from the psychological trauma and brain looping, as this time I was able to recognize how traumatic it had been for me. It's traumatic to be so ill and incapacitated, feeling there is no one who can help you, and your entire being needs great care to recover fully. I have found any kind of brain retraining to be extremely beneficial in alleviating stress associated with trauma, changing my unconscious thoughts, and creating better health and a better life for myself.

I had gone to this town in Northern California because I intuitively felt it right for me to be in a strong, positive, and grounded energy field, and I knew I would find that there. It is known to be the root chakra of the planet. I actually felt this very grounding and peaceful energy come over me when I was about thirty minutes away from arriving in town. I did spend a lot of time alone there, which would not have been my mind's logical choice for myself, but I surrendered to it because it was what it was, a decision based on my intuition. I knew I had no energy to make it any different, and I knew that to get myself through this time, I needed to be alone and inwardly focused to as large a degree as possible.

The reason I decided after two months of being there to move to southern Oregon was because I found there were many dance groups and classes there. Even in the midst of what I was dealing with, I was learning on a deeper level to transcend my suffering by following my bliss. Dance is definitely one of those things for me. The things I love and that bring me joy, as well as bring me into that altered space of consciousness, were an important part of my healing once again. In Ashland, I found NIA dance, African tribal dance, and ecstatic dance classes almost daily.

I also found it fabulous to be in the vibrational energy of others who were loving the dance, movement, and music as much as I was. On a personal level, the foundation of my life now is always to check in about whether what I'm doing is in alignment with what my spirit wants. Societal standards, or even what someone else thinks would be beneficial for me, is a definite recipe for misalignment with Spirit and therefore dis-ease. The human spirit and its connection to the planet, Gaia, or Pachamama is such that if we let it guide us, it will bring us our salvation, our bliss, and our healing.

The entire time I spent in the Pacific Northwest, I was in the hard-core midst of my second Saturn return. Also, Saturn falls in my sixth house of work and health. It was during this time that I realized a big part of my life's work *is* my health, like it or not. I may not like it, but I found I had best learn to accept it and concentrate on it fully and with everything in my being; otherwise, it would be very difficult for me to remain here on the planet. Yes, good old karmic taskmaster Saturn.

You do begin to realize that your spirit has some things it must've signed up to learn in this lifetime under Saturn's effects. And, yes, as I have told many people, I start my day by adhering to my health regimen, which includes not only physical but emotional, mental, and spiritual aspects, which takes hours. If I don't, I may as well sign on for having the universe beat me upside my head with a two-by-four until I do. It's easier this way. Most of you probably don't have this Saturn placement and will not have to work as hard at it. I fully understand that many have other commitments in life that prohibit spending this amount of time and being so regimented with it. You do not need to spend as much time as I did necessarily, but like anything, the more you are able to devote yourself to it, the better your results will be.

One reason I love astrology is that you can actually see in the natal chart that there are likely some areas of your life that will not submit to human control and that you may have great difficulty changing, regardless of attempting to change these issues in a variety of ways and numerous times. The key to peace, happiness, and joy can be found in acceptance of these particularly difficult areas, if not all areas of your life. It is a major benefit of meditation, as it helps tremendously in arriving at that place of acceptance and peace and a greater sense of connection with everything as it is.

Meditation can bring us to a place of greater peace within, from which more good can begin to come our way … such as the body healing itself more easily, or a key to your healing suddenly pops into your mind, or we begin to understand how important it is to love everything, regardless of its outer appearance. And I do mean that in the literal sense. Love everything. It's all here for you, and that is the truth. No one said it was going to be easy or that you had to like it. I know I sound like your mother telling you to eat okra or liver. The truth is acceptance and love are key ingredients to a happier, more peaceful existence.

This is why the gurus stress meditation the way they do, they have a secret they've been trying to teach for eons. Meditation opens us to universal life flow. It grounds us in truth and who we really are at the core of our beings.

Who we really are is love, and from this place all life force flows. It opens every cell to the flow of universal energy, and all the flow wants is for you to have everything you want and need, including your physical well-being. It's as simple as opening and flowing with life instead of shutting down to universal life force in fear and restriction. I do not watch or pay attention to mainstream media news, as I do not allow my thoughts to sink into negativity and doom. I will not allow people or media programming that persist in spreading that or anything low vibratory in my environment. What you allow in your space emotionally, mentally, spiritually, and physically have a great effect on your being.

Astrology has helped me understand some of these things in my life that have just proven to be unavoidable. My north node sits right smack on my descendant angle, which can indicate the unfortunate energy of attracting people to me who will in some way try to victimize me or blame me—the proverbial scapegoat. Also, I began my life's plan by being born into a family where my experience was that of feeling neglected. It made my first experience in life that of feeling like a victim, with very little power or control. So, what looks like a rather unfortunate area of my chart has actually turned out to play an important part in my life's purpose and plan. Now I know it was for me to learn to practice greater discernment and step out of the role of being a victim in this life, to become empowered and then to show others how to do the same.

I still have difficult moments, as we all do, of course. Recently, after a long period alone at home, I went into town. I had been trying to arrange to see several friends, as I had been alone in my rural home and had seen no one in that time. Unfortunately, no one was able to connect that day, and for some reason, that day, I went into a downward spiral of depression that seemed to come up out of nowhere. I felt myself shattering into pieces, and when it was over, I could see that it was my ego trying like crazy to hold onto all the darkness and pain still left in me, oozing out like lava from a volcano.

I was driving, so I pulled over to a safe spot where I could continue venting and sobbing. It was an insanely intense for a few moments. But it stopped as suddenly as it had begun, and I just sat there in a very detached sort of way, and this was so calming that I couldn't continue and saw it all for what it was. It was my true self (spirit) just watching the ego in me fighting to hold onto all the old negativity and pain, needing to make it mean something about me. It was my pain from childhood or perhaps even other lifetimes of not feeling wanted. I saw that Spirit had used exactly what I needed to bring me to my knees once more. This process of surrendering the ego and pain my ego clings to has happened in layers and stages for me, not all at once.

Also, speaking of how we may be affected energetically, once when I was ill with MCS, I was watching a program on TV with my family, and one of the people on the show was smoking a cigarette. I suddenly realized I could smell the cigarette smoke as if I were engulfed in a cloud of smoke right there in the living room of my chemically safe home. It was beyond real. They all watched in amazement as I swore repeatedly how the smell was so strong it was as if it were in the room with us and not just a picture on the television.

This led me to the understanding that if something I see or hear can affect my olfactory perception in such a profound way, there is clearly a connection between the energetic and the physical that we *don't* completely understand. And if our sensory perception can be affected in this way, how many other things on an energetic level can possibly be affecting our physical perception of what is happening? Many are aware there is such a thing as a psychic attack, which has the potential to affect someone in a very negative way. A psychic attack is most often not a conscious or premeditated form of aggression. However, it usually results from someone who focuses strong energies of jealousy, resentment, anger, or even fear on their unsuspecting target. The power this has to disrupt your well-being and life force energy is often invalidated or just ignored.

Thoughts and feelings are energy, and if this energy is directed at you in a negative way, you are going to feel it, especially if you are a sensitive being. It has the strength to disrupt your life in a multitude of ways. It can be very confusing and make you feel as if the problems you're having are originating from within yourself. For an empathic being, this is not always the case. Another form of psychic attack is the limiting and damaging thoughts and beliefs we are all taught as children, either by parents, the school systems, or others with authority over us. This is the type that can be the most difficult to recover from since it is so ingrained in us from an early age, but you most certainly can recover and move past it. This can be where brain retraining is quite helpful, or working with a quantum or shamanic healer. A huge way of dealing with these types of attack lies is learning how to generate your own positive energy.

This can be done by taking the best possible care of yourself—doing things like yoga or daily exercise, eating healthy, meditation, positive thinking, and reframing all outmoded and negative belief systems or any negative thoughts. It's also good to balance and align your chakras, as these are your personal energy centers. The more out of whack or filled with negative energy they are, the more you will feel it, and this also has a negative effect on your overall mental, emotional, physical, and spiritual health. This is a truth and such an important one. It is sad that we are not taught this as young children. Also, it's important to clear your living space and body on the energetic level regularly.

Saging your home environment and your body are great ways to clear space energetically. If you can't tolerate burning sage, placing a bowl of sea salt in the center of every room works too. Sprinkling sea salt all around the outside perimeter of your home is something many energy-sensitive people do regularly. Playing high-vibrational solfeggio frequency music in your home is great, and there are many of those on YouTube. Putting any kind of rock or stone in every corner of your home and on every windowsill and by every door is an effective negative energy absorber.

The power of prayer is energetic and can affect people and situations in a very *positive* way. There is more going on in any given situation than we are able to know with our intellect alone. We may not ever understand or be able to explain everything on a rational or scientific level, because there are so many other levels of life. When we accept this as a part of life, on a spiritual and emotional level, and without fear, there is so much more that becomes available to us for our healing.

If there was only one major spiritual law to fully know and practice, it is that whatever you focus on, amplifies in your life. We are far more powerful as creators than we understand and can choose to create from a place of fear or love. Often, when we are doing it from fear, it's because we are simply unaware and continuing to operate robotically from what we have been taught in our childhoods—what humanity as a whole has been taught for eons. It has become encoded in the cells of our being. The good news is that we are capable of breaking this code, wiping the slate clean, and starting afresh with anything we choose.

These unwanted encodings can be broken or released in numerous ways. One way is through shamanic journeying. I was supposed to sell my house and property after my divorce. I put it on the market dutifully and went through three different Realtors over five years. It simply would not sell. Finally, I did a shamanic journey with the intention to find out what I needed to do to sell my house. In the journey, an Indian chief appeared over my entire seven-and-a-half-acre property and said to me, "You are not supposed to sell this property." In spite of that, I still continued to try to sell it—to no avail. I finally gave up trying. I had to change the way I thought around it, realizing that if one has done all in one's power (and trust me, I did all I could do) and still, there are no results, one must come to a different realization. That, for me, was the fact that I wasn't going to be able to adhere to a rule, legal or not. Fortunately, it has all worked out in my favor and for the best. The shamanic journey helped me to accept it all.

Thoughts are also a form of energy and have so much more power than most realize. So, based on this truth, why would anyone want to continue along the path of negative, fear-filled, denigrating, cynical, mean-spirited thinking? And, if this is truth, you have far greater control over creating your life than you may have previously thought possible. You *will* create your world from your thoughts. First, the thought you're having, or, letting your mind think, will have an effect on your emotional body or emotions. You are truly hurting or helping yourself and others moment to moment with your very thoughts.

Let's say you're having a fear-based thought. A typical one for me was, *Every time I go into a big-box store, I feel so sick from the chemicals in there.* Then look to see where that thought leads … maybe to another like, *I am progressively getting worse and worse from all these exposures. I hate my life. I am so limited in what I can do, I may end up super debilitated more than I already am if I do almost anything or go almost anywhere.* You see how it spirals downward? One negative thought invites a slew of them in. It's a negative, vicious downward spiral. Then notice how you feel after this onslaught of negative thoughts. Are you happier? More joyful? More present in your current life situation? I seriously doubt it. Most likely, in fact, you are feeling just the opposite.

From here, the negative thinking leads into negative emotions. Sadness, fear, overwhelm, exasperation, frustration, resentment, bitterness, despair, you name it. Your emotional state has a strong impact on the state of your physical being/body. If you think this is not so, you are deluding yourself. Watch while you have a negative thought and see if you can't feel your heart sinking, your stomach churning, your muscles tightening, your mood plummeting. This is just what you can feel. There are vast amounts of chemical reactions between every atom, cell, and neuron in your body that happen from this change in homeostasis. You can decide if you want to change this and make your mind your garden. You get to decide which thoughts are planted, which to prune, and exactly how to watch over and care for or nurture the garden of your mind.

You must go within or intuit and decide whether you are ready to do this work. Then decide you will do the work to turn this around for yourself. No one else can or will do this for you. The only way is to become conscious of what is going on in that head, which is connected to your body. Once you are conscious, you can choose what thoughts you would like to replace the negative, fearful ones with. It's really as simple as that. The hard part is getting past your resistance to doing it or thinking it cannot be done. I am here to tell you otherwise from my own experience.

So, again, once you decide which new positive thoughts to create to replace the old ones that are not working so well for you anymore, practice them repetitively, as often as possible until they become your new thoughts. Our brains are so similar to a computer that needs to be programmed. So, instead of the previous low-vibrational thought process, what if you changed it to something like …*Wow, this body feels some side effects when I go into a big-box store. I think I will try to figure out how I can get my needs met in another way that is more conducive to my physical and emotional health. I am so smart. I can actually feel love and acceptance for myself that I have this sensitivity to so much of what is low vibrational on the planet. I am a highly sensitive being, and I love myself for that.*

So you see, instead of fighting or resisting what's going on, you have changed your perception of what is and are now choosing to go with the flow and not make it mean the same things. See how you feel and how your body feels after you've made the change in thought. If it relaxes you and you feel a big sigh of relief or expansion, you will know your thought is coming from a state of love, as opposed to fear. Nothing has to mean what we think it does or what we have been taught it does. Literally nothing really does. You can find ways to rephrase almost anything. This is the power of the human mind. This power to reframe or recreate whatever we want to is our God-given birthright.

When you are able to run more than half of your thoughts from that space of love, you will start to notice a definite decline in the number of negative-thought-inducing things and occurrences in your life. In fact, you will notice the opposite happens. At first, you will be amazed, and after a time, it will simply become your new world and life. Many fewer things will come into your existence to cause you to want to go into a negative or fearful thought mode. Although it will sometimes still happen, you are now armed with the awareness that it is actually happening and see that it is for you to practice as well as to see how far you've progressed on your new path. This is a spiritual truth.

We have trouble believing it because it's operating on the spiritual level, where we cannot see with our eyes what is happening. But it is happening nevertheless. So what if you don't understand how something works. Why not just try it and see if you get the same results that everyone else who has tried it has gotten? What do you have to lose, except the old way, which no longer works and you are probably not enjoying? Who wants to keep something in their lives they are not enjoying? Who said we had to do that? Why? Self-inquiry is especially helpful in this whole process. Ask yourself these questions as much as you need to. Really seek to know the truth—the truth of who you really are within, your full-on power. The truth of what you have quite possibly come here to master.

I did not have what I considered a happy childhood. I was the oldest child and expected to carry a lot of responsibility for which I was not prepared. I was also neglected emotionally and not recognized for who I really was. Nor was my sensitivity held in any esteem. More so, I was ostracized for my sensitivity and eccentricities. Can you imagine the effect of this on a highly sensitive being? Being so sensitive did not help, as I took all this to be truth and hence felt I was the cause of my own neglect. If I was smarter, prettier, different somehow, more outgoing, or less sensitive, I would be honored as the beautiful and perfect divine being that I was and am, and I would have been given the emotional sustenance I so desperately craved and wanted.

I have since realized it was part of my life's plan. I was born with the numerological life path number eight, which is considered to be about developing strength, achievement, success, and power. Yes, the number eight is not supposed to have needs, God forbid. Thank God I had the parents and the family I did, as they helped me to fulfill my life's path just by being who they were. I am not making light of it, not by a long shot. What I'm saying is I have learned to reframe my thoughts about my past. Instead of being bitter or angry about what I did not receive as a child, I now have gratitude for the way I was raised, as it has made me the person I am today.

I choose to love that person deeply and completely. And I do see now how it has helped me develop incredible strength and power. It has also helped me to become empowered to be fully and authentically who I am with no apologies. I have also been successful in healing myself, and I hope to inspire as many others as I possibly can on their own healing path. There is a grander scheme at play that is quite noticeable once you slow down, reflect, and ask to receive more awareness about what is actually going on. You must be willing to ask for change to be brought into your life and then have the courage to grab the reins for the crazy, beautiful ride.

It is crucial to uncover the meaning or purpose of your life's journey here, however you do that—whether it is through meditation and prayer, shamanic journeying, astrology, numerology, the birth cards by Robert Camp, Human Design astrology, Vedic astrology, or the Gene Keys. Or you could go to several psychics and ask them to get an overall concurring picture on what your life path is. I have used all of these, as they seem to dovetail, and it has helped me to get a fuller picture of myself. We are very complex beings, and many of us are operating on a multidimensional level.

It will help you to understand more about why you have suffered and endured the particular traumas and circumstances in your life. There is a definite pattern, purpose, and rhythm to all of it. It makes it so much better if we can piece it all together and know what our purpose is. When there is meaning to everything that has been particularly difficult, there can be a deeper understanding, growth, and transformation. One of my purposes, as I now understand it, in part, has been to learn through much trial and error, using myself as a guinea pig in essence, and to share the knowledge and wisdom I have gathered with as many others as possible, or with those for whom it would ring true.

I have the overall goal of helping people to free themselves and live with more spaciousness and possibility to their lives. To realize my strength and abilities, I chose not the easy way in this life (oh, how I wish) but ways that would hone and refine that gift of strength and make it as durable, resilient, and unbreakable as possible, so that I would be able to become the empowered version of myself, raising myself out of supreme victimhood or a place of zero empowerment. I wanted to best be able to lead others in the way of their own empowerment and out of victim consciousness—into the light and power of their true beings so that a new kind of earth can begin to manifest for us all.

We are all our own alchemists, creating and flowing with the magic that is our lives. We are blessed to be here at this time in history. If you only knew how brave your soul has been in choosing to come here and try to uplift humanity for the evolution of humans and the planet. We have been the recipients of a holy mission, and it is so very important that you take heed and be in gratitude about *all of it*. Everything that happens is in divine alignment, and all we need to do is get ourselves out of the way, especially the ego or mind control that we've let run the show for eons.

Let go of every last negative thought about any of it. Accept it all. Let go of all judgment, worry, doubt, fear, jealousy, regrets, guilt, and anger. None of that is helpful. All of it creates blocks to your evolution and the upliftment of yourself and the planet. What if you just blessed everything and everyone? What if it was all OK? Meaning, you shine your bright light on all of the darkness—and poof, it simply begins to vanish. Bring the dark into the light of day. When these negative feelings arise, simply accept them for what they are and sit with them. Make yourself sit with them.

That is you giving yourself the gift of being present for yourself. It is truly one of the kindest, most loving things you can do for you. It is the very thing we want to run from, push back down into the dark, and pretend doesn't exist. What I have learned is that the second we accept and acknowledge that which we abhor, judge, and want to resist and get rid of, that is when it is healed. Love for self and acceptance of all is what heals.

When you are suffering with seemingly unbearable aspects of your life, I ask you to say to yourself, "I acknowledge you, fear, judgment, and anger, and I am OK with your presence here. In fact, I am just going to sit here and let you rise up in me and *feel* you. I will no longer resist that which I judge as bad, uncomfortable, or scary. In fact, I will allow your presence in me right now, and I will breathe deeply into this feeling." Even when it is physical pain or a symptom that makes you feel pure terror, breathe into the exact place of pain or the symptom. Then, ask for your spirit guides, regardless of whether you know exactly who they are, to help you to sleep, breathe, eat, or whatever it is you need to do at that moment. I have used this innumerable times for help with sleeping in particular, and it has not failed me once.

Many times in the past, I have been too stubborn or too caught up in my own victim mentality in being miserable to remember. This mental hardness has to be released. We have been taught it is the thing that will get us through and the thing that makes us strong. It most definitely is not. It is the thing that will keep you so stuck. It requires a certain amount of humility and surrender to give up the mental rigidity. It helps to open to another possibility that there is another aspect of our existence that very few of us have been taught. Most who have learned about it or experienced it have come to it through extreme hardship, trauma, or the last straw. Or, there are those lucky few who just always knew and therefore have had access to this alternate world of surrender to Spirit.

Any illness, any insurmountable obstacles or traumas in life, can be alchemized into a consciousness-raising event or segment of our lives, if not to actual enlightenment. Part of this involves being willing to let go of what you once thought you needed to be happy and secure in your life here on this earth. What you've been taught you need is not necessarily truth. It will help you to understand and see this when you question the things you've been taught instead of blindly accepting it all. Reconnect with your sacred inner self—the truest, most authentic part of you. Accept that much of your life may look quite different from what you originally thought, hoped, or planned.

These ideas of how your life should be have mostly originated from your mind, your ancestors' minds, and the false paradigms and constructs with which we've all been raised. When you've opened to letting your authentic connection to your own spirit transform you, it can and most certainly will. What seems at first be incredible losses can lead to incredible transmutation, ultimate victory, and a true knowing that your spirit is utterly invincible and can rise above anything. That is where it always has been; you just needed to stop and take the time to connect with it to be able to see and feel it.

In order to reach this place, I would suggest a practice of quieting your mind, such as beginning to meditate for just a few minutes daily, learning how to do shamanic journey for yourself, journaling, dancing, doing art, spending time in nature, or praying. Share with that power that is greater than yourself, God, your spirit guides, your animal totem guides, or your higher self what you want to let go of, achieve, or know the answers to in your life. Then do your practice to quiet your mind. This is how you begin to get into the zone or connect with your own spirit.

When you are very empathic, you often take on others' thoughts or feelings or even physical symptoms as your own. It pays to become aware of when you have done this. Most often, for me, it happens when I am in a group of people, especially those who are not very aware or highly conscious. I will come home and notice that I am not feeling as good as I normally do. I used to attribute all of this simply to chemical exposures. I now know that many times, I have actually taken on others' thoughts and sometimes even physical pain or maladies. A good example of this has been during this coronavirus pandemic. Going into town and grocery shopping right now can be a somewhat painful and exhausting experience. I come home and realize I am very sad, angry, or totally drained. I know that I have most likely picked up on others' feelings while there. As soon as I do my energy hygiene practices—take a sea salt bath, smudge with sage, or spend time outdoors grounding—I feel back to myself.

Not everyone does this unconsciously or at all, but I am so aware of this now, as I notice my vibration dropping and am no longer in as high a space of joy, peace, and happiness. When this happens, I immediately set the intention to clear these thoughts and change what I am thinking to be in alignment with how I want to be feeling, and this brings my vibration and feelings of happiness and joy back up. This is key to changing your whole experience of life so that you are more empowered and living in higher states of joy and bliss. This alone is amazingly healing. It is also crucial to learn how to set good emotional boundaries for yourself. Think of this as being as beneficial to your health as eating properly, getting enough sleep, and doing whatever protocol you are doing to improve your health—because it actually is.

If you have friends or family who drain your energy regularly, you must learn how to set limits for yourself so this is no longer an issue. A good example of this is when you have a very draining friend who consistently dumps all their problems on you, without showing any responsibility for trying to resolve their own issues, and then refuses to listen to you at all. This shows a lopsided and dysfunctional energy exchange. It will behoove you to limit your contact with such a person either partially or completely. Forget any stories your mind tries to tell you, such as you owe them, or they don't have anyone else they can talk to. No, because *you* have to make yourself the most important person in this case. It is the opposite of being selfish. It is you being loving to you. When you love yourself in this way, you are actually capable of loving others in a more profound way. Never feel guilty for doing what you need to do to take care of yourself. You are the only person around who is going to take good care of you. You would never feel guilt for taking the best possible care of your own child, so why should you be any less worthy?

Grounding is another hugely important thing to do every day, if not several times every day. I cannot stress the importance of this enough. It keeps you centered within your own being. Therefore you become stronger within yourself, and your physical and spiritual boundaries are less permeable. When you are grounded, it is less likely you will be receptive to toxins of any kind—chemical, electromagnetic, or energetic. It is similar to electrical wires being grounded versus not. If they are not, this is when they can electrocute you. It is the same with your body; when it is not grounded, you become fried much more easily, mentally, physically, emotionally, and spiritually. We are the body electric for sure. Also our bodies are mostly water, so we are conductors for electricity. It just makes good sense.

Many folks with chemical sensitivity issues and many other autoimmune illnesses are actually highly sensitive beings, super empathic, and psychic. If you look at the deeper spiritual self, we are just extremely sensitive to all the ills of society. We really need to become aware of all that is coming in through us, meaning everything emotionally and spiritually, not just chemicals. Seeing things from a more spiritually intuitive space is a way to reframe what is going on at a deeper level.

It is my opinion that most illnesses, including MCS and Lyme, are multifaceted dis-eases. *As above, so below* holds great meaning here. Reconnecting to our spiritual beings is a major part of returning to wholeness and a life of more ease. If I can convince you of this one concept, my purpose in writing this book will have been served. This has been my saving grace. It has also been the foundation for continued improvements in my health and every aspect of my life. Once you put this concept into practice daily in your life, abundance in life is truly yours. Life becomes an unlimited, bountiful cornucopia just waiting for you to experience in this newfound way.

Most of society has yet to understand that all illness is a result of living out of alignment with the world of the spiritual. That is a truth I learned the hard way, and I know I am here in part to help guide those who are open to hearing this truth. Yes, we are told by our government and science how illness happens, and it is ingrained in all of us. They are sadly lacking the entire truth. So, I cannot in authenticity write this book on the premise that some diseases just happen and the people it happens to are victims. That's too easy and will not lead to true healing or long-term health. In my way of thinking, nobody needs to be a victim.

And, indeed, it is not my goal to blame. No, it is to help you empower yourself to discover the deeper underlying reasons for what you are experiencing or dealing with, and to educate about your full ability to maintain good health, regardless of outer circumstances that are painted as truth but are not spiritual truth at all.

Part of the reason it can take so long to heal from any dis-ease comes is the old thought paradigm that our power, our help, our salvation comes from outside ourselves. Nothing could be further from the truth. You have everything you need inside yourself. Everything. It is true. And it is true that your best help will come from within you. I am not saying it's easy to learn to go within; it's usually the very last thing we will do, and we only do when we are truly between a rock and hard place. It isn't very hard though.

You just have to be open and willing to put in the time. It's basically your time for you—you loving and gifting yourself time with you. Give yourself the love you so deserve. Once you accept that doing this is your key to health, joy, peace, and happiness and that this work is yours to do and no one else's, you will begin to feel powerful beyond what you could have imagined. This is the best part of the whole deal, aside from watching your health, vitality, and well-being skyrocket. You get to know and stand in your own power. There simply is no better feeling on earth.

In my journey, I have grown past the need for any religion to tell me what to do or how to live my life. I believe that many ascended masters have walked this earth and have given us many tools and concepts with which to live our lives by. We are all one, regardless of religion. I believe that Jesus was trying to impart to humanity that whosoever believes in the things He did and the ways He walked in love and has that same level of faith or trust, this person will do the same and greater things. He was trying to let humanity know we all have the same power, to help us come to a place of self-empowerment.

We all have God in us. We are all *one*. Many of us are now realizing this. We have awakened to the truth, to who we really are, and stepped into our power. We are all evolving, just at various rates. Some are awake, and some are not yet, and this is all fine. People awaken and transform themselves when they are ready. Long ago, when people were much less evolved, they needed to find an evolved and enlightened person they could believe in and follow, something or someone outside themselves.

Many have now realized the truth that Jesus spoke and have been able to apply it directly to our lives, so we no longer need an ancient text or ascended master to guide us, as we have begun to embody the Christ consciousness ourselves. As we realize that God is living within us and we are walking in alignment with Him, we don't need to ask what would Jesus do anymore, because we are in alignment with our own Source connection, our God sparks, our spirits. We *know*, as we are in direct connection all the time. Almost everyone has the power to reach this place. I ask each day for God to go before me and show me the way, and it is given because I ask and I trust. I have seen miracles and magical synchronicities in this life.

And, eventually, being angry at the world will lose its charge for you, because it is an inside job. Self-love and care and being in touch with your intuition moves you into a space in which you lose all judgment for yourself, and hence judgment for others. You will learn what an inside job means the more you put all your focus on you, your internal landscape. The outside world and other people are just where they're at. There's no right or wrong. It all just is what it is, until awareness happens—and then change or release and forgiveness.

The more we work on ourselves from the inside out, the more we are able to attract things of a better quality. Our outer circumstances get better and better as our inner self heals. We begin to see that other people are just where they're at, and there's no right or wrong, no reason to judge anything or anyone. It all simply is what it is.

I'm sure many have done inner child work and then had better relationships with their families. It helped me tremendously to learn astrology, as then I had real evidence in front of me as to why people behaved in certain ways that I previously judged as bad. It helped me to stop judging anyone, as I could now see how very different we all came in to be and how we each had our individual lessons to learn. As a result of this inner work, others around us benefit from our newfound radiance and self-love. So, in a seeming paradox, like so many things, this is how we inspire. The positive energy ripples outward. This is how an individual reaches greater and greater awareness, which leads to change, release, forgiveness, and ultimately even enlightenment. This is how we begin to change the world.

Healing is truly an inside job and therefore not something to be left up to anyone other than yourself. By all means, search out the help of others along the way, but do not leave the responsibility for your health in their hands. Step into your power more fully and stop the business of being anyone's victim. You are not anyone's victim *unless that is what you choose to be*. Own the responsibility for yourself and your life. It truly doesn't belong to anyone other than you. When you make someone else responsible for you, you give your power away and become a victim to them or your seemingly undesirable set of circumstances.

It's a big step, but it feels so good to act from your own seat of power and not blame anyone or anything outside yourself. Doing this is part of growing up spiritually and taking responsibility for yourself completely, forgiving and releasing your issues from the past. Blame is the handy, easy, irresponsible way out of taking charge of your life. To end the blame game requires looking within first to see why you feel anger or frustration being triggered in you and then direct it outward. This is a huge fallacy we've all been taught, that if anything is wrong, there must be someone else to blame for it. The reality is, if you find anything wrong, it is originating from within and your own unhealed wounds.

That is the absolute truth as I know it, on a grand scale. It does beg for a certain level of introspection and self-honesty. If you are not willing to go there and deal with yourself on this level of seriousness and feel that pain in yourself, you will not be able to heal much of anything. It will always be a struggle between yourself and others—a sad game of separation and division instead of unity, peace, and intimacy. All the latter are those things that lead to healing, happiness, and joy—the proverbial Garden of Eden. It's so worth the work and digging up of the old pain to heal on the deepest levels. Not only does it have individual rewards, but it's the ultimate key to healing our planet.

We can more fully love others when we refrain from judging them, as we can never fully know or understand the path the other is walking, as that is truly only between them and their Creator. Anytime we find ourselves standing in a place of judgment or blame, it's because there is a lesson for us to learn about ourselves, the part of self we'd rather not notice, as we are in judgment of that very part of ourselves, which we have kept hidden. And then along comes a person who operates as a mirror standing in front of us. This is always the case with judgment. It is called projection. It is done primarily when you are unwilling to look at yourself and deal with the pain within.

I saw this in operation with Aragon and myself. I saw such ego in him and was so repelled at first by this. Then, little by little, I began to realize I had my own ego I needed to learn to contend with. And, along the way, I learned where a huge ego comes from. Often it comes from childhood trauma, such as being abused or neglected, and to survive it at all, one must develop an amplified sense of self-importance. It's just part of what happens when you are given no sense of self by your primary caretakers. It's a survival mechanism. Now, when you come across someone with this seeming character defect, you may feel a greater sense of compassion for them.

Learning to do this will contribute to you growing on the emotional and spiritual levels. I cannot begin to describe to you how it feels to be in a place of nonjudgment for not only yourself but your fellow human beings. It is so freeing and results in abiding love, compassion, and true understanding without having to know and comprehend every detail. In essence, it is complete surrender into love for all that is. It gives you more freedom to move through the wild unknown, with a deep knowing that you will be safe, that all will be as it should be. It is an enlightenment of sorts to find yourself able to do this. As a result of learning to practice looking within and healing all that you have previously deemed unlovable in yourself, you will feel safer and more secure within yourself.

You will gain the feeling of being on solid ground within yourself, having loved yourself first and foremost, instead of casting stones at others and hence yourself. This can bring about a feeling of having one's light body activated and being fully present in it—a state of living in higher consciousness, a feeling of being one with all that is. You might even realize that in past lives, you have been a murderer or any number of things you have judged in this life as wrong, and here you still are, growing and learning and evolving, joyfully and sometimes painfully. Living life fully, integrating both light and dark, accepting it all, loving it all. No judgment. Fully free. Old paradigms melt away. Rigidity is a thing of the past. Fluidity and life and movement can all operate, in divine alchemy, to create whatever you believe you can create. We can actually create a Garden of Eden together if that is what we choose to do. But we must believe it is true. You will be able to glimpse that truth when you've done some of your own internal healing.

Life now becomes a fertile growing ground from which the new and inspirational constantly spring forth. There is no *having to be anything, do anything, or say anything.* There is only the here and now, all ripe and ready for the next creation, which springs forth from a nurtured spirit and psyche. I have so lovingly created and written this from that place of my own inner knowing. When you can clear out enough of the old garbage to see it all from a higher perspective, you will know this is true. A spiritual awakening can result from simply giving yourself this time to clear out all your old wounds, paradigms, and negative thoughts. There is nothing like it to bring about a higher state of health and overall immunity.

To have greater life force or kundalini energy moving through you creates a greater sense of aliveness (one reason why it may be called an awakening), of being more awake, more conscious, and it also opens you up intuitively. This helps to create not only better health but a sense of flowing, moving, melding, and collaborating with life. A spiritual awakening makes you aware of our own courage, power, and vitality, which can be used for good to transform everything in your path. It is sacred. It is pure strength—powerful and creative beyond measure. It is this life force energy that connects you to your higher self and Source, which expands horizons and leads to higher spiritual awakenings. Everything I have shared with you in this book is designed to help you create more life force energy and healing for yourself.

It is why the church, government, media, and things like the pharmaceutical industry would prefer that the masses remain unaware of this innate power and wisdom each of us has within us. And these institutions that are currently crumbling have done everything in their power to keep us squelched and ignorant of truth. They can control us more easily when we are asleep and unconscious. They can no longer control or have any impact on those who are consciously awake. You will increase your life force energy simply by doing some or many of the things I suggest in this book, as well as by listening to your own intuition, which is as simple as being quiet and still for a small amount of time every day. This will also serve the purpose of connecting you to Spirit, which is where your intuitive self resides.

To illustrate this, the government in place would prefer that you obey them and the mandates they put into place. They have told us what to think, what to believe, and how to live our lives. And most just go right along with it. They haven't awoken to their internal power and ability to know what is best for them personally. They have not been taught that they can do this and instead have been taught that others with more experience, knowledge, or authority over them are needed to help them be successful and safe in life. Unfortunately, nothing could be further from the truth. This has all been a facade on a grand scale, and that is why we are now in what is known as a massive Great Awakening. You came here to do this. You are ready. Otherwise, you would not be here in the midst of it all—an exciting, tumultuous time of chaos. It always leads to awakening and something that is healed and works far better. It may not seem like it while you are in the thick of it all, but this is truly a period during which all that is of the dark and unhealed is being purged from each of us individually and on a planet level. Those unwilling to do the internal individual work will not fare as well. But those who are, they are the ones who will be creating a new, higher-vibrational earth. Wake up and take your power back!

Start to really pay attention to the joy in your life. Make it your main concern to notice. It lifts your vibration and everyone else's around you. It's such a seemingly illusory paradox. You can be in the depths of despair over all that has gone "wrong" in your life yet still have the ability to experience profound joy around the simplest things, such as the fragrant perfection and sweet juiciness of a ripe summer peach, enjoying the beauty of brilliant, colorful, exquisitely designed flowers and nature, the breeze, a child laughing, beautiful guitar chords being strummed, and the Zen sound of a hang drum. Begin to pay attention to the smallest things.

If you are so inclined, I recommend reading something like *The Pleiadian Agenda: A New Cosmology for the Age of Light* by Barbara Hand Clow. It explains much about spiritual concepts that can ultimately be very helpful in your spiritual journey. It is here you can learn many things that are never discussed in the mainstream world. People are now hungering to know and understand things on a more spiritual level, and they want and need to know more of what is really happening on the deeper levels. Many of us now understand that all this healing is taking us toward ascension and into our light bodies, which are free of karmic heaviness, toxic chemicals, heavy metals, and everything, including ancestral family lineage karma. There are many books written to help you gain a greater understanding of the metaphysical and spiritual world, books that are more understandable to our current culture and do not need as much decoding as the Bible does.

All that does not belong in our field and which will no longer serve us at a different level of being will be released during the coming age. It is all part of the three-dimensional world, and we are now moving beyond 3-D, rapidly moving or ascending into 5D. Many more are feeling very symptomatic with maladies that doctors have no way to diagnose or help with. Much of it is due to this huge change happening at a cellular level and is nothing to be afraid of. It is nature's way of detoxifying us and letting us know we are living out of alignment with our spirits and the natural order of the universe. It is bringing us back into alignment and can seem as if it is forcing us as long as we are in resistance to the rhythm.

This is happening due to our solar system moving deeper into what is known as the Photon Belt or Kuiper Belt. It is an area of space with a higher density of photon light particles than we are used to. This has been improperly called a conspiracy or new age theory. However, since my kundalini awakening, my body has been gifted with the ability to be a sort of Geiger counter in a different way. Instead of lower-density chemicals, it is now very sensitive to incoming planetary energies, and I can most definitely feel these surges happening more frequently and more intensely. This is just part of the process of truly waking up for many. An earlier part of this is becoming sensitive to many of the toxins in the 3-D world, which helps you to awaken to what is not serving you or our world.

It is painful and very trying at times, but understand it is all part of a process we agreed to before we came here, and there is nothing to fear and everything to gain from it. Those experiencing the most discomfort are the ones going through it very rapidly, and some, like myself, agreed for the love of humanity to take on others' dis-ease to make it easier on them. It is very hard to understand why one would do this, but the spirit understands quite differently from what our earthly bodies and minds comprehend. I have been experiencing many unexplainable symptoms since 1987 that started near the time of the Harmonic Convergence on the planet.

Once you know that you've been releasing much illness and dis-ease for the collective, or are an empath and take on too much of others' toxicity, emotional, and mental traumas that they are unwilling or unable to release, you do not need to continue doing it, as you are truly only responsible for yourself and your own ascension and healing. There are many ways to energetically protect yourself and clear yourself of this type of negative energy, and as I've said, you should make it your practice to do so daily, even several times a day. Little by little, your recall of many amazing things will come back to you as you heal, things you knew from previous lives or your ancestors. We are the ancestors actually, as we carry their genetics, life wisdom, and traumas in our DNA.

It is all truly an amazing process and web of life. I suggest that you begin asking questions if you are curious about learning more. The internet and YouTube are loaded with information. Books, too many to count, have been written on all kinds of spiritual topics with fascinating, new, cutting-edge information. You need only use your intuition to guide you as to what resonates or is right for you. Far better to use this than to have some misguided or even malevolent authority tell you what is right for you. We are sovereign beings, with free will, moving into a new earth, a new way of being and doing things. I am here simply as a guide, helping you move into your own freedom and sovereignty and claim what is rightfully yours.

I want to say a bit more about the protective spiritual layers surrounding our physical bodies. Being ill alters the etheric and auric bodies, many times making them weaker (even creating perforations in these spiritual bodies) and more subject to violation by unwanted energies. This can be draining to our energy field and levels. The etheric body is the first layer in the human energy field or aura. It sustains the physical body and connects it with the higher bodies. It is important to be as healthy as possible, to keep these bodies stronger and less permeable to outside energies. These energies can come from many places. It can be as simple as easily absorbing others' negative emotions, which actually infiltrate these openings in your auric and etheric fields and drain you of your vital life force energy.

If this goes on for long enough, it can start to cause pain in the area of the openings and end up affecting your health negatively. These negative energies can also come from what energy healers commonly call cordings, or karmic ties to other people, places, or events. A good energy healer will be able to help clear your field of these drains on your energy. I highly advise all who are ill to learn techniques to clear themselves energetically. Often a good energy healer can teach you what they are doing if you ask.

Again, there are videos all over YouTube on how to do this. Some techniques include grounding, visualization, breathing through your chakras, brushing yourself off all over, bathing in sea salt water, burning sage, rubbing yourself all over with a smooth, round, flat stone (yes, stones will absorb negative energy!), asking for your spirit guides to clear you energetically of any energy that is not your own, and asking them to close up the holes in your auric and etheric fields. To recharge your stone, just put it on the ground outside for a day or night.

Profound healing can result from letting go of the need to heal. Ponder that for a moment. That is how I began my healing on the spiritual level. Healing from that level is the top of the hierarchy in healing, as all illness or dis-ease begins on the spiritual level. This is similar to one of the sayings of spiritual twelve-step programs, "Let go and let God." In other words, let God have the control in your life, even more so when things are not working for you. There is so much power in doing this, as God is all-powerful. Our lives work better when He is put at the helm.

I felt so trapped for so long, feeling like a victim of all that was happening outside me. I'd say that feeling of entrapment was Spirit's way of attempting to get me to face myself and the darkness, negativity, and heaviness within. That's a very hard thing to do, and most of us will never do it willingly or without kicking and screaming and huge resistance. However, astrologically and otherwise, this is an unprecedented time for the entire world to do just that. It is almost as if the energies are going to force many to do that. Those who don't may suffer much greater misery. Not that it will be easy for those who do, but they will be able to come out on the other side with much greater understanding, strength, and lightness of being.

I fought doing this for a very long time—until I could see my fighting was doing absolutely nothing, and the universe was going to pretty much force me to be alone and learn to love myself. It became much easier when I surrendered to that force, which I realized was greater than myself and was trying like crazy to sweep me up in its loving arms and hold me and love me like I had never been loved before. Learn to surrender and trust that every negative feeling that arises within you just wants to be acknowledged and loved. As Matt Kahn, a spiritual guru you can find on YouTube, has said, "Whatever arises, love that."

Make it your daily intention to surrender to whatever is, and stop resisting anything you think should be different. Doing this opens the flow of the universe for you. Resistance shuts down all flow and brings you to a place that can begin to feel like hell on earth. The second you decide you are just too tired to fight or resist any longer, it all seems to change. You begin by simply making it your daily intention. It soon becomes rote, easy to do, and one of the fastest ways to align with your spirit, which is connected in every way to universal life force. You will find a different world waiting for you. It will enable you to see how everything is a blessing and all is happening for you and just as it should be happening, even though we cannot always see the logical reasons or understand at the time why certain things are taking place.

As I have said previously, I pay attention to my thoughts. If they have become negative ones, I change them to more positive ones that will create the higher-vibratory emotions that I wish to be feeling instead. I pay no mind to whatever might be right in front of me, presenting itself as my current reality. This is how alchemy and transformation of any situation are created. We will all be learning about this concept more and more as our planet evolves and raises in consciousness. It's the same thing as the law of attraction. It all changes here and now with your thoughts. We have far more control over our thoughts than what we have been taught to believe. Of course, we all think our thoughts must reflect what is right in front of us in reality. But this is not true; we get to choose what we allow as thoughts in our minds.

This is part of our God-given ability to create. And, oh yes, it makes a huge difference—maybe not right away, as it does take time to create something new and different. You will notice immediately you feel uplifted emotionally, and this will reflect for you physically, sometimes fairly quickly but often down the road a bit. It says in the Bible in Hebrews 11:3, "By faith we understand that the worlds were prepared by the word of God, so that what is seen was not made out of things which are visible." And Psalm 33:6 says, "By the word of the Lord the heavens were made." So we know that thought precedes that which is spoken. I have at times been in a very dark place and have pulled myself out of it by telling myself how happy I am and how grateful I am for the blessings in my life.

Reframing negative thinking when these thoughts come up, to be acknowledged and released, and being in gratitude for as much as you possibly can helps lighten your load, lifting things in ways you couldn't have imagined, not the least of which will be your mood. You get to choose whether to stay stuck in a downward spiral of heavy, self-pitying, victim-like, negative thoughts or to free yourself. What do you have to lose? Once you learn to do this and use it regularly, you will be amazed at the difference it makes in your life, bringing a flow of extra blessings.

In the course of having my illness, I lost pretty much everything. I lost almost my entire past, I lost my toxic ways of living, and I lost many of the false paradigms I'd been taught to believe. Of course, I lost friends, and at times I felt I lost family. I lost the ability to work a regular job, I lost a social life and most of my contact with society, and I lost the ability to do many things that most healthy people take for granted, even going places and being out and about anywhere other than remote places in nature. I became a mandatory hermit on this planet. With the current corona pandemic, I have been known to say, "I've already been through my own personal apocalypse with this." And because of all the healing work I've done, I no longer will submit to any type of fear or guilt tactics from others. I've experienced the deep, dark hole of an abyss in life, and I no longer will willingly put myself there.

Once you've faced your worst fears head-on and transmuted them, nothing has that power over you anymore. You are empowered by the healing and in your power. No one in their right mind would choose to go back, regardless of what the rest of the world may be doing. I have seen people who haven't done their own inner healing work and are still operating from the logical, left/ego brain and how it keeps one in a perpetual state of fear. From my experience, this cannot lead to a higher-vibrational healing state and is not love at all.

Through it all, I can see that the course of my life changed from what I had thought it would be, and it has absolutely been for my highest good. This can be a consciousness-raising illness or time in one's life, one that can lead to a state of spiritual enlightenment if that is one's path. It does take being willing to let go of any notion that anything needs to be a certain way for you to be happy and live a fulfilling life. It may just look different from what you had hoped for or thought your life would be.

This is the place I've come to thirty-five years after first becoming sick. Yes, it was an incredibly tough row to hoe, with an unbelievable amount of blood, sweat, and tears. Because I'm so damn strong and stubborn, it may have taken me much longer to soften my resistance. When you can open to letting it transform you, it can and will. Incredible loss can sometimes lead to incredible victory and a true understanding that the body may not be invincible, but the spirit is.

There is something happening on the earth right now that many who are suffering with alleged incurable or difficult diseases many not be aware of. It is a process known as ascension, which is the process of spiritual awakening that moves one into a higher level of consciousness. It is nothing to fear at all, although it can be accompanied by many undiagnosable symptoms of what amounts to a physical detoxification. That is precisely what is happening in many people. A good explanatory article called "Ascension, Nutrition and Disease—Aligning with Earth" can be found at aligningwithearth.com. This happens when the earths resonance rises (something called the Schumann resonance, or the earth's vibratory heartbeat) as it has been doing quite rapidly in the past few years. "Tuning into the Earth's Natural Rhythm" at brainworldmagazine.com can help you better understand what the Schumann resonance is and how it affects life. People's vibratory rate has to also rise to keep up with that, and the process requires the body to let go of all that is toxic, heavy, or negative to stay in alignment with the planet.

This process is going to happen, and there isn't much we can do to stop it—nor would we want to. It is leading us into the period spoken of in the Bible, the thousand years of peace. I encourage you to change your perspective on your dis-ease to that of your body simply releasing all that will not serve your higher-vibratory light body on a planet of light and love, which is what is rapidly happening here. I may not happen tomorrow, but we are definitely moving in that direction and much faster than previously. And right now on the planet, just as with the body, when it looks as if chaos has ensued, this is actually just what is needed to uncover, release, and reorganize to create a higher-vibratory body and a more functional structure for a new society. What happens on the microcosmic level is also happening on the macrocosmic level. You will reap so many benefits during this time by purifying yourself on the mind, body, and soul levels.

So, fear not and allow. Assuming that what many of us have experienced could be the symptoms of ascension, it follows that our bodies and spirits are on a higher-vibratory level than many toxic chemicals, screaming at us to remove them not just from the planet but from our bodies as well. The vibratory rate of the planet and many humans is increasing all the time, so it makes sense that more and more people need to detoxify in order to survive here. And the more people detoxify and purify themselves, physically, mentally, emotionally, and spiritually, the closer we move to creating heaven on earth. The process will work more smoothly if we can all do our own part and stop looking at what is happening outside ourselves so much.

So, instead of looking outside yourself and wondering why everyone else doesn't help to create a safer environment for you and the whole planet, look within and do your own healing work. Then you will be that example to such a degree that others will want to follow suit. When you have done all you can to raise your own vibration, everyone and everything you come into contact with is elevated. This is a universal truth. It may not happen in the way you think it should or hope, but I do believe you will be pleasantly surprised by the results. It will be more than what you could've planned yourself.

The symptoms people are now having of ascension are eerily similar to those of MCS, Lyme, and just about every other disease known. Many of them have also gone to numerous doctors, with little to no help or diagnosis. Below is a list of some of the symptoms of ascension, although there are many others:

- digestive issues
- loss of appetite
- ravenous hunger
- unexplained nausea
- sudden body temperature changes
- intolerance to heat or cold
- exhaustion beyond what is normal
- insomnia

- excessive sleeping
- frequent headaches (can be pineal gland decalcifying)
- increased sensitivity to smell and sounds
- heightened emotions
- changes in vision or perception, including flashes of light, sparkles, or swirling forms of energy (you should always call your eye doctor for any changes in vision just to be safe)
- difficulty keeping track of time and getting normal tasks done
- body aches and pains
- clumsiness
- sporadic bursts of increased energy or inspiration
- anxiety or panic attacks
- a need to spend more time in nature and with creative activities
- abrupt changes in interests or friends
- a need for more personal space and time
- feeling invisible or detached from others and the world around you
- feeling ungrounded or scattered
- moments of heightened spiritual connection
- increased telepathy or empathy with others
- bizarre or intense dreams
- increased psychic awareness
- profound feelings of love, peace, understanding, and connectedness with all
- sudden divine revelations, flashes of insight, or rushes of energy

Now that I practice, teach, and attune others to kundalini Reiki, a form of energy healing, I have noticed that many endure a few uncomfortable symptoms that are very similar to detox or ascension symptoms for a short period of time after the attunements. They are being elevated to a new level of consciousness, and in the process, their bodies begin shedding toxicity of all types—chemical, emotional, mental, and spiritual.

When you are elevated to a new level of consciousness, you suddenly become more sensitive to things that didn't seem to faze you before. That is because the higher-vibratory rate of your physical vessel is no longer compatible with the lower-vibratory rate of the toxins. People who realize this do not necessarily fall prey to identifying with being sick. They may not be feeling well or 100 percent; that is true. It is an old paradigm to believe you are sick or must be diagnosed with some malady if you have an abnormal or uncomfortable symptom. They just do what they need to do to take the best possible care of themselves without going into a state of fear, which is so detrimental to every biological process related to life.

I do not judge those who identify with being sick. I'm simply trying to point out that there may be another perspective to adopt, one with more hope. Our bodies speak to us, and it is not to worry us or make us fearful but to make us more aware of the need to tune in with compassion and care and to be proactive for ourselves and subsequently the planet and every human we are connected with. It creates a ripple effect. So, I encourage you to discern for yourself what your body is trying to let you know about your life that is not in alignment with your spirit or what needs healing on an emotional level. There is usually a connection.

A huge block to ascension and therefore healing on any level comes from feeling that help will come from someone or something outside of ourselves. It comes from within yourself and your connection to God, Source, or spirit. Many assume that God is an entity outside oneself. I have experienced God differently, as being part of myself. God or Spirit lives in each of us, and it is evident when you have made that personal connection. First and foremost, there must be this. Most often, what I've found is that the right person or circumstance will show up in your life as a result of this connection. You must first ask and intend, then be quiet and still and listen for your personal answers. You will receive what you need. Everyone has this ability. To receive a personal connection and be filled with God or the Holy Spirit, you must simply set your intention for this. Ask for it and trust. Do not doubt for a moment that you will be heard and that what you ask will be given.

It is like a muscle that must be exercised to function well. You just have to be willing to do the work, and you must make the intention to be present with all of your being to receive what is so rightfully yours. When I wake up in the morning, I lie quietly for fifteen to twenty minutes, and it is from this space of stillness, when I haven't yet started to think yet, that I often receive answers. This is a practice, just like setting aside the same amount of time or longer to meditate daily. Once you truly decide to accept the challenge, that this work is yours to do and no one else's, you will feel powerful beyond measure. This is the best part of it. You get to know yourself, your personal power, and stand in it. There is nothing I have found that comes close to creating such a sense of wholeness and strength.

In reality, all illness is based on spiritual dis-ease. Once you truly understand this, you will no longer be willing to live as thought your spirit is separate from your mind and your body, because you will understand that when you do this, you become dis-eased. You will understand that a spiritual practice is just as important as your daily hygiene routine, even if it is just a daily gratitude practice.

One of the spiritual truths I have learned along the way is to stop putting my needs for security or safety first and trying to figure out life with my mind or intellect. I have learned to simply ask, "What does my heart want? What does my spirit want?" Your mind just tries to keep you alive, and other than keeping your bodily functions performing, it is not able to perform the way your heart—or heart and mind together—can. Your heart always knows what is best for you, for it is the most connected to Spirit.

Yet another truth I have experienced directly is that whenever you have someone in your life who is triggering you or upsetting you in some way, they are a gift for your transformation and evolution. They are showing you the place and parts of yourself you have yet to forgive and love. That can be a tough concept to wrap your mind around at first, but if you are willing to look closely and dig deeply, you will begin to understand how every single person in your life who has triggered you is doing so as a gift to you, for your own evolution and healing.

Here is an exercise you can do to help you get in touch with this concept and hopefully see how healing it is not only for you but also your relationships with all people. In a column, write down the difficult people who have been or currently are in your life, and then in a second column next to the person, write the parts of them you don't like. Then honestly look at yourself to see if you have ever shown that characteristic in any way and how you felt about yourself when/if you did. Write that down in the third column.

It takes being vulnerable enough with a willingness to drop your ego to perceive this truth. This phenomenon shows us the process of duality at play, or shadow and light coming into wholeness, unity, or oneness. What we have viewed or judged as negative about another, is always something we hold against ourselves as well, and now it is having light shown onto it so that it can be forgiven, loved, and made whole within us, or integrated. This is the essence of shadow work. Once you understand this concept, you will see how there is only love.

We can love and forgive anything. It's a choice. Forgiveness creates the highest level of healing work. When I first had my kundalini awakening, which was profound, I started to be faced with some of these things. I was so horrified at first. I wanted to run screaming from myself! To a large degree, it boils down to dropping all resistance and learning to accept and love what has seemed unacceptable or unlovable. The fear and horror created a form of resistance or nonallowing. It took me a while to soften that resistance and realize that all of those parts of me were what made up the whole, and it would help nothing to keep denying my shadow side.

How could I not be in love with all of me? It would be like saying to your child, "I don't love the part of you that I judge or view as negative." It's much more holistic to love the whole, to bring it all into the light of love. Then one can see the alchemy and beauty that is actually possible. It's a process and takes time, so be gentle with yourself. It is from here that we go more toward being able to love what has seemed unlovable not just in ourselves but in everything and everyone.

You will then begin to see how self-love and acceptance is how we begin to heal and create peace and harmony here on this planet and in the universe. Have great gratitude for these parts of yourself because they have played their grand part in the overall scheme and in making you who you are. And, if you ask, they will let you in on what their message is for you, which can be an opportunity for you to experience greater compassion, understanding, and love not only for yourself but for others as well. It truly does manifest in this way. What you give to yourself, you give to others as well.

Here are some steps to accepting your shadow self:

"Beneath the social mask we wear every day, we have a hidden shadow side: an impulsive, wounded, sad, or isolated part that we generally try to ignore. The Shadow can be a source of emotional richness and vitality, and acknowledging it can be a pathway to healing and an authentic life" (C. Zweig and S. Wolf).

First, you must let go of the shame, realizing everyone has what they consider unacceptable thoughts, impulses, personality characteristics, and desires.

Journaling is an excellent tool. You can write all of your thoughts out in a journal, things you would never tell another soul. It can be like therapy, only it is more or less therapy with your higher self. I guarantee you will start to have more compassion toward yourself when you see your thoughts expressed on paper or your computer screen, as well as new insight on how to deal with things that are difficult for you.

Meditate with the intention to accept yourself fully, flaws and all, to understand deeply that it is part of being human.

Focus on your good qualities, while knowing that the opposite is also likely to be true. I once had a therapist who told me that most people's good characteristics had a flip side, the opposite in reality, as well. Understand that your shadow side is where you may find your power once it's accepted by you, your honesty and passion.

Try talking to a therapist, life coach, or spiritual healer, such as a shaman or energy healer.

A fabulous article on the shadow self can be found at lonerwolf.com. It is titled "Shadow Self: How to Embrace Your Inner Darkness (3 Techniques)."

Mindfulness or Being Present

My spiritual path has taken me to a place where I realize that worry, anxiety, and fear take me out of the present, where I always have everything I need, and places me in the future, which is not happening yet. It is so pointless to worry or be in fear about things that may or may not happen. Most of them never do happen, if you think about it. This greatly diminishes your ability to be present to what is happening right here, right now. Be present, to yourself, for yourself, always. It is the best gift you can give yourself. It is this very presence that will help you to trust surrendering to your higher self.

You can become more present by simply taking some deep breaths until you feel calm and in your body. Another way is to place one hand on your lower abdomen and the other on your heart for a few minutes. It does take commitment to yourself to begin to practice these new ideas, but if you don't do it for yourself, who will? The rewards are a life of peace, joy, gratitude, supreme well-being, higher energy and vitality, wisdom, incredible inner strength, better health … all things that bring you a life more worth living, nothing short of phenomenal.

Gratitude

I feel good all the time, no matter how my body feels. There is so much to be grateful for here on earth. There is so much love, life, positive energy, vibration, and magic. All it takes is to move your focus to it and make it a practice. Discipline yourself to do so. I focus on seeing the beauty, synchronicity, and magic in everything. And because of that, life tends to show me more of itself in that way. Now I see how life is truly a wondrous alchemy of beauty. I have long since come to the realization that this was Spirit's way of guiding me along my path of awakening, greater communion with my true source, joy, and bliss.

There is nothing that can come close to that. And in the past few years, I've been so excited to see so many more people beginning to awaken to truth, and those who've been awake for some time now are feeling more free to come out completely and help guide others on this path of healing, ascension, and evolution that we are all on together on our beautiful planet, Mother Gaia.

You can choose to practice gratitude regardless of any amount of seeming lack, chaos, or turbulence going on in the world around you. It's much easier to do if you choose not to focus on all that happens outside of you in the world. Your mind/ego will have you believe that you need to keep your focus out there in order to remain safe. This is not true. The ego mind doesn't know truth; it just knows how to keep us physically safe and alive. It's good for some things, although not nearly as much as it would like to have you believe.

I am a huge fan of breath of fire as used in kundalini yoga, as this is a key method in which energy blockages are removed and life force energy is allowed to flow through the body unimpeded. There are also breath workshops offered in many places now. The results of having all energy channels open to life force moving through are nothing short of profound. It energizes everything; everything can then move. Body, mind, and spirit flow and merge as they are intended to. Life purpose becomes evident, one has boundless if not limitless energy when one is fully connected to universal life force energy, and, best of all, the breath provides essential prana or vital life force and is crucial for vibrant good health.

While traveling in Europe, I was constantly barraged by new experiences and consistently on the move, to the point I didn't have the time or resources to always pay attention to my body, mind, and spirit as much as I would've liked to in my daily routine. Once I returned to the States, it was easy to see why one can have so much resistance to opening those channels to the life force energy flowing through. It is not easy work. It involves a lot of time and effort and letting go of what does not serve one's higher interest. That can mean physical detox work. I feel this needs to be first in the order of affairs, because without the physical and energy body being cleared, the mind and spirit do not function as they are meant to.

I know there have been miraculous overnight spiritual healings, but it often works the other way too. My first day back from Europe, I woke up and knew I needed to juice, meaning I needed to take at least a day or two to consume only juices. It was to start the cleansing process from all the wheat, dairy, coffee, and sugar I'd consumed on my trip. The next morning, I got all my vegetables out for juicing—carrots, celery, cucumber, swiss chard, beets, and fennel root. Then I looked at them and, with dismay, thought, *I have to chop all these up to go into my juicer?* The amount of work required felt overwhelming. Then, afterward, I had to clean my juicer. To be honest, I didn't even make it through that first morning without some whole food. I had some fruit. I knew my body was screaming for nutrients. What had become quite routine and simple before my trip now seemed daunting. I tell you this to let you know it can feel seriously difficult and troublesome getting started on a new way of eating or taking care of yourself. I promise that, after a short while, it becomes your new routine and is easier to carry out with time.

I knew in part this was the wheat in my system playing tricks in my head, but the memory of the easy wonder of grabbing a croissant and stuffing it down mindlessly seemed so inviting by comparison. It's the initial difficulty of getting started or restarted with your healthy protocol after ingesting too many toxins that slow your energy down and make your brain more sluggish. Then the mental part of you, which is in truth under siege, just wants to say no, that it's too hard. So, I do promise, once you get started, very shortly you will wonder why you thought it was so hard. Part of that is because your energy will surely begin to dramatically improve, giving you newfound vitality.

I had more than just a couple days after reentering my world of healthy living where I was incapable of doing much aside from lying on my bed and wandering around my house aimlessly, while toxins being released affected my ability to think and my motivation to even unpack. I know some would call this jet lag, but I know myself, and jet lag alone is almost inconsequential when one is detoxed and eating raw or at least in a very healthy way. There is a reason experts tell you to eat lightly to avoid jet lag, because it works, and it's the best thing for overall health of the body, mind, and spirit.

The hardest part of the resumed detox and return to super healthy lifestyle was over within a few short days, and I was again bursting at the seams with fresh energy. It is for this reason I continue to live this lifestyle of primarily raw food consumption (and for anyone, whatever healthy eating works best), with a focus on detoxifying the body, mind, and spirit. If not for this, I would never have been able to do what I did, which was to travel Europe on my own, staying in a variety of places, where I never bothered to think about the toxicity level. It was not something that I felt I needed to concern myself with or put a lot of focus on.

When my girlfriend asked me how long I felt I could continue to live in this traveling manner, I responded with, "Oh, I could do it another year if I needed to." Not that I wanted to, but that's how strong I felt in terms of my body and spirit. So, I press on with this lifestyle, as it has brought me numerous benefits I never imagined possible.

After Europe, I consumed about sixteen ounces of juice three times a day, along with herbal teas and maybe some miso soup if I felt the need or desire. I do put a small amount of lemon juice in my green juices, as it makes them more palatable. Also, I sometimes put a bit of garlic, cilantro, or ginger. The days in between are my norm, which is a breakfast of fresh organic fruit, cut up, with raw granola (sprouted sunflower seeds, sprouted flaxseed, coconut, and dried fruits) or a super smoothie with frozen fruits, banana, frozen chard, kale, or spinach, stevia, Chloroxygen, sunflower lecithin, aloe, collagen powder, maca root powder, lucuma, cacao powder, cilantro, bee pollen, hempseed, chia seed, super greens powder, and/or camu powder and water. I don't use all of those ingredients every time. Sometimes it's just two or three of them.

You may want to experiment with barley grass or super greens powder or cilantro for heavy metal detox. I have made my own protein powder by grinding up flax, chia, hemp, pumpkin seed, and pea protein powder. From all the variations, some amazingly delicious combinations have resulted. I cannot say enough good about super herbs and foods, as they are totally natural, and instead of a ton of supplements, you are just including a few things into your diet to get what your body needs. But as always, test even these with small amounts first to be sure your body tolerates them.

Dinner is often a salad, one of many different varieties. One of my favorites is a bed of spring mix or baby salad greens with strawberries, almonds, cranberries, and avocado with balsamic or lemon vinaigrette. I have turkey or salmon a couple times a week, or root vegetables, especially when I am feeling the need to get more grounded. Another simple salad is radishes, cucumber, avocado, and spiraled beets with sprouts, sunflower seeds, almonds, crushed-up flax crackers, or pine nuts top, along with lemon juice and olive oil. A dressing I love is maple syrup, lemon juice, and coconut aminos, with a little sesame or olive oil. Sometimes I make a Thai coleslaw or put some sprouts or fermented vegies on top, like sauerkraut or some organic kimchi. Or I add guacamole or a sprouted sunflower, pecan, or pine nut pate.

Sprouted nuts are really important, as the enzymes are released, making them easier to digest and enabling you to absorb more of the nutrients. I also like to sprinkle royal bee pollen on my fruit salads, smoothies, or dinner salads for the B vitamins. I really like to focus on whole foods and super herbs for obtaining as many vitamins, minerals, and nutrients as I can. I feel these are far easier for my body to assimilate than any synthesized supplements or products. I pretty much focused just on this regimen after Europe and no other detox, just to get my intestines and digestive tract back into the best shape possible first. I also did a series of colonics to help speed the process, several a week for a couple weeks. Yes, perhaps it seems a nuisance, but the results are generally outstanding—more energy, clearer brain, and just a bit faster loss of that muffin top I gained in Europe. Once my energy got back to normal, I began to rotate doing different things, like I was in a bakery choosing the most delicious treat to consume! All I know is the cleansing vastly improves the quality of my life, to the degree that I don't want to stop. Also, I went back to dance, kundalini yoga, qigong, and tuning into myself to see what I need on a daily basis.

The longer I've lived this lifestyle, the more I've developed my inner sense of power. A lot of this can be helped along and even done with energy work, as well as informing my DNA and body what I want it to do and asking my spirit guides for energy healing while I sleep. There are ways to reactivate your DNA, the original twelve strands that all humans have, ten of which have been called "junk" DNA. Nothing could be further from the truth. There are light language videos on YouTube specifically for reactivating or recoding your dormant DNA. We are meant to be evolving to the point that all humans can have this DNA activated if they choose. I do a lot of intention setting to help manifest my goals and desires, leaving exactly *how* that happens to the universe.

I do understand that many cannot spend this amount of time on healing. The fact is that if you are able to work a full-time job, you most likely don't need to spend this much time on your healing process. Life is like that; you are given what you need always. So, please do not be discouraged if you can't do everything I speak of in this book at all times. Do the things that fit into your life the best, what you feel will be the most helpful to you personally, and make it your own. I simply share what worked for me in the hope that you may gain inspiration for your life and healing and that some of what I've laid out here works for you. Do what you are able to do, what feels right or resonates, and you will get the benefits for sure. It's not a contest, and there are no hard and fast rules. You can even do different parts at different times and not all the time. You can do it full-on once or twice a year when you have the time to devote to it. As you can see, we are all so different, and there are a vast number of ways and paths to accomplish the same thing.

I was so discouraged when I began the Marshall protocol for Lyme because everyone else was able to manage much higher doses of the medications and much more often than I could. And the truth was I improved far more and even more rapidly than a lot of those people I was comparing myself and my journey to. This is strong validation for doing only what is right for you and making no judgment on it, trusting that you will be given what you need, no more and no less. Making your connection with Spirit and your intuition is like gold for you, as this is the most important part of the journey.

I had a conversation with a woman who was at a very low point in her life, feeling there was no way out. I told her the idea that she was in a trap was completely an illusion. I said the only trap is your mind insisting that you are in a trap. So, in reality, she was in a trap, that of her own mind and making. I then told her, "If you were in a house that was burning down, and you'd die if you stayed in that house, I am sure you would get up and walk out without a logical thought of trying to figure out where you'd go next or what you would do. This is the way Spirit works through you. You don't always figure everything out in advance when you are operating from a spiritual place, and this is always in your highest good! You go with what you feel, because to not do so is to stay put in the burning house and go down with it." And then Spirit most always presents you with even harder lessons if you try to ignore that aspect of life. This is the most important aspect of life that we must begin to accept and relearn as valid.

Spirit will help you if you let it! Your fear, which is mind/ego based, is keeping you trapped. Becoming aware of the illusory nature of the mind will help you tremendously. It's unfortunate that we've been taught the exact opposite, that the intuition and spiritual world is the one of illusion, when it's the other way around. Fear helps to create more situations and people that bring more circumstances that are fearful to you. This strong adherence to false, outdated beliefs does nothing for your state of mind, body, or spirit. It's not life affirming or health giving to live your life in this manner, regardless of this false paradigm we've all been taught from early on, that we must logically think through and plan out every step of our lives in order to keep ourselves safe and for things to go well for us.

Nothing is further from the truth. You will not know this unless you try something different. Stop telling yourself how so many things are impossible, and then you will begin to step out of the role of victim and into your true power. I am by no means invalidating the horror or difficulty of what you're dealing with, or how difficult it may be to rise above it. I am here to let you know it *can* happen. You begin first with the messages you tell yourself to empower yourself. Yes, when you are sick with an illness that society and families fail to understand, support, or validate, you are most ripe for growing in your self-esteem and strength and stepping into empowerment.

There's nowhere to go but up from there. Having an illness of this nature is something that can make or break you spiritually, and you get to decide. Which will it be? I don't believe you will be sorry if you decide to step into your power. You do this by refusing to need anything to be a certain way to be able to claim your happiness. When you focus on what's happening outside you, you cannot access your own power and happiness. That's right, true happiness and peace have nothing to do with anything happening outside you. Your peace and happiness come from within you. We've just been taught otherwise. When you give up this illusion that anything outside you gives you happiness, peace, control, or power, you are on the road to standing in your own power. I see that as being what this world needs more than anything else at this time. By doing your own healing and shadow work and taking full responsibility for it, you are doing your part to heal this planet.

From this will come acceptance and true understanding that you have everything you need within yourself. This is the truth, that you have the universe within you, waiting for you to recognize, acknowledge, and accept it. This is true power—to stand back and create space for our desires to come about, not in our limited consciousness way but in the way Spirit and the universe are capable of providing, which our limited thinking cannot begin to match. Being attached to outcomes and refusing to let go are two of the greatest stumbling blocks. It seems so scary to just let go of our perceived needs being met in a certain way. Holding on with attachment creates constriction and impedes energetic flow or the flow of the universe. Visualizing your highest creation and intending that, while letting go with detachment to a specific outcome to any scenario, allows energy to move and flow in ways that are unimaginable to the human mind. Once we accept Spirit as part of ourselves, we become magical and have abilities we once thought belonged to only the gods.

In tying this all together, I've come to understand that so much of what happens in our lives is actually predestined, and there is so much that will happen that seems beyond our control, but it is really all there for our specific lessons and learning. Therefore, it makes sense to become very close to or in touch with Spirit, God, your higher self, whatever you choose to call it. It is only from here that we can see from a higher view and know that Spirit has always got our back. Make the effort to see from that vantage point and let it guide you every step of the way. Set your ego mind aside and live from your heart, as this is where Spirit/ God is closely connected and will speak to you.

Although so much is predestined, by choosing a positive and joyful mindset about all that is happening and what you wish to happen, you will most definitely create a better, more joyful life for yourself. You will be able to see what is happening from a higher level, as if you have transitioned to the other side. Things are so much more understandable and easier to accept when you see from this greater perspective in love, at which point your life becomes a meditation of peace, love, joy, and trust.

Everything is more beautiful and enjoyable from this place. With persistence, emotional resilience, and the help of Spirit, you will succeed. How can you not? You will certainly improve your life and evolve, which brings huge spiritual gifts. If all you end up doing is creating a stronger bond with God or your higher self, it will all be worth it. This much I know is true.

I do not live from a place of fear any longer, as fear is the opposite of love. Fear is far too limiting. It constricts every cell of your being and does not allow life and life force energy to flow through your being. How can your body be physically healthy if you are doing and thinking things that stop this flow? It can't, plain and simple.

First, you want to address how you are living and make the decision to live from your intuitive knowing about what you need diet wise for your best health. What we put into our bodies—or not—is crucial. Then look at your environmental surroundings. Is the place you live in suited to you and your health? If not, how can you make it so? This includes not only the physical toxins but also toxic people and your own possibly toxic mindset and way of thinking. Next, you may want to address the shadow side of yourself and make sure you receive the healing you need to resolve old wounds and ways of thinking. And finally, the spiritual side of yourself and life does not want to be neglected. This is the part that pulls it all together.

The benefits are numerous when you take on the responsibility for your life, well-being, and happiness. All bitterness and thoughts of lack begin to dissipate and are replaced with joy, compassion, love, enthusiasm for life, wonder, and abundance. You begin to feel a greater sense of power and control in your own life when your focus is primarily on yourself and improving yourself and your circumstances in all the ways possible. The horizons open up for you in so many more ways. You may be able to travel, work at something you love doing, and socialize in ways you haven't been able to, due to being incapacitated with exhaustion or fear of becoming overly toxic. Fear and anxiety decrease dramatically, since you are doing all you can to improve your health, mind, body, and soul, and you see improvements along the way.

If you fall down even after great success, you can get back up repeatedly, with a lifelong commitment to listen to yourself and your body and surrender to Spirit. Life has not been easy on this planet for many of us, but there are ways to make it much easier. I think of Kevin Costner's last line in *Dances with Wolves*, "Do you see that I am your friend? Can you see that you will always be my friend?" Know that your own spirit is this to you, always.

Learn to trust, know, live in communion with, and love your spirit. This is the greatest gift anyone can find here. My mission is to help lead you back to yourself, where true freedom is and a new earth is created. I love all of you so very much.

Out of suffering have emerged the strongest souls.
—TheHealingCenterPalmBeach.com

Radiation, Vaccine and Pathogen Detoxification

Any or all of the following can be used as part of a protocol for any kind of radiation detox, detox from vaccines or vaccine exposure and pathogen elimination. Use your own judgement as to which ones to use or not. Doses and how to take can be found online.

High doses of vitamin C ascorbates to bowel tolerance. If it includes sodium, it is buffered.
Coenzyme Q10
Vitamin D or daily sunlight exposure
Betaine
Ginger and cayenne pepper tea for blood clotting issues
Binders such as sea moss, nano zeolites, bentonite
Diatamaceous earth which has minerals such as boron and silica in it
Boron
Silica
Nano Soma – www.thenanosoma.com
Pine needle tea
Colloidal gold/platinum
Lauricidin
Elderberry
Candex

Capryl
Colloidal silver
Cinchona bark
Sea salt/baking soda/clay baths
Lymphatic massage and/or Lymphomyosot
Kidney and Liver detox herbs or homeopathy
Castor oil liver packs
Qigong – great for keeping energy meridians open and flowing

Bibliography

Arcturianlight.com.au/index.php/about-us/the-arcturians.

Asur 'Ana. 2018. Ascension, Nutrition and Disease—Aligning with Earth. www.aligningwithearth.com.

Basheer, Fahad. 2015. *The Science of Emotions*. Panchsheel Park, India: Partridge India.

Bernstein, Gabby. 2020. "A Meditation to Get into Spiritual Alignment." February 23, 2020. www.gabbybernstein.com/spiritual-alignment.

Clow, Barbara Hand. 1995. The Pleiadian Agenda: A New Cosmology for the Age of Light. October 1, 1995. Rochester, VT. Bear and Company.

Cousens, Gabriel MD. 2003. Rainbow Green Live-Food Cuisine. August 22, 2003. Berkeley, CA. North Atlantic Books.

Emoto, Masaru. 2004. "The Hidden Messages in Water: Dr. Masaru Emoto and Water Consciousness." www.thewellnessenterprise.com/emoto/.

Fraser, Cheryl. 2020. "Alright Tell Me More about Tantric Sex." www.besthealthmag.ca.

Gabriel, Roger. 2016. "What Is Oneness?" www.chopra.com.

Guenter, Dale. 2019. "McMaster University Observational Study Shows Significant Changes in Health Outcomes with Dynamic Neural Retraining System (DNRS)." www.retrainingthebrain.com.

Guzman, Isabel. 2017. "Tuning in to the Earth's Natural Rhythm." October 4, 2017. www.brainworldmagazine.com.

Hardick, B. J. 2016. "The Relationship between Genetics and Detox (It's All About Methylation)." November 16, 2016. www.drhardick.com/genetics-detox-methylation.

Landis, Ronnie. 2016. Holistic Health Mastery Program. June 28, 2016. Scotts Valley, CA. Create Space Independent Publishing Company.

Mooji. www.mooji.org.

Nature Healing Society. www.naturehealingsociety.com.

Schur, Maxine Rose. 2019. "How I Came to Fear French Doors." April 10, 2019. www.bonjourparis.com.

Sol, Mateo. 2014. "Shadow Self: How to Embrace Your Inner Darkness (3 Techniques)." www.lonerwolf.com.

Urban Monk. "Attachment: Understanding the Origin of Human Suffering, Part 1." www.urbanmonk.net.

Young by Choice. 2020. "9 Reasons to Throw Out Your Canola Oil and What to Use Instead." January 29, 2020. www.youngbychoice.com.